W9-CAX-307

2 to 22 DAYS IN EASTERN CANADA

THE ITINERARY PLANNER

FELICITY MUNN

John Muir Publications
Santa Fe, New Mexico

Acknowledgments
Thanks to all the tourism officials who helped out, including Tracey Arial, Gilles Bengle, Deborah Cook, Kay Coxworthy, Liz Fauteux, John Hamilton, Judy Hammond, Valerie Kidney, Helen Jean Newman, Chris McCarney, Paula Nichols, Paul Nix, Peggy Pelletier, Barbara Quarry, and Marjorie Ruddy. Special thanks to Richard Abbott, Roger Cameron, Ann Duncan, David Gersovitz, Kathleen Hickey, Laura Jack, Sylvie Lavoie, Maria Thomas, and Ina Warren for their tips, advice, and moral support; to Roger Rapoport and Peter Beren for starting the process and to Elizabeth Wolf and Richard Harris for their patience in seeing it through; to Dave Munn for being such a great traveling companion; and most of all, to Adrian Robertson for keeping me sane.

John Muir Publications, P.O. Box 613, Santa Fe, NM 87504

First printing March 1995
ISSN 1070-0617
ISBN 1-56261-204-2

Typeface Garamond
Maps Holly Wood
Cover Photo Leo de Wys Inc./Bob Krist
Typography Sarah Johansson
Printer Banta Company

Distributed to the book trade by
Publishers Group West
Emeryville, California

CONTENTS

2 to 22 Days in Eastern Canada

From the heady rush of Niagara Falls to tiny fishing out-posts along the rocky Newfoundland coast, from the bustle of big cities to the soothing serenity of oceanside vistas, eastern Canada holds the promise of infinite discoveries.

This book tells you how to get the most out of your visit, whether you want to tour the wineries of the Niagara Peninsula, sample as many of Montreal's marvellous restaurants as possible or meander along New Brunswick's Fundy Shore, where the tides are the highest in the world.

In Ontario, Canada's largest city likes to think of itself as New York City, only without the crime and grime. That's why some wags call Toronto The Big Lemon. In the Thousand Islands, you'll find islands so small they scarcely have room for a house, a dock and a couple of trees, but you'll also find islands with mansions on them, and one that has a magnificent castle on it. Ottawa, the national capital, comes gloriously alive in spring, when thousands of tulips burst into bloom all over the city.

In my home province of Quebec, Montreal, the so-called Paris of North America, offers wall-to-wall summer festivals, a great nightlife, and several unique museums, including, would you believe, a humor museum. Up the road a piece, Quebec City's remarkable clifftop setting is dominated by the stately Chateau Frontenac, one of the most photographed hotels in Canada.

Atlantic Canada, made up of New Brunswick, Nova Scotia, Prince Island and Newfoundland, has some of the most magnificent scenery in the country and also one of its most visited natural attractions, namely Magnetic Hill in New Brunswick. Prince Edward Island is all gently rolling hills, rust-red soil and sweeping beaches. The Cabot Trail on Nova Scotia's Cape Breton Island provides so many wondrous vistas of cliffs and ocean that there's a danger of scenic overdose. In Newfoundland, known affection-ately as The Rock, the people are the most unaffected, hardy and humorous anywhere. Offshore, huge, luminous icebergs float serenely past even in the summer heat.

In three weeks, this is a lot to take in—but it's manageable, and this book will guide you through the trip. If you have less than three weeks or want a leisurely tour, whittle your itinerary down to one area and spend more time there.

The itinerary format is divided into 22 daily sections, each containing:

1. A **suggested schedule** for each day's travel and sightseeing.

2. A detailed **driving route** description for each driving segment of your trip.

3. **Sightseeing highlights**, rated in order of importance: ▲▲▲ Don't miss, ▲▲ Try hard to see, and ▲ See if you get a chance.

4. Selected **restaurant**, **lodging**, and **camping** recommendations.

5. **Helpful hints** and **insights**—random tidbits that will enhance the trip.

6. User-friendly **maps** designed to show you what the road up ahead is really like.

Because Newfoundland is so large, the itinerary leaves time to see only the Avalon Peninsula area on the east coast. For travelers who would rather tour the province's west coast or who have enough time to tour the entire island, I've added a chapter at the end of the book that lays out a suggested west-coast trip.

When to Go

June, July, or August is the best time to go, given the climate; but in southern Ontario, for example, April and May aren't bad, and September is a fairly safe bet—except maybe in Newfoundland, which can have pretty gruesome weather. Visually, the most stunning period is late September and early October, when the changing leaves paint a sublime tableau of scarlet, yellow, and orange as far as the eye can see. It's been called the greatest natural show on earth, and it's worth seeing. The height of the colors varies depending on a number of factors, but

Canadian Thanksgiving, the first weekend of October (Columbus Day in the U.S.), is often when they peak.

Winter is characterized by sub-zero temperatures and bone-numbing cold. However, there are always winter sports, from skiing and snowshoeing to skating and ski-dooing. A lot of cities have winter festivals of one sort or another. Among the best are Ottawa's Winterlude, centered on the frozen Rideau Canal, billed as the longest skating rink in the world, and Quebec City's winter carnival, mainly an excuse to ward off the cold with copious amounts of an alcoholic concoction called Caribou.

Canadian temperatures are measured in Celsius, not Fahrenheit. Officially, to convert Celsius to Fahrenheit, you multiply the Celsius figure by nine, divide the result by five and add 32. (Don't forget your pocket calculator, eh?) Or, to figure out approximate temperatures in Fahrenheit, double the Celsius temperature and add 30; 20°C, for example, becomes 70°F. The chart of average lows and high includes Celcius rounded to the nearest degree and Fahrenheit conversions in brackets.

Climate Chart

	Ont.	Que.	N.B.	P.E.I.	N.S.	Nfld.
Jan.	-3 (27)	-6 (21)	-3 (27)	-3 (27)	-2 (28)	-1 (30)
	-11 (12)	-15 (5)	-13 (7)	-11 (12)	-10 (14)	-7 (19)
Feb.	-2 (29)	-4 (25)	-2 (28)	-3 (27)	-2 (28)	-1 (30)
	-11 (12)	-13 (7)	-13 (7)	-11 (12)	-11 (12)	-8 (18)
March	3 (38)	-2 (28)	2 (36)	1 (34)	3 (37)	1 (34)
	-5 (23)	-6 (21)	-7 (19)	-7 (19)	-6 (21)	-6 (21)
April	12 (54)	10 (50)	8 (46)	6 (43)	8 (46)	5 (41)
	1 (34)	1 (33)	-1 (30)	-2 (28)	-1 (30)	-2 (28)
May	18 (64)	18 (64)	14 (57)	13 (55)	15 (59)	10 (50)
	6 (43)	7 (45)	4 (39)	4 (39)	4 (39)	1 (34)
June	24 (75)	24 (75)	19 (66)	19 (66)	20 (68)	16 (61)
	12 (54)	13 (55)	8 (46)	9 (48)	9 (48)	6 (43)

	Ont.	Que.	N.B.	P.E.I.	N.S.	Nfld.
July	27 (81)	26 (79)	22 (72)	23 (73)	23 (73)	20 (68)
	14 (57)	16 (61)	12 (54)	14 (57)	13 (55)	10 (50)
Aug.	26 (79)	25 (77)	22 (72)	22 (72)	23 (73)	19 (66)
	14 (57)	14 (57)	12 (54)	13 (55)	13 (55)	11 (52)
Sept.	21 (70)	20 (68)	17 (63)	18 (64)	18 (64)	16 (61)
	10 (50)	10 (50)	8 (46)	9 (48)	9 (48)	8 (46)
Oct.	15 (59)	13 (55)	12 (54)	12 (54)	13 (55)	10 (50)
	4 (39)	4 (39)	3 (38)	4 (39)	4 (39)	3 (38)
Nov.	7 (45)	5 (41)	6 (43)	6 (43)	7 (45)	7 (45)
	-1 (30)	-2 (28)	-2 (28)	-1 (30)	-1 (30)	0 (32)
Dec.	0 (32)	-3 (27)	0 (32)	-1 (30)	1 (34)	2 (36)
	-7 (19)	-11 (12)	-9 (16)	-8 (18)	-7 (19)	-5 (23)

Money Matters

All prices in the book are in Canadian dollars. One-dollar bills were phased out a few years ago in favor of a $1 coin. It has a loon on it and so is known as a loony.

The Canadian dollar varies in value against U.S. currency but normally the U.S. dollar is worth anywhere from $1.17 to $1.40 Cdn. So right away, American visitors get more bang for their buck.

Prices for just about everything in Canada tend to be higher than in the United States, though. And there is also a little something in Canada called the GST, or goods-and-services tax. The seven-percent tax was brought in by the federal government in early 1991, just as the recession really took hold. Canadians loathe the GST and grit their teeth whenever they have to pay it— as they do on virtually everything, be it a haircut, a hotel room, or tampons. Visitors have to pay it too, but they can get a rebate on goods purchased and transported out of the country within 60 days as well as on short-term accommodations, i.e. less than 30 days.

You can apply for a rebate as long as the GST paid is $7 or more; in other words, you need only buy $100 worth of goods and/or accommodation to be eligible for the rebate. So remember to keep all original receipts, which must clearly show that the GST was paid. You have one year from the day you bought the goods and/or accommodation to claim the rebate. GST rebate application forms are available at participating Canadian duty-free shops, tourist information centres and, in other countries, Canadian embassies and consulates. Fill out the form and attach original bills of sale. You can hand it in at a participating duty-free shop, in which case you'll get a cash rebate on the spot (to a maximum of $500 per day), or mail the whole thing to Revenue Canada, Customs and Excise, Visitor Rebate Program, Ottawa, Ont., Canada K1A 1J5. Proof that you are not a Canadian resident and a sample signature are required.

Rebates for the GST are not paid on the following items: services other than short-term accommodation; alcoholic beverages; tobacco, motor fuels, or basic groceries; goods left in Canada; meals and restaurant charges; prescription drugs; medical devices; agricultural and fish products; and certain used goods and collectibles that tend to increase in value, like paintings or jewelry.

For more information on GST rebates for visitors, call 1-800-66-VISIT toll-free from within Canada or (613) 991-3346 from outside Canada, or write to Revenue Canada at the above address.

The provinces also have assorted sales taxes; again, rebates are available for visitors. Call provincial tourism departments for information (see the end of this chapter for toll-free phone numbers).

When filing for sales tax rebates from both the federal and provincial levels, keep in mind that since both require claimants to provide original sales receipts, you should claim the federal GST first because your original receipts will be returned to you.

Lodging and Camping

The selection is pretty much similar to what you get in the United States. For the budget-minded, there are campgrounds and no-frills motels. From there, the options rise through to the ritziest downtown hotels, which in Canada include properties in the Four Seasons chain, the

Intercontinental chain, and Canadian Pacific Hotels and Resorts. The latter operates some famous old hotels, including the Chateau Laurier in Ottawa and the Chateau Frontenac in Quebec City.

Bed and breakfasts are another option. Ten years ago they were a novel concept in Canada, but since then have proliferated. B&Bs are usually reasonably priced, especially considering the ample breakfast served; they offer comfortable, homey surroundings; and, best of all for travelers, they provide a ready-made opportunity to meet locals. Try to book at least 24 hours ahead. Would-be guests rolling up at 8:00 p.m. with no advance notice make life difficult for the people who run B&Bs. There are a variety of B&B reservation services in the larger cities; contact numbers are included in those sections. For guidebooks on B&Bs in Canada, see the Recommended Reading section below.

I've included a cross-section of interesting accommodations to suit all tastes and budgets. The recession of the early '90s has hit Canadian hotels hard, so potential guests have more bargaining power than usual. Before making hotel reservations, always ask about special or weekend rates, which can be much cheaper than the so-called rack rate, the official published rate. Similarly, I've included a wide range of restaurant selections. Don't let what's in the book limit you, especially since new restaurants are opening—and others folding, alas—all the time. Ask local residents for recommendations and check the restaurant-review sections of local newspapers.

Transportation
Travel by car is the best bet for this itinerary. Visitors from the United States should know up front they'll be paying more for gasoline than they do at home. Most of the difference is taxes.

Otherwise, driving in Canada shouldn't hold any major surprises, but there are a few things to keep in mind. Canadians measure distances in kilometers, so a speed limit of 100 does not give you license to floor it. The 100-kilometer highway speed limit is roughly 60 miles an hour. In town, the 50-kilometer speed limit is roughly 30 miles an hour.

Radar detectors are illegal in all six provinces covered in this itinerary.

Roads in Ontario, Prince Edward Island, and Nova Scotia tend to be better maintained than in the other three provinces. In the Newfoundland countryside, you also have to beware of wandering animals.

Public Transportation

If doing it all by car isn't feasible, virtually all the cities and towns on the itinerary are accessible by public transporation of one sort or another.

Air Canada and Canadian Airlines International are the major air carriers. Each is also affiliated with half-a-dozen feeder airlines, or regional carriers, serving smaller centers. All the major centres on this itinerary, from Toronto to St. John's, Nfld., are served by one or another of the airlines. For information on schedules and fares aboard Air Canada or its feeder carriers, call 1-800-361-8620 from within Canada or 1-800-776-3000 from the United States. For information on Canadian Airlines and its feeder carriers, call 1-800-665-1177 from Canada or 1-800-426-7000 from the United States. In summer, a number of charter airlines offer discount flights on domestic routes; see a travel agent to book.

If you love train travel, look to Via Rail, the national passenger railway service. There is regular train service among Toronto, Ottawa and Montreal, with the express train between Toronto and Montreal doing the trip in four hours flat. From Montreal, Via runs trains to Quebec City (an express train does it in two hours and 45 minutes), to the scenic Gaspe peninsula and to Halifax. The latter trip takes 24 hours. Via is owned by the federal government, which chopped the railway's operating subsidies and services by half in 1990, claiming not enough people were using it. Yet the railway has somehow managed to make some major improvements since then. The interiors of all its trains have been refurbished, personnel are much more welcoming than they used to be, on-time service has

improved dramatically and the express trains have been
added on the aforementioned Montreal-Toronto and
Montreal-Quebec City routes. Via has also upgraded its
first-class services, and traveling first-class on Via is now
actually worth the extra money, where for years, frankly,
it wasn't. Passengers in coach class can book five days
ahead to get a 40-percent discount for travel on off-peak
days, meaning any day except Friday, Sunday, and holiday periods. First-class fares are the regular coach fare
plus a flat surcharge. Between Toronto and Montreal, for
example, a one-way first-class ticket costs $115, including
a $36 surcharge. The regular one-way fare is $79, the
advance-purchase fare $47. For extensive train travel, con-
sider a Canrailpass. The 1994 low-season prices for adults
were $373 for any 12 days of unlimited travel in a 30-day
period and $340 for seniors and youths. High-season rates
were $545 and $492 respectively. Via has ticket offices in
all the major cities on this itinerary. Otherwise, see a travel
agent for information on Via's rates and schedules.

Towns not served by either the airlines or Via are usually on the network of intercity bus routes. Buses are
operated by different companies depending on the area.
In Ontario, the major ones are Greyhound Canada (1-800-
661-8747 from Canada) and Voyageur Colonial (1-800-668-
4438 from Canada); in Quebec, Voyageur Colonial; in
Nova Scotia, Acadian, at (902) 545-9629; in Newfoundland
and Labrador, Road Cruisers (1-800-563-6353 toll-free from
within the province, or (709) 737-5916 from elsewhere);
and in New Brunswick and Prince Edward Island, S.M.T.
(1-800-567-5151 toll-free from New Brunswick, (506)
859-5060 from elsewhere).

Customs

Adult visitors from the U.S. entering Canada may bring in
50 cigars, 200 cigarettes or two pounds of tobacco duty-
free, plus 1.1 liters (40 ounces) of liquor or wine. After a
minimum of 48 hours in Canada, returning United States
residents can take back, duty-free, $400 worth of articles
for personal use, including up to 100 cigars (as long as
they're non-Cuban), one liter (33.8 ounces) of alcoholic

beverages (if the bearer is at least 21) and 200 cigarettes. If the stay is less than 48 hours, the allowance shrinks to $25 worth of goods, which can include 50 cigarettes and 10 (non-Cuban) cigars.

A trip to Canada, by the way, provides cigar smokers with a rare chance to find out whether the mystique surrounding Cuban cigars is really justified. Specialty smoke shops sell them individually or in boxes; prices begin at $4 per cigar.

Dealing with the Metric System

Canada is a metric country, which can be terribly confusing for U.S. visitors. Some user-friendly conversions:

1 U.S. gallon = approximately 4 liters.
1 liter = about 1 quart.
1 Canadian gallon = approximately 4.5 liters.

1 pound = approximately ½ kilogram
1 kilogram = about 2 pounds

1 foot = approximately ⅓ meter.
1 meter = about 1 yard.
1 yard = a little less than a meter.

1 mile = approximately 1.6 kilometers.
1 kilometer - about ⅔ mile.

90°F = about 30°C
20°C = approximately 70°F.

Safety

Crime rates in Canada are nowhere near what they are in the United States. Just take the usual precautions, especially in cities. Don't walk alone at night, and stick to well-lit, well-populated streets. Use a fanny-pack rather than a purse, leaving your hands free to take photos and point excitedly at things.

Language

It may cause much bickering within Canada, but for English-speaking visitors it shouldn't be a problem. Oddly

enough, New Brunswick is the only one of the 10
provinces that's officially bilingual. The federal government
is also officially bilingual. Quebec is officially French and
it's the one place visitors may have language problems.
Most traffic and commercial signs are in French only. Some
merchants around Montreal post "F/E" stickers in their
shop windows, indicating that they will serve you in
French or English, whichever you prefer. When driving, try
to remember that *est* means east, *ouest* means west, *sud*
means south and *nord* means north.

Generally, Quebeckers seem more willing these days to
speak English if necessary; recent figures from Statistics
Canada show that 83 percent of Quebeckers speak French
at home but fully 35 percent are bilingual. In any situation,
there ought to be someone around who can translate.
Quebec City is such a tourist mecca that people working
in the tourism industry routinely speak English to visitors
from elsewhere in Canada and the United States.

National Holidays
New Year's Day, Jan. 1, is a holiday across Canada. In
Quebec only, where New Year's is a big family holiday,
businesses also remain closed Jan. 2. At Easter, some businesses take Good Friday, some Easter Monday and others
both days. The Monday closest to May 24 is a holiday
known as Dollard Day in Quebec and Victoria Day in the
other provinces. Quebec alone celebrates St-Jean-Baptiste
Day on June 24, while the whole country marks Canada
Day a week later, on July 1. The first Monday in August is
a civic holiday in all the provinces except Quebec. The
first Monday of September is Labor Day and the second
Monday in October is Canadian Thanksgiving. Nov. 11,
Remembrance Day, is a semi-holiday in that some businesses close and some don't. And December 25-26,
Christmas and Boxing Day, are holidays for everyone.

Recommended Reading
Jan Morris casts her discerning eye on ten Canadian cities,
including Toronto, Montreal, Ottawa, St. Andrews, and St.
John's, in *City to City* (Toronto: Macfarlane Walter and

Ross; published in the U.S. by HarperCollins under the title *O Canada: Travels in an Unknown Country*).

As an apt counterpoint, check out *Welcome Home—Travels in Smalltown Canada*, by Stuart McLean (Toronto: Viking). McLean spent two years traveling across Canada and in the end wrote about seven small communities, including Dresden, Ontario, St-Jean-de-Matha, Quebec, Sackville, New Brunswick, and Ferryland, Newfoundland. McLean says he's always most interested in people stories, and this book reflects that.

Local Colour (Toronto: Douglas and McIntrye), an anthology devoted to contemporary travel in Canada, covers most of the country via articles and book excerpts by Canadian writers. For example, Wendy Penfield tours along the St. Lawrence River from Montreal to the Saguenay, while Margaret Laurence visits small towns in southern Ontario, Eugene Cloutier explores New Brunswick, and Clare Morvat voyages along the New-foundland coast with husband Farley.

The Story of Canada (Toronto: Lester Publishing/Key Porter Books) is meant for kids aged about 10 and up, but in fact is a delightfully readable overview of Canadian history and culture for adults too. The bright, anecdote-filled text by Janet Lunn and Christopher Moore is complemented perfectly by Alan Daniel's lavish illustrations. The book chronicles everything from the first people to cross the Bering land bridge thousands of years ago to Roberta Bondar's 1992 flight into history as the first Canadian female astronaut.

Oh Canada! Oh Quebec! (Toronto: Penguin) is Mordecai Richler's take on why Canada seems on the verge of fracturing. Richler's sharp eye and acerbic wit have won him international critical acclaim, and this book paints an often devastating portrait of pettiness, paranoia, and anti-Semitism in Canada, particularly Quebec. Subtitled *Requiem for a Divided Country,* the book created a big brouhaha when it was published, to which Richler replied, "There is nothing like pointing at childish behavior to make people even more petulant."

Niagara—A History of the Falls (Toronto: McClelland & Stewart), is by Pierre Berton, a prolific writer and well-known Canadian personality. Berton's use of memorable characters—stuntmen and women, explorers, artists, power brokers, suicides, love-sick bridegrooms—makes for a lively social history of the falls.

The Canadian Book of the Road (Montreal: Reader's Digest) is a marvelous companion for road trips, replete with brightly written nuggets of information, illustrations and photographs on the history, culture and sights along Canada's highways and byways. It covers just about every part of Canada that can be reached by car.

Another very helpful Reader's Digest book is *Backroads and Getaway Places of Canada*, published in a similar format to *Book of the Road*, but concentrating, as its title suggests, on areas outside big cities. It features suggested drives, national park closeups, places to see, regional maps, and so on.

The Canadian Bed and Breakfast Book, by Gerda Pantel (Toronto: Fitzhenry & Whiteside) is billed as the most comprehensive guide available to the rapidly growing B&B scene in Canada

Tourist Information

The addresses and phone numbers for tourist information on each province are:

Ontario: Ontario Travel, Queen's Park, Toronto, Ont., Canada M7A 2R9; 1-800-ONTARIO.

Quebec: Tourisme Quebec, C.P. 20,000, Quebec, Que., Canada G1K 7X2; 1-800-363-7777.

New Brunswick: Economic Development and Tourism, P.O. Box 12345, Fredericton, N.B., Canada E3B 5C3; 1-800-561-0123.

Prince Edward Island: Visitor Services, P.O. Box 940, Charlottetown, P.E.I., Canada C1A 7M5; 1-800-463-4PEI.

Nova Scotia: Nova Scotia Tourism and Culture, Box 130, Halifax, N.S., Canada B3J 2M7; 1-800-565-0000 from Canada; 1-800-341-6096 from the United States.

Newfoundland and Labrador: Department of Development, Tourism and Promotions Branch, P.O. Box 8730, St. John's, Nfld., Canada A1B 4K2; 1-800-563-6353.

2 to 22 Days in Eastern Canada traces a path from Niagara Falls, Ontario eastwards to St. John's, Newfoundland, but the trip can be started at almost any point en route and traveled in either direction. Travelers arriving from the United States by road can begin in Ontario, Quebec, New Brunswick or Nova Scotia. For example, people coming north on New York's Interstate 90 can begin with Day 1, but those arriving via Interstate 87 or 89 in Vermont can start with Day 6. Travelers entering New Brunswick from Maine at the Calais crossing can begin with Day 13, while those crossing by ferry from Bar Harbor or Portland in Maine to Yarmouth, Nova Scotia, can start with Day 17.

For vacationers with less time, the itinerary also divides into suitable shorter trips. For example, people with two weeks' travel time could concentrate on Ontario and Quebec (Day 1 through Day 11), or on Atlantic Canada (Day 12 through Day 22). One week would be sufficient for either the Ontario or Quebec parts of the itinerary, or for any two of the four Atlantic provinces.

DAY 1 Begin by visiting Niagara Falls, one of the most popular draws in Canada. View the falls from afar by going to the top of the Skylon Tower, from closer by exploring the Table Rock Tunnels and from nearer still by taking the Maid of the Mist boat ride. Cap it all off by going right over the falls on a simulator ride.

DAY 2 Drive through the Niagara Peninsula region, pausing to visit a winery and the picturesque town of Niagara-on-the-Lake. Continue to Toronto, where a trip to the top of the CN Tower and a walk along the harborfront provide an introduction to Canada's largest city.

DAY 3 Explore more of Toronto, including the peaceful Toronto Islands and, by way of contrast, the busy downtown core with its lively neighborhoods and endless shopping opportunities. Stop in at the Royal Ontario Museum and the Art Gallery of Ontario en route to Casa Loma, Toronto's enormous "castle on a hill."

DAY 4 Visit Old Fort Henry and wander the waterfront in Kingston before taking a cruise of the scenic Thousand Islands, where eerie Boldt Castle on Heart Island is a must stop-off. Back on the highway, take a short side trip to Athens to see the attractive murals painted on many of the village's buildings.

DAY 5 Start a tour of Ottawa with a visit to Parliament Hill. Then stop off at the National Gallery of Canada before exploring the Byward Market, a trendy shopping and dining area. Visit the massive Canadian Museum of Civilization across the river in Hull and, back in Ottawa, stroll along the picturesque Rideau Canal.

DAY 6 Get an overview of Montreal from a lookout on Mount Royal before exploring Sherbrooke and Ste-Catherine Streets, the heart of the city. Sherbrooke has grand mansions and museums and Ste-Catherine has shopping complexes, many connected to Montreal's "underground city."

DAY 7 In the city's east end, visit the Olympic Stadium, which has the world's tallest inclined tower, and the unique Biodome ecological museum. Spend the afternoon in Old Montreal, which has cobblestone streets, a lively riverfront promenade and the fascinating Pointe-à-Callière Archeological Museum.

DAY 8 In Quebec City, tour the Citadel, wander the Plains of Abraham and walk along the Promenade des Gouver-neurs, which offers a spectacular clifftop view. Wander through Old Quebec, the historic area that's on UNESCO's world heritage list.

DAY 9 Explore Lower Town and the Old Port, including the Civilization Museum. Then drive along the St.

Lawrence River to Tadoussac, stopping en route at the artists' colony of Baie-St-Paul and at Pointe-au-Pic, billed as the birthplace of tourism in Canada.

DAY 10 Take a cruise from Tadoussac to see the whales and the Saguenay fjords before catching a ferry across the St. Lawrence. Drive along the north coast of the Gaspé peninsula, one of the most scenic areas of the province.

DAY 11 Tour Forillon National Park, a dramatic product of erosion, before continuing around the Gaspé coast on a route highlighted with stops at towering Percé Rock and the Île Bonaventure nature reserve.

DAY 12 Drive south to Fredericton, the capital of New Brunswick. Take a walking tour of the downtown area and a short sidetrip to see Kings Landing, a recreated Loyalist village on the banks of the Saint John River.

DAY 13 Explore the Fundy coast, including the chocolate-making center of St. Stephens, the venerable summer resort of St. Andrews, and Compobello Island, where U.S. President Franklin D. Roosevelt spent summers as a youth. In Saint John, wander the city's attractively restored water-front area.

DAY 14 Visit Fundy National Park and Flower Pot Rocks Provincial Park, where towering rock formations that look like small islands at high tide resemble giant flower pots at low tide. Experience Moncton's Magnetic Hill, where your car is pulled magically backwards up a hill, before catching the ferry to Prince Edward Island.

DAY 15 Take a walking tour of Charlottetown and then explore the rest of the island. Green Gables House is a major attraction, but there is much else to see, from the 40 kilometres of beach in Prince Edward Island National Park to peaceful villages and lighthouses on windswept bluffs.

DAY 16 Start a tour of Halifax, N.S., with a visit to the Citadel on a hill overlooking the city. On the waterfront, stop in at the Maritime Museum of the Atlantic before taking a harbor cruise and exploring Historic Properties, a picturesque waterside complex of boutiques, restaurants and bars.

DAY 17 Tour some of the attractive towns and villages of the southwest shore, beginning with Peggy's Cove, renowned for its picturesque setting. Other highlights along this coastal route to Annapolis Royal include Mahone Bay and Lunenburg.

DAY 18 Drive through the heart of the tranquil Annapolis Valley, taking short sidetrips to the fishing village of Halls Harbour and to The Lookoff, which provides a dramatic view over the valley's patchwork fields. Continue to Cape Breton Island.

DAY 19 Tour the Cabot Trail, which winds along the coast of upper Cape Breton Island and is one of the most scenic drives in Canada. Then head for North Sydney to catch the ferry to Newfoundland.

DAY 20 Travel from Argentia to St. John's at a leisurely pace, stopping at Cape St. Mary's Seabird Ecological Reserve, where soaring cliffs are blanketed with thousands of nesting birds, and at Salmonier Nature Park.

DAY 21 Explore St. John's, beginning with Signal Hill, where North America's first transatlantic radio transmission was received. Follow up with a visit to the Newfoundland Museum and a walking tour of the downtown area, including the historic waterfront.

DAY 22 Take a whale- and bird-watching cruise from Bay Bulls south of St. John's. Then drive in a circuit around the souteast arm of the Avalon peninsuala, where the scenery ranges from tiny fishing villages to windswept heathlands dotted with grazing caribou herds.

NIAGARA FALLS

Niagara Falls is billed as the honeymoon capital of the world. It is breathtaking in its aggressive garishness, especially on Clifton Hill, the tourist center of town. Fortunately, the Niagara Parkway and a wide expanse of the riverbank across from the falls themselves are on Niagara Parks Commission land, and thus kept pleasantly green and unspoiled. The parklands extend from Lake Erie to Lake Ontario, parallel to the Niagara River on the Canadian side of the border; entry to the park is free. Be prepared for crowds. Niagara Falls, a city of 73,000, attracts somewhere between 10 and 12 million visitors annually.

Suggested Schedule

10:00 a.m.	Niagara Falls Imax Theater.
11:30 a.m.	Skylon Tower for a panoramic view of the falls.
12:30 p.m.	Lunch.
2:00 p.m.	Table Rock Tunnels.
3:00 p.m.	Maid of the Mist boat ride.
4:00 p.m.	Ride Niagara for a simulated thrill.
Evening	Check out Clifton Hill. Summer nights, when it's packed, it's like a carnival.

For the record, the Canadian Horseshoe Falls—the more spectacular of the two waterfalls—drop 52 meters (170 feet) into the Maid of the Mist pool, while the waters at the American Falls plunge between 21 and 34 meters (70 to 110 feet) onto a rocky slope at their base. More than 168,000 cubic meters (six million cubic feet) of water go over the Horseshoe Falls crestline every minute—or about a million bathtubs full of water every second. The torrents of waters are eroding the rock underneath at the estimated rate of 36 centimeters (about 14 inches) every 10 years. Some 12,000 years ago, the falls were 11 kilometers (seven miles) downstream from where they are now. But the erosion rate has actually slowed since the early 1950s,

thanks to major water diversions for a generating plant
and construction of something called an International
Control Works, which spread the flow more evenly over
the entire crestline of Horseshoe Falls.

Getting Around
Arriving by road from the United States, the access points
are four bridges across the Niagara River. Starting south of
Niagara Falls, the Peace Bridge links Buffalo, N.Y., and
Fort Erie, Ont.; after crossing the bridge, drive north on
the Niagara Parkway for the scenic route or, for the fastest
route, go north on the Queen Elizabeth Way highway
(widely known as the QEW). Either way, the drive is only
about 20 kilometers (12 miles). The Rainbow Bridge and
the Whirlpool Rapids Bridge each link Niagara Falls, New
York, with Niagara Falls, Ontario. North of Niagara Falls,
travelers entering Ontario via the Queenston-Lewiston
Bridge can drive south on the Niagara Parkway. Arriving
from Toronto, the most direct route is via the QEW, which
links Toronto with Niagara Falls.

In Niagara Falls itself, the major attractions are within
walking distance of each other. For instance, the scenic
tunnels are about a 10-minute walk along the Niagara
Parkway from the Skylon. Since none of the attractions
except Ride Niagara involve sitting down a spell, you may
want to get a pass for the Niagara Parks People Movers—
buses that shunt back and forth all day among the various
attractions along the parkway and operate between May
and October. The passes cost $3.50 for adults and $1.75
for children. If you've parked in the Imax parking lot, you
can also hitch a ride to the scenic tunnels on a doubledecker bus that shuttles from the theater along the southern part of the parkway and back. The ride is free, and
the bus looks just like a London doubledecker except that
it's covered in coins, which give it a glittery gold look.

Sightseeing Highlights
▲▲▲**Niagara Falls Imax Theater**—To learn about the
falls and their history, stop first at the Imax Theater, a
pyramid-shaped building on Buchanan Avenue behind the

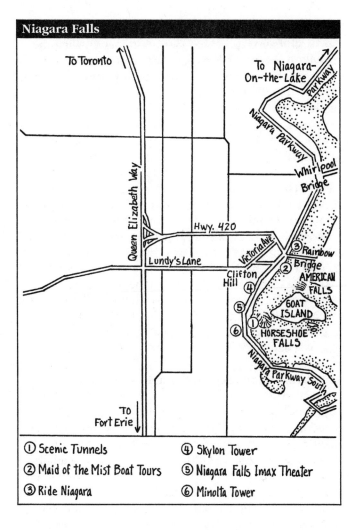

Niagara Falls

To Toronto

To Niagara-On-the-Lake

Niagara Parkway

Parkway

Whirlpool Bridge

Queen Elizabeth Way

Hwy. 420

Victoria Ave.

③ Rainbow Bridge

② AMERICAN FALLS

Lundy's Lane

Clifton Hill

④

⑤

BOAT ISLAND

①

⑥

HORSESHOE FALLS

Niagara Parkway South

TO Fort Erie

① Scenic Tunnels   ④ Skylon Tower

② Maid of the Mist Boat Tours   ⑤ Niagara Falls Imax Theater

③ Ride Niagara   ⑥ Minolta Tower

Skylon Tower, to see the 45-minute film on a screen so
enormous—six stories high, they say—that it makes you
feel like you're right there. The movie, *Niagara: Miracles,
Myths and Magic*, wondrously conveys the power and
beauty of the falls, as well as their strange allure for
assorted eccentric daredevils. The building also houses a
display on the history of the falls, complete with some of
the barrels and other contraptions in which people have

gone over the edge. The film is shown daily on the hour, so stroll the exhibit either before or after viewing the movie. The exhibit takes about half an hour to see properly. In summer, Imax opening hours are 10:00 a.m. to 9:00 p.m. in spring and fall 11:00 a.m. to 8:00 p.m., seven days a week. From October to March, the hours are 2:00 and 3:00 p.m. weekdays, 11:00 a.m. to 8:00 p.m. Saturdays and 11:00 a.m. to 4:00 p.m. Sundays. Admission is $7.50 for adults, $6.75 for seniors 60 and up and youths aged 12 to 18, and $5.50 for kids. Parking is free.

▲▲**Skylon Tower**—It's next door to the Imax Theater. Leave the car in the parking lot at the theater, walk across to the tower and head up to the observation deck for a panoramic view of the falls, the river, and the entire surrounding area. On a really clear day, you can see Toronto across Lake Ontario. The observation deck is open from 8:00 a.m. to 1:00 a.m. from early June through early September, and from 1:00 a.m. to 9:00 p.m. the rest of the year. Entrance fees are $6.25 for adults, $3.75 for kids 12 and under, and $5.25 for seniors. There are souvenir shops aplenty both on the ground level and at the observation deck level.

▲▲▲**Table Rock Scenic Tunnels**—Well worth seeing, particularly since entrance fees are relatively low. After entering, you're given a cheap plastic raincape. You'll need it. Then you get on an elevator, descend about 45 meters (125 feet) and emerge into a long, damp tunnel, filled with the dull roar of the falls. The tunnel leading away from the elevator ends on an open bluff jutting from the cliff next to Horseshoe Falls—hence the term Table Rock. Another tunnel to the right ends right under the falls; all that's visible is a thundering torrent of white water. For a drenching, get close to the railing. Open mid-June to early September from 9:00 a.m. to 11:00 p.m.; the rest of the year, 9:00 a.m. to 5:00 p.m. Entrance fees are $5.25 for adults and $2.65 for kids aged 6 to 12.

▲▲▲**Maid of the Mist**—It's almost a cliche, but it's also a must; if you have time to do nothing else in Niagara Falls, take the *Maid of the Mist* boat ride. The *Maid of the Mist* building is at the foot of Clifton Hill. After walking down a winding ramp and riding an elevator down still further to the base of the cliff, passengers are handed oil-skins before going out on the dock. On board the *Maid of the Mist*—there are actually several of them, operating from both the Canadian and American sides of the river—the best vantage point is the bow of the lower level. Otherwise, head for the front of the upper level. There is a recorded commentary, but you probably won't be able to hear it over the roar of the falls. The boat hovers briefly opposite the American falls, then heads up into the Horseshoe Falls basin and hovers there, too, for a couple of minutes, its powerful engines fighting the raging cur-rent. Throughout the day you've been getting closer and closer to the falls. This is the closest you can get, and from here, they're awesome—a wall of water soaring into the sky. Boats depart about every 15 minutes and the trip lasts roughly half an hour. The cost is $9.25 for adults and $5.60 for children aged 6 to 12.

▲**Ride Niagara**—You've seen the falls; how about going over them in a space-age capsule? Ride Niagara, a simula-tor ride that takes you over the falls in safety and comfort, is both fun and funny. Take a People Mover shuttle bus or walk along the parkway to get to the Ride Niagara build-ing under the Rainbow Bridge. Like most simulator rides, there's a preamble, in this case involving a film followed by an elevator ride to the "abandoned hydro tunnel" where space-age shuttles await. Actually, they're the motion simulators. You climb in and are propelled through the tunnel system to emerge above the falls. You're surging towards the brink now. . . . I won't give it away; suffice it to say it has some surprises and some entertaining narration. The whole experience takes about 20 minutes, but the ride itself is probably under five min-utes. Entrance is $8.50 for adults, $6.95 for seniors 55 and up and $4.25 for kids aged 6 to 12. The show runs every half-hour between 10:15 a.m. and 8:00 p.m. daily. For information, call (905) 374-RIDE.

▲**Clifton Hill**—At night it looks like Vegas, only the attractions are mainly kitschy "museums" instead of casi-nos. The Guinness Book of World Records museum vies for attention with Ripley's Believe It or Not! museum, the Movieland Wax Museum and other such attractions, which can be entertaining if you're in the right mood. Admission prices are fairly steep, running around $6 to $10 a person. If nothing else, absorb the atmosphere by strolling the length of the hill. It's only a couple of blocks.

▲**Tivoli Miniature World**—If you're travelling with young kids, this might be an evening alternative to the brassy lights of Clifton Hill. Miniature World is impossible to miss in a Victoria Avenue building fronted with massive Greek columns. Inside are miniature recreations of more than 90 landmarks and buildings from around the world. It's open until quite late in the evening, with the display floodlit. The Eiffel Tower is here, and so is the Statue of Liberty, and the Acropolis, the Kremlin, the pyramids, the White House, on and on and on. Some of the models look pretty slipshod, but others are magnificent. Most impressive of all is the recreation of the Vatican, the last display before the exit. Miniature World is in an open-air compound, so forget it if it's raining. Admission is $10 for adults, $8 for seniors, and $4.27 for kids aged 5 to 12.

Lodging

Although Niagara Falls is often viewed as an expensive destination, accommodation costs vary depending on the season and even on the numbers of visitors, which in turn can depend on factors like the weather. Most hotels and inns have honeymoon suites with Jacuzzis, and many also offer assorted promotions, including packages for families that allow kids under 12 to stay and eat for free. Overall, there's a vast range of accommodations to choose from. *Guide Niagara*, published by the Niagara Falls Visitor and Convention Bureau, lists some 70 hotels and motels and provides basic information on each. In June, July, and August, reserve ahead. The rest of the year, except for holiday weekends, just drive around and pick and choose.

At the budget end of things, the main motel strip is along Lundy's Lane. Generally, the farther from the center of town, the cheaper the rates. They begin around $40 a night in-season. I found a clean, basic motel room for $22 a night in early autumn, at the time only about $4 more than camping in a tent would have cost. The motel manager said that at the height of the season, the same room could run $80.

There are also numerous, more expensive hotels in the downtown tourist core. Hotels with rooms that have views of the falls include the **Oakes Inn** at 6546 Buchanan, 356-4514 locally or 1-800-263-2577 toll-free from Pennsylvania, Ohio and New York or 1-800-263-7134 toll-free from Quebec and Ontario; the **Sheraton Fallsview Hotel** at 6755 Oakes Drive, 374-1077 locally or 1-800-267-VIEW; and the **Skyline Foxhead Hotel** at 5875 Falls Avenue, 374-4444 locally or 1-800-263-7135 toll-free. In Niagara Falls, naturally, rooms with a view are among the priciest in town. Expect to pay $100 and up per night.

There is a string of bed-and-breakfasts in Victorian-era houses along River Road, part of the Niagara Parkway that overlooks the Niagara River Gorge. Try **A Rose and A Kangaroo** at 5239 River Road, (905) 374-6999; **Park Place B&B** at 4851 River Road, (905) 358-0279; **Butterfly Manor** at 4917 River Road, (905) 358-8988; **White Night Inn** at 4939 River Road, (905) 374-8767; **Gretna Green** at 5077 River Road, (905) 357-2081; **Glen Mhor House** at 5381 River Road, (905) 354-2600; **Bed & Breakfast with Friends** at 4877 River Road, (905) 374-4776; **Rainbow Hospitality** at 5239 River Road, (905) 358-2861; or **Bedham Hall** at 4835 River Road, (905) 374-8515. Roughly, rates range from $40 to $60.

It's also possible to reserve accommodation at selected hotels and resorts through Ontario's toll-free tourist information line at 1-800-ONTARIO.

Camping
There are eight campgrounds in the immediate area, four of them on Lundy's Lane: **Campark Resorts** at 9387 Lundy's Lane, (905) 358-3873; **Niagara Falls K.O.A.** at 8625 Lundy's Lane, (905) 356-CAMP; **Orchard Grove Tent & Trailor Park** at 8123 Lundy's Lane, (905) 358-9883; and **Scott's Tent and Trailer** at 8845 Lundy's Lane, (905) 356-6988. Other campgrounds include **Niagara**

Glen-View Tent and Trailer Park at 3950 Victoria
Avenue, (905) 358-8689, and **Yogi Bear's Jellystone Park
Camp-Resort** at 8676 Oakwood Drive, (905) 354-1432.

Restaurants

Niagara Falls has dozens of restaurants of every variety. The
ones that stand out are mainly those with views of the falls,
like the **Table Rock Restaurant**. A good bet for lunch on
this schedule, it's right next to Horseshoe Falls and has floor-
to-ceiling windows. Duck into the Table Rock Fast Food
downstairs for burgers, pizza, or salads, or try the Table Rock
Restaurant upstairs for a more leisurely meal. You can get in
without reservations during the off-season, but even then you
may have to wait about 20 minutes. Prices are reasonable,
given the dramatic location, and the food quite good. Main
dishes at lunch run from $7.95 to $10.95. The restaurant
opens at 11:30 a.m. Phone 354-3631 for reservations.

The Table Rock is operated by the Niagara Parks Commission, which also runs a couple of other scenically situated
eateries in the area. The **Victoria Park Restaurant** in Queen
Victoria Park faces the American falls and is open for lunch
and dinner. Phone 356-2217 for reservations. The **Whirlpool
Restaurant**, a short drive north along the Niagara Parkway, is
next to a public golfcourse and you can watch golfers from
your table. Phone 356-7221.

If budget is irrelevant, try one of the restaurants in
either the Skylon or Minolta Tower. In the **Revolving
Dining Room** at the top of the Skylon, for instance,
luncheon main courses run from $12.95 to $17.50 and
dinner main courses from $25.50 (for chicken cordon
bleu) to $37.95 (lobster tails). A second Skylon restaurant,
the **Summit Suite Buffet Dining Room**, is less pricey but
still not cheap. For reservations in either establishment,
phone 356-2651. Or try the **Top of the Rainbow** in the
Minolta Tower, which overlooks Horseshoe Falls. For
reservations, call 356-1501.

Helpful Hints

A particularly dramatic way to see the falls is by helicopter. But I hesitate to recommend it for two reasons: it's

expensive, and the flights may be greatly restricted by the time you read this. As many as five helicopters hover over the falls at once. A fatal collision of two sightseeing helicopters over the falls in September of 1992 has given rise to heated debate on the issue, and it's possible the flights will be limited. If you're game, call **Niagara Helicopter Rides** at 357-5672 the day or evening before. Rates are $70 for adults, $130 for couples, and $25 for children age 2 to 11.

Besides the attractions highlighted here, there are literally dozens of others in and around Niagara Falls, from the **Marineland** theme park, featuring assorted aquatic shows and midway rides, to the **Great Gorge Adventure**, a tunnel that leads to the edge of the lower Niagara Gorge Rapids. One of the lesser-known attractions worth checking out is the **Niagara Parks Greenhouse**, where a flock of 50 Peruvian hummingbirds fly free among the seasonal floral displays. Best of all, admission is free. The greenhouse is located just south of Horseshoe Falls on the Niagara Parkway. It's open from 9:30 a.m. to 7:00 p.m. in July and August and until 4:30 p.m. the rest of the year.

Nor does the town shut down in winter. From late November until mid-January, the Winter Festival of Lights is a miles-long, $800,000 lighting extravaganza centered on a "motion light" display from 5:30 to 11:30 p.m. each evening in Queen Victoria Park. Trees and buildings along the Niagara Parkway and in the city itself are also festooned with lights during the festival, which organizers say is the largest holiday lighting display in the world. The seven-week festival has a full calendar of family-oriented activities, including alcohol-free festivities on New Year's Eve, plus theater, symphonies, and craft shows.

For more information, contact the Niagara Falls Visitor and Convention Bureau, 5433 Victoria Avenue, Niagara Falls, Ont., Canada L2G 3L1, phone (905) 356-6061; or the Festival Country Travel Association at 1-800-267-3399 toll-free.

THE NIAGARA PENINSULA TO TORONTO

Winston Churchill once described the Niagara Parkway as the "prettiest Sunday afternoon drive in the world." Stop en route for a winery tour and a visit to picturesque Niagara-on-the-Lake. In Toronto, check into your hotel and then go up the CN Tower, the tallest free-standing structure in the world, for a dizzying overview of Canada's largest city. Right next door is the Skydome, the city's pride and joy and home turf to 1992 and 1993 World Series winners the Toronto Blue Jays. Take a tour of the stadium. Notice that the Skydome Hotel abuts the stadium, and some hotel rooms with big picture windows actually look out onto the playing field. Shortly after the complex opened in 1989, the hotel got more publicity than money can buy when a couple in one such two-level suite took time out from watching the game to play some games of their own on the bed upstairs. They neglected to draw the curtains, and the incident was all over the newspapers the next day.

Suggested Schedule

9:00 a.m.	Head north up the parkway from Niagara Falls, stopping at Queenston and at one of the wineries along the way.
11:30 a.m.	Explore quainter-than-thou Niagara-on-the-Lake and have lunch there.
1:30 p.m.	Drive to Toronto.
3:00 p.m.	Check into a hotel, then explore the harborfront.
4:00 p.m.	Visit the CN Tower.
4:30 p.m.	Take a tour of the Skydome.

Driving Route: Niagara Falls to Toronto (130 km/78 miles)

Follow your nose northward along the Niagara Parkway, which runs lazily along the Niagara River and ends at Niagara-on-the-Lake. It's only 22 kilometers (13 miles) from Niagara Falls to Niagara-on-the-Lake, but with the rolling, scenic parkland on either side you'll probably want to take your time. From Niagara-on-the Lake, take Highway 55, also known as Niagara Stone Road. About 12 kilometers (seven miles) along, it's intersected by the Queen Elizabeth Way, widely referred to as the QEW.

Head west on the QEW and follow it right into Toronto. The QEW runs through a densely populated area that wraps around the western end of Lake Ontario, on through Toronto and past it. The largest city en route is Hamilton, at the tip of the lake, and its most remarkable feature, visible from a long stretch of the QEW, is the massive steelworks looming over Hamilton Harbor's south shore. Sunlight slanting across the smokestacks and harbor makes for a striking sight.

Getting into downtown Toronto, the QEW becomes the Gardiner Expressway and runs east-west, parallel to the harborfront. Turn off it depending on where your hotel is. There are exits at Spadina Avenue, York Street and Jarvis Street, each of which gets you quickly into the heart of downtown. The whole route from Niagara Falls to Toronto is only 130 kilometers (78 miles), so how long it takes to drive depends on how often you stop to admire the sights en route.

Sightseeing Highlights
▲**Queenston**—A sleepy but historic village on the Canadian side of the Queenston-Lewiston Bridge, Queenston is a stop mainly for history buffs. Here, during the War of 1812 in which the Americans tried to conquer British North America, Sir Isaac Brock routed the enemy in the Battle of Queenston Heights. Today in Queenston Heights Park, open daily from mid-May to Labor Day, there is a towering monument to Brock, the commander of the British forces in Upper Canada, as Ontario was then called. Brock died in the battle. On Partition Street in Queenston, the Laura Secord Homestead honors a Canadian heroine who saved the British from American attack at one point in the same war. She walked 30 kilometers (18 miles), skirting the enemy, to warn the British

The Niagara Peninsula to Toronto

of an impending American attack. The Secord homestead is open 10:00 a.m. to 6:00 p.m. from the Victoria Day weekend in May until Labor Day.

▲▲▲**Winery Tour**—The Niagara Peninsula is a major wine-growing area, thanks to the rich soil and temperate climate, and some of the wines produced here are pretty fine. Personally, I recommend Inniskillin because I like some of their wines so much. The 45-minute guided tours, offered twice daily in the summer, conclude with free samplings of two wines. Go easy on the tasting if you're driving. There is also a nifty boutique with wine and wine paraphenalia housed in an attractive old barn that also showcases original art by Canadian painters. Inniskillin is on the Niagara Parkway a few kilometers south of Niagara-on-the-Lake. Watch for the sign on the left-hand side of the road as you drive north. Tours are offered daily at 10:30 a.m. and 2:30 p.m. between June and

October, and at 2:30 p.m. on Saturdays and Sundays only
from November to May. The store is open daily from
10:00 a.m. to 6:00 p.m. from May to October and 10:00
a.m. to 5:00 p.m. the rest of the year, except in January,
when it's shut altogether. The phone number is (905)
468-3554. Also recommended is Hillebrand Estates on
Highway 55 between Niagara-on-the-Lake and the QEW.
It offers free tours and tastings at 11:00 a.m., 1:00, 3:00,
and 4:00 p.m. weekdays and, on weekdays and daily
throughout the summer, adds a 2:00 p.m. tour too. A
"wine information centre" and the winery store are open
10:00 a.m. to 6:00 p.m. daily year-round. The phone number is (905) 468-7123. Altogether, there are some 15
wineries in the Niagara wine region; the provincial
tourism department has a brochure called *Wine Route*
describing all of them.

▲▲▲**Niagara-on-the-Lake**—From 1791 to 1796, it was
Upper Canada's first capital. In those days it was called
Newark. Nowadays it has a preserved 19th-century main
street that the town modestly refers to as "the prettiest
street in the world," its back streets boast 200-year-old
mansions, and it is home to the annual summer Shaw
Festival. It's also expensive.

The four-block stretch of Queen Street that is the
tourist hub of town is choc-a-block with trendy country-
style shops and restaurants, and it's seriously crowded on
most weekends except in winter. Prices are pretty high
but if the street's not too busy, it's a lovely place to
browse and window-shop. Chocoholics should stop in at
Renaissance, a shop and factory where workers hand-
make chocolate on vast marble slabs behind the counter.
For reasonably priced food, get away from Queen Street,
where a cup of coffee costs $1.95. The tourist information
office at 153 King Street can supply information and
brochures.

The Shaw Festival, running from April to October every
year, highlights the plays of George Bernard Shaw and his
contemporaries with daily performances in three theaters—the
Festival Theater, the Royal George and the Court House. The
box office is at 468-2172 locally or 1-800-267-4759 toll-free.

Helpful Hint
The Niagara peninsula is the kind of place you could
spend one day or one week in. There are forts and scenic
riverside drives and canals and all manner of things to
explore if you have the time. For more information, call
the Region Niagara Tourist Council at (905) 984-3626 or
1-800-263-2988 toll-free, or the Festival Country Travel
Association at 1-800-267-3399 toll-free. For information
on Niagara-on-the-Lake, call the Niagara-on-the-Lake
Chamber of Commerce at (905) 468-4263 locally.

Toronto
Toronto, a sprawling city of 3.5 million perched on the
north shore of Lake Ontario, lies farther south than most
of Michigan and all of Minnesota, at the same latitude as
the northern California border. The huge Lake Ontario
keeps the climate temperate; summers are clear and hot,
winters cool with little snow. "Toronto" is the Huron
Indian word for "meeting place," which is how American
Indians used the site before a French fur-trading post was
established here in 1750. The British colonized it in 1793
and named the town York, which later reverted to
Toronto when the city was incoporated. During the War
of 1812, an American force of ships raided York, burned
the parliament buildings, and ransacked the village. In ret-
ribution, the British invaded Washington and tried to burn
down the President's residence. The building remained
intact but its scorched outside walls had to be white-
washed—hence, the White House.

At Canada's Confederation in 1867, Toronto was the
capital of Upper Canada, now Ontario. The seat of government is at Queen's Park, on land that was once used as
an asylum for the mentally disturbed. The left-leaning
New Democratic Party is currently in power.

Over the years, Toronto has grown into a manufacturing and industrial powerhouse because of its proximity to
natural resources, agricultural land, inexpensive energy,
and the nearby markets of the American heartland. But
even Toronto has been hit hard by the recession in the
last couple of years. Banking and financial services are the

biggest industry, followed by tourism, manufacturing, and communications.

Toronto is sometimes called Toronto the Good, a nickname arising from the city's strict puritanism in the late 19th century. Perhaps out of envy, other Canadians still tend to view Toronto with some suspicion—it works too well, something must be wrong—and its residents as being uptight and driven, motivated mainly by the urge to make money.

In reality, Toronto has a thriving cultural life. For example, it has the third-largest theater industry in the English-speaking world, behind London and New York. It also has a panapoly of ethnic communities to enliven things; in fact the United Nations deemed Toronto the most "ethnically diverse" city in the world in 1989. It was originally settled by English and Scottish immigrants, but today is home to more than 80 different ethnic groups speaking 100 different languages. It claims relations between the ethnic communities are good, but Toronto was the only Canadian city in which there was rioting and looting after the Los Angeles riots in 1992, and relations between police and ethnic communities are not the best. It has particularly large Italian, Chinese, Greek, Korean, and Portuguese populations, each with its own area—Little Italy, Chinatown, Little Athens, Koreatown, and Kensington (Portuguese and West Indian).

Pearson International Airport, the busiest in Canada, handles more than 35 airlines in three terminals. Terminal 3, with its soaring, atrium-like main hall, opened in early 1991. Pearson is connected to the city by airport bus every 20 minutes, taxi and limousine. The Toronto Island Airport in Toronto Harbor handles short-haul commuter flights and is minutes from downtown. Via and Amtrak trains stop in Union Station right downtown. Union Station, magnificently cavernous, is worth seeing even if you're not arriving by train.

Getting Around

Traffic is dense in metro Toronto and a nightmare at rush hour. Parking can be hard to find and expensive when you do find it. The city has a strict ticketing and tow-away policy. As a visitor, forget getting around by car. Leave your vehicle at the hotel and use the efficient public transit system of subway, buses, and streetcars—or walk. The major sights and activities are mostly downtown within walking distance of each other. If you get hungry, you can stop to buy a hot dog from the street vendors.

Toronto is laid out in a grid pattern and it's quite easy to orient yourself. Starting at the waterfront and moving north, the major east-west streets are Queens Quay, Front Street (CN Tower and the SkyDome), King Street, Queen Street and Dundas. Farther north, Bloor and Eglington are big cross streets.

The major north-south artery is Yonge Street (pronounced Young), reputedly the world's longest street. It runs from the Toronto riverfront to Rainy River, Ontario, near James Bay, 1,900 kilometers (1,140 miles) away. Yonge also divides cross-street addresses into east and west. Bay Street (Canada's Wall Street), University, Spadina, and Bathurst are to the west of Yonge, Jarvis and Parliament to the east.

The main subway artery runs in an elongated U along Yonge Street and University Avenue, looping through Union Station, at the base of the U. The other line runs east-west along Bloor Street. Ticket costs for the subway, streetcars, and buses are $2 per ticket, $6.50 for a strip of five tickets, 13 for a strip of 10 tickets or $5 for a day pass which can be used after 9:30 a.m. Pick up a copy of the "Ride Guide" at subway entrances, or call the Toronto Transit Commission information line at 393-INFO between 7:00 a.m. and 11:30 p.m. daily.

Sightseeing Highlights

▲**Harbourfront**—Harbourfront is a combined recreation and shopping area that stretches from the foot of York Street west to Bathurst Street. Walk from Union Station down to the ferry docks next to the Harbour Castle Hotel and then go one block west. Harbourfront encompasses craft studies, art galleries, an antique market and the Queen's Quay Terminal shopping complex of trendy boutiques, and the whole area hums with activity in summer.

▲▲▲**CN Tower**—Toronto's most famous landmark provides a bird's eye view of the terrain for miles around. It's at 301 Front Street West, and you can get to it from the street or walk through the Skywalk from Union Station, a vast glass-encased walkway lined with shops on one side. The very tip of the tower is 553 meters (1,815 feet) high—the equivalent of 187 stories—and the observation level is about three-quarters of the way up. The elevators go up and down the outside of the tower and naturally have glass walls. The ride up or down takes 58 seconds. From the observation decks, you can look straight down through glass. Look for some of Toronto's more architecturally striking buildings, such as the wedding-cake-like Holiday Inn, the colorful new CBC building, and the Royal Bank Plaza—the one that glints gold in the sunlight. Several million dollars' worth of gold flakes are embedded in its windowpanes. The gold acts as an insulator, reducing heating and cooling costs. Entrance to the CN Tower observation level costs $12 for adults, $9 for seniors, and $6.50 for children aged four to 12. For information, or to make dining reservations at the Top of Toronto Revolving Restaurant, call 360-8500.

▲**The SkyDome**—The SkyDome, next door to the CN Tower, is billed as the only stadium in the world with a fully retractable roof. The 32-story-high roof opens and closes in about 20 minutes, at a cost of $500 per time. It's home to the Toronto Argonauts, Toronto's football team, as well as the Toronto Blue Jays baseball team. Seating is 53,000 for baseball, 54,000 for football and up to 64,000 for other events. The SkyDome took three years to build and cost $550 million. A guided tour, available when events schedules permit, includes a film on its construction and visits to a dressing room, the press box and a "Skybox." For information, call 341-3663. One-hour tours begin most days at 10:00 a.m.; the cost is $9 for adults and $6 for children and seniors.

Lodging
We're only here for a day and a half and it's a big city, so staying downtown makes particular sense. The trade-off is that it's generally more expensive, although even

downtown lodging comes in all price ranges, from budget to deluxe.

Expensive but noteworthy hotels include the grand old **Royal York Hotel** at 100 Front Street across from Union Station. The Royal York recently underwent a multi-million-dollar renovation and is looking better than ever. Room rates average $160-$200 for doubles; phone 368-2511 locally or 1-800-441-1414 toll-free. The **King Edward Hotel** at 37 King Street East, a relatively small, luxurious European-style hotel, has rooms from $160; phone (416) 863-9700. Seventy of the **SkyDome Hotel**'s 300-plus rooms, including 31 luxury suites, have stadium views. Rates begin at $109; Call 360-7100 locally or 1-800-441-1414 toll-free. The **Westin Harbour Castle** at 1 Harbour Square is right on the waterfront and has a revolving rooftop restaurant; for rates, phone (416) 869-1600 or 1-800-228-3000 toll-free.

More moderately priced downtown hotels include the **Quality Hotel** at 111 Lombard Street, between King and Queen Streets. Rates run from roughly $85 to $95. Phone 367-5555 locally or 1-800-4-CHOICE toll-free. The **Executive Inn** at 621 King Street West, the fashion district, has rates running around $75. Call (416) 362-7441. The **Strathcona** at 60 York Street, one block from the SkyDome, offers rooms ranging at $78 for a double. Call 363-3321 locally or 1-800-268-8304 toll-free.

There are also various motels off some of the major highways into Toronto. Off the QEW, for instance, **Motel 27** at 650 Evans Avenue offers comfortable rooms starting around $40 for a double. Take exit 138 or 139 from the QEW. The phone number is (416) 255-3481.

Toronto has several hotel accommodation services that will book a room for you in your preferred area and price range. Try **Accommodation Toronto** at (905) 629-3800 or **Econo-Lodging Services** at (416) 494-0541. Both services are free and offer economy, moderate, and deluxe hotels. If you're calling the province's toll-free tourist information line (1-800-ONTARIO), ask about reserving lodging in Toronto.

Bed and breakfast registries include **Bed and Breakfast Homes of Toronto**, P.O. Box 46093, College Park Post Office, 444 Yonge Street, Toronto, Ont., Canada M5B 2L8, (416) 363-6362; **A Downtown Toronto Association of Bed and Breakfast Guest Houses**, P.O. Box 190, Station B, Toronto, Ont., Canada M5T 2W1, (416) 977-6841; and **Metropolitan Bed and Breakfast of Toronto**, at (416) 964-2566. If you're thinking B&B, one particularly attractive area to stay in is The Beaches, a mere 10 minutes east of downtown but seemingly a world away. A former resort community whose summer cottages have been converted to permanent homes, The Beaches boasts a beach that runs along the shore of Lake Ontario, a two-mile long boardwalk along the beach, and, along Queen Street, trendy restaurants, cafés, bars, and boutiques. On weekends, The Beaches is a favorite place for brunch.

Camping

There are several campgrounds within 50 kilometers (about 30 miles) of Toronto. The closest is **Indian Line Tourist Campground** in Brampton, open from mid-May to mid-October. The phone number is (905) 678-1233. Alternatives include **Toronto West KOA Kampground** in Campbellville, open April to October, phone (905) 854-2495; the **Milton Heights Campground** in Milton at (905) 878-6781; **Grangeways Trailor Park** in Mount Albert, (905) 852-3260; **Ponderosa Campground**, also in Mount Albert, (905) 473-2607; **Glen Rouge Park** in Scarborough, (416) 392-2541; **Cedar Beach Park Ltd.** in Stouffeville, (905) 642-1700; and the **Heber Downs Conservation Area** in Whitby, (905) 655-3978.

Restaurants

There are more than 5,000, serving every variety of food imaginable. Here are just a few recommendations.

Ohh Kitchen serves Chinese food with entirely fresh ingredients, including Szechuan snapper or melon shrimp. It's at 23 Baldwin, phone 977-1255. Another widely recommended French restaurant is **Encore SVP**, serving moderate to expensive seafood, grilled meats, and other Continental dishes at 4 Front Street East; call 947-0655. For steak and seafood, try **The Senator**, a retro-style diner and steakhouse at 249 Victoria Street, phone 364-7517.

The **Bofinger Brasserie** is a tavern-style place at 1507 Yonge Street, 923-2300. **North 44** serves a wide selection of dishes described as "new-world Italian with Californian-Asian undertones" at 2537 Yonge Street, 487-4897. The menu at **Oliver's**, a Mediterranean-style bistro at 2433 Yonge Street is likewise wide in scope, but at budget prices; call 485-8047. **Bemelmans** at 83 Bloor Street West also serves a wide selection; phone 960-0306.

Whitlock's Restaurant at 1961 Queen Street East in The Beaches serves a mix of Continental and Canadian dishes at moderate prices; call 691-8784. The **Kensington Kitchen** at 124 Harbord Street is a popular place with a moderately priced menu and a rooftop patio that gets crowded in summer; call 961-3404.

Meyer's Deli at 69 Yorkville serves up deli food and jazz; call 960-4780. Another branch, **Meyer's Bar & Deli**, is at 185 King Street West downtown, 593-4190. Also downtown, **Shopsy's Deli & Restaurant** at 33 Yonge Street features 1930s decor and has been a Toronto institution for some 70 years; phone 365-3333. **Movenpick** is a trendy cafeteria-style establishment whose decor makes it unlike any other cafeteria you've ever seen. It serves reasonably good food at reasonable prices, but you'll have to line up. It's at 165 York Street.

Baralo at 193 Carleton serves good Italian food in the moderate to upper price range; call 961-4747. **Pronto Ristorante** at 692 Mount Pleasant is a moderately priced Italian restaurant; call 486-1111. **La Grolla** at 195 Merton is another Italian restaurant in the mid-price range; call 489-7227. For Italian nouveau cuisine at higher prices, try **Centro Grill & Wine Bar** at 2472 Yonge Street, 483-2211.

Ouzeri is a lively Greek restaurant at 500a Danforth Avenue; phone 778-0500. **Penelope Restaurant** at 33 Yonge Street is another Greek place, with prices running from moderate to expensive; call 947-1159.

The **Hunan Palace** at 412 Spadina Avenue is one of the more popular Chinese restaurants in Chinatown; call 593-9831. Also in Chinatown, try **Champion House** at 480 Dundas Street West, 977-8282.

Bamboo is a Caribbean place that's a good bet for lunch and also has entertainment in the evenings. It's at 312 Queen Street West, 593-5771.

Nightlife
The first thing to know about the nightlife in Toronto is that the bars shut at 1:00 a.m., which means last call is at 12:30 a.m. A tram-ride away from the center of the city, **The Beaches** at the eastern end of Queen Street East is a festive mix of stately homes, beach, boardwalk, bars, and boutiques. The area is a favorite for people-watching, and on weekend nights the bars are hopping. The **Queen Street West** area is for the younger crowd, while **Yorkville**'s bars attract an older, wealthier crowd. There is lots of live music in Toronto; for up-to-date listings, check one of Toronto's three daily newspapers (*The Toronto Star*, *The Globe & Mail* or *The Toronto Sun*) or pick up a copy of *Now* or *Eye*, both weekly news and entertainment guides distributed free.

Toronto's busy theater community has received a boost in recent years thanks to major restorations of several old theater buildings and the opening of a new venue. The Pantages Theater, which had been divided into a multi-screen theatre, was restored to its original opulence at a cost of $20 million. The Elgin and Winter Garden complex, one of the few remaining "stacked" theaters (with one theater on top of the other), has also been restored. The Elgin is a large velvet-and-gilt theater, while the Winter Garden upstairs features tree trunks for pillars and foliage on the ceiling. The Royal Alexandra Theater frequently offers blockbluster productions like *Phantom of the Opera*. A new entry on the theater scene, opened in 1993, is the Princess of Wales Theater, a 2,000-seat venue built especially for *Miss Saigon* and owned by the same family that owns the Royal Alexandra. Many other, smaller

theaters offer innovative performances of classical, contemporary, and Canadian plays. The city's theater district
lies east of Union Station, girded by Front, Jarvis, King,
and Parliament streets. For discounts on same-day theater
tickets, try the T.O. Tix booth outside the Eaton Centre at
Yonge and Dundas streets. For concerts and musicals, Roy
Thomson Hall is a shimmering circular building on the
outside, while the interior has state-of-the-art acoustics
and a lobby that encircles the concert hall. It is home to
the Toronto Symphony.

Shopping

Toronto is one of those cities where you really could shop
'til you drop. The **Eaton Centre** on Yonge Street between
Queen or Dundas has more than 350 boutiques, services,
and restaurants on five levels, anchored by two department stores, Eaton's and The Bay. The nearest subway
stops are Dundas or Queen. **Queen's Quay Terminal** on
the waterfront is a renovated landmark building with
some 100 specialty boutiques and restaurants that are
open seven days a week. The nearest subway stop is
Union. If money is no object, check out the **Yorkville-
Bloor** area, probably the most exclusive shopping area in
the city. Yorkville was a rundown hippie haven 25 years
ago, the Toronto equivalent to San Francisco's Haight-
Ashbury at its peak; now it's home to tony shopping
centres like **Hazelton Lanes** and the **Holt Renfrew Centre**
(Holt Renfrew being a Canadian-owned chain of extremely
upscale clothing stores). The nearest subway stop is Bay.
To soak up some atmosphere while shopping, visit the
Kensington Market, a multi-ethnic bazaar of foodstuffs,
clothes and streets vendors in a hectically busy Chinatown
enclave of small streets west of Spadina and south of
College. The nearest subway stops are St. Patrick and
Queen's Park. **Queen Street West**, Toronto's answer to
Greenwich Village, is lined with funky shops, offbeat
restaurants, and trendy bars. MuchMusic, the Canadian
equivalent of MTV, is housed here in a building that's
hard to miss. You can look through large street-level win-

dows directly into the studio, and an old City TV news car literally juts out of the side of the building at about the third-story level. (MuchMusic is owned by the same people who own City TV.) During the campaign leading up to the national referendum on the constitution in 1992, there was a big billboard on Queen Street West that said: *125 Reasons for One Canada—The Queen already has enough breakups on her hands.* The nearest subway stop to this area is Queen.

Helpful Hints

Year-round, the Metropolitan Toronto Convention & Visitors Association operates a Visitor Information Centre on Yonge Street south of Dundas, outside the Eaton Centre. Seasonal visitor information centres are located throughout Toronto from late May to Labor Day. For travellers coming in to Toronto on Highway 401, there is a computerized tourist information center, the Shell Info Centre, on the 401 west of Winston Churchill Boulevard; or contact the association's main office at Queen's Quay Terminal at Harbourfront, 207 Queens Quay West, P. O. Box 126, Toronto, Ont., Canada M5J 1A7, (416) 203-2500. The toll-free tourist information line is 1-800-363-1990. Ontario Travel has a travel centre on level two in the Eaton Centre.

Stratford

The main itinerary doesn't leave time for Stratford, a pretty town 90 minutes west of Toronto that's famous for its annual Shakespearean summer theater festival. If you include Stratford on your itinerary, put aside at least 24 hours and plan to take in a play, which is what Stratford is all about. Book both lodging and theater tickets well ahead. Stratford is an extremely popular destination; its permanent population of 28,000 swells by half-a-million visitors during the Stratford Shakespearean Festival, which runs from May to November each year.

To get there from Toronto, take Highway 401 West to Kitchener and turn onto Highway 8, which runs northeast from the 401. Stay on Highway 8 until you get to Stratford.

To get there from the Niagara Peninsula, get off the QEW
onto Highway 403 between Hamilton and Burlington and
after about six kilometers (four miles) on the 403, turn
onto Highway 6, which cuts north to Highway 401. Head
west on the 401 until you get to Highway 8. The driving
distance is about 150 kilometers (90 miles) from Toronto
and slightly longer from Niagara-on-the-Lake.

Stratford, established as a village in 1854, was named
Stratford because its setting reminded settlers of Statford-
upon-Avon in England. And yes, the river that runs
through Stratford, Ontario, is the Avon. Stratford was initially an agricultural center, then a railway center until
Canadian National Railways announced in 1953 it was
closing down its local shop. With the economy desperately
in need of a boost, it was decided it would be a great
location for a theater festival.

Each year the festival offers about a dozen plays on its
three stages, ranging from the Bard to contemporary
works. Ticket prices range from about $35 to $50. Along
with the festival plays, there is a variety of theater-related
activities available, including backstage tours and post-
performance discussions with actors and actresses.

Aside from the festival, the tranquil and extremely pretty
town of Stratford has lovely parks all along the edge of
the Avon River, dotted with gardens and picnic tables.
Picnicking is made ridiculously easy by local take-out
places specializing in picnics-to-go. All summer, majestic
swans float on the water and wander the parks (don't get
too close; they can be agressive). Pathways lead from the
river's edge to the Victorian downtown area, where an
abundance of small shops along York and neighboring
streets offer everything from antiques and collectibles to
souvenirs and books.

Similarly, there are restaurants to suit most tastes and
budgets, from fast-food to pub fare to seafood. For lodging, B&B is big in Stratford, although there are also hotels
and motels. Again, there are places to suit most budgets,
but it must be said that Stratford is so popular that its
room rates tend to be on the high side.

Accommodations and theater tickets must be booked well ahead—two to three months in advance, especially for weekend stays, if you'll be there in July or August. Even in spring and autumn, you should reserve two to three weeks ahead.

To make visiting easier, call Tourism Stratford's toll-free number for tourist information, lodging reservations, and festival tickets. The number is 1-800-561-SWAN, or 271-5140 locally. A comprehensive guide to the city is sent out in the mail with your theatre tickets.

About 10 kilometers (6 miles) east of Stratford on Highway 8, a hamlet called Shakespeare boasts 10 antique shops.

TORONTO

Escape this morning to the Toronto Islands, small oases that sit in the harbor practically within shouting distance of the downtown waterfront but seem a world away from the city bustle. Follow up with lunch and a wander through the heart of downtown, but remember to warm up your shopping muscles first. In the afternoon, absorb some culture and history by visiting the Royal Ontario Museum, the Bata Shoe Museum—strange though it may sound—and Casa Loma, a massive castle built at great cost by a wealthy entrepreneur who later had to give it up because, curiously, he couldn't afford the taxes.

Suggested Schedule

9:00 a.m.	Catch a ferry to Ward's Island and wander at will.
11:00 a.m.	Shop and explore downtown; check out the Eaton Centre, Chinatown, Kensington Market, and the Art Gallery of Ontario, pausing en route for lunch.
2:00 p.m.	Stop in at the Royal Ontario Museum to see the bat cave and the dinosaurs.
3:00 p.m.	Visit the nearby Bata Shoe Museum.
4:00 p.m.	Explore Casa Loma, a landmark castle on a hill.

Sightseeing Highlights
▲▲Ward's Island—A series of interconnected islands in Toronto Harbour, the Toronto Islands are accessible by ferry year-round. The ferry terminal is next to the Harbour Castle Hotel; round-trip fares are $3 for adults,$1.50 for students and seniors, and $1 for kids under 15. Departures are frequent. (Call 392-8193 for ferry information.) On the island chain's western tip, at Hanlan's Point, the Toronto Island Airport serves commercial and private flights. Centre Island with its small amusement park, picnic grounds, and bicycle rentals, is the most popular destin-

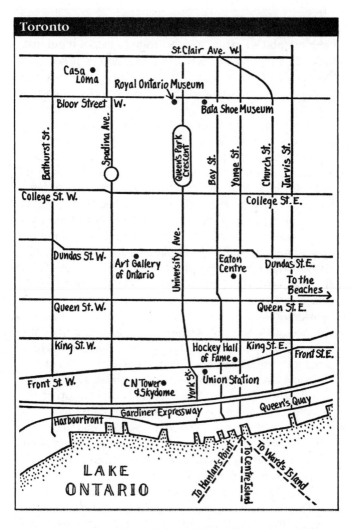

ation among the three islands. My favorite spot is the
charming Ward's Island at the eastern end of the islands.
It remains relatively uncrowded even on summer weekends. About 300 people live in a tiny community of tiny
old houses on Ward's Island. As you get off the ferry,
you'll see small houses nestled in a clump to the left, dis-
sected by tiny streets that are actually more like pathways
but have street names. Some of the houses look pretty

rundown, but in spring, summer and fall there is so much greenery and so many flowers around most of them that they still look lovely. There is a beach and boardwalk on the other side of the island. Ward's Island also has lots of parkland and picnic tables, and ducks wandering around at will. It's like being in another world, yet just across the water is a magnificent view of the heart of Toronto.

▲**Hockey Hall of Fame**—Back in the city, this new attraction will have hockey fans in heaven. It's billed as the world's most comprehensive collection of hockey artifacts, displays, and memorabilia. Both King and Union Stations are connected underground to the Hall of Fame, whose entrance is in the concourse level of BCE Palace (at the corner of Yonge and Front streets). Admission is $7.50 for adults and $5.50 for seniors and children. Call 360-7765 for more information.

▲▲**The Art Gallery of Ontario**—Take the subway to Queen or Dundas and browse through the Eaton Centre, Kensington Market, and Chinatown, all within walking distance of each other downtown. Art lovers, stop in at the Art Gallery of Ontario. At any given time, about 10 percent of the gallery's collection of 16,000 works of Canadian and international art is on exhibit. Highlights include a wealth of Canadian works by the Group of Seven and others, the Henry Moore Sculpture Center, and a collection of Inuit art. The AGO, as it's commonly called, is now the tenth largest public art gallery in North America following a massive renovation and expansion project; art and architecture critics alike lauded the results when the project was completed in 1993. The AGO is at 317 Dundas Street West, two blocks west of University Avenue; the nearest subway stop is St. Patrick. Admission is $7.50 for adults and $4 for seniors and children, except on Wednesday evenings, when admission is free. Call 977-0414 for current exhibition information.

▲▲▲**The Royal Ontario Museum**—Take the subway to Museum, the stop (logically enough) for the Royal Ontario Museum, one of the five most popular museums in North America. It's Canada's largest, home to an enormous variety of treasures. The most visited displays are the dinosaur hall and the bat cave, the latter being a dark, eerie, and quite fabulous exhibit in which the bats seem creepily alive. There is also a large gallery of life-sized animals, from musk ox and caribou to lions, tigers, and reptiles. All these exhibits are on the second floor. On the ground floor, the museum houses Chinese collections renowned for their range and quality. The third floor has a permanent display called *Caravans and Clipper Ships* which recounts the history of east-west trade, plus exhibits on the history of the Mediterranean world, from ancient Egypt to Islamic civilizations. There is a free self-guided audio tour. Regular hours are Tuesday to Sunday, 10:00 a.m. to 6:00 p.m., but it's open until 8:00 p.m. on Tuesday. Closed Mondays between Labor Day and May 20. For 24-hour recorded information, call 586-5551. The museum is at 100 Queen's Park. The entrance fee is $7 for adults, $4 for seniors and students, $3.50 for children, and $15 for families.

▲**The Bata Shoe Museum**—A shoe museum? How bizarre. I thought so too until I saw it. It has more than 450 shoes and related artifacts that provide remarkable insight into history. Although we rarely think about it, shoes are a personal artifact that reveal the owner's social status, habits, culture, and religion. The display spans 4,000 years, from platform boots worn by Elton John, cowboy boots worn by Robert Redford, and silver evening shoes worn by Elizabeth Taylor, back through to four-inch shoes worn by Chinese women after their feet were bound and ancient sandals worn by Australian Aborigines. As the display explains, the Aborigines were always barefoot except when it came time to execute someone. Because footprints were an identity giveaway, the executioner would wear sandals in order to remain anonymous. The shoe museum is at 131 Bloor Street West. That's its temporary site; the collection is eventually to be housed in a permanent site to be built at the University of Toronto. Opening hours are 11:00 a.m. to 6:00 p.m., Tuesday to Sunday, closed Mondays. Entrance is $3 for adults, $1 for seniors and students, and $6 for families. Call 924-7463 for information.

▲▲**Casa Loma**—Toronto's spectacular "castle on a hill"
was originally constructed as a private residence. Toronto
entrepreneur Sir Henry Pellatt built it as his dream home
between 1911 and 1914, importing craftsmen from Europe
to assist. With the economic downturn after the first World
War, Sir Henry found himself in arrears on his city taxes.
He was forced to turn the 98-room castle over to the City
of Toronto. The building is still owned by the city and
operated by the Kiwanis Club. The outstanding rooms
are the Conservatory on the main floor and, on the second floor, Lady Pellatt's Wedgewood-blue suite next door
to Sir Henry's suite. The shower in Sir Henry's bathroom
is pretty remarkable too. When first built, Casa Loma
was the only castle in the world to have an electrically-
operated elevator and an indoor swimming pool. The
pool is on the lower floor and was never actually completed, but original plans called for it to be surrounded
by cloisters, marble arches, and gold swans. The lower
floor also contains the entrance to the 450-meter (1,470-
foot) tunnel that connects the castle with the stables.
From the third floor of the castle there is access to some
of the towers above. Seeing everything takes at least 90
minutes. Entrance fees are $8 for adults and $4.50 for
seniors and children aged 6 to 16. Self-guided audio
tours are provided. Casa Loma is at 1 Austin Terrace, off
Spadina between Davenport and St. Clair Avenue West.
The nearest subway stop is Dupont. The box office is
open daily from 10:00 a.m. to 4:00 p.m., but you can
wander around until 5:00 p.m. Phone 923-1171.

▲**Neighborhoods**—Besides the neigborhoods already
cited (Chinatown, Kensington, Queen Street West, The
Beaches), consider strolling through **Cabbagetown**, a
trendy yuppified area replete with charming Victorian
houses; **Little Italy**, humming with trattorias, sidewalk
cafes and boutiques; **The Annex**, west of Yorkville on
Bloor Street, an area populated with students, writers and
artists and consquently featuring budget bookstores, specialty shops and cafes; and **High Park**, not so much a
neighborhood as a large oasis of rolling greenery located

still further west on Bloor Street. All these neighborhoods are pretty much in the downtown-midtown core of the city.

▲**Ontario Science Centre**—Consider a visit to the Ontario Science Centre, whose hands-on displays will entrance children and adults, science fans and neophytes alike. It's open daily at 770 Don Mills Road; phone 696-3127 for more information. Open daily 10:00 a.m. to 6:00 p.m. Admission is $7.50 for adults, $5.50 for youths, and $3 for children and seniors.

▲**Metro Toronto Zoo**—If you're with children, a visit to this highly rated zoo should keep them enthralled; it has more than 4,000 animals housed in eight tropical pavilions. The zoo is in Scarborough on Highway 401 at Meadowvale Road, 16 kilometers east of the Don Valley Parkway (exit 389 eastbound, exit 392 westbound). Call 392-5900 for information. Open daily, mid-May to Labor Day, from 9:00 a.m. to 7:00 p.m. Admission is $9.75 for adults, $7 for youths age 12 to 17 and seniors, and $5 for children age 5 to 11.

▲**Canada's Wonderland**—Another good possibility if you're with children, Canada's Wonderland, located just north of Toronto, features more than 50 rides and a waterslide theme area, plus live shows and assorted other attractions. Call (905) 832-7000 for information. Open 10:00 a.m. to 10:00 p.m. daily, late May to late September. A day pass covering all rides costs $28.95 for ages 7 and up, $14.45 for children under age 7 and seniors.

▲**McMichael Canadian Art Collection**—One art gallery that's virtually a must-see, even though it isn't in central Toronto, McMichael Canadian Art Collection in nearby Kleinburg features an impressive collection of works by the Group of Seven artists, the most famous landscape painters in Canada, with paintings by other Canadian artists and works by Indian and Inuit artists as wel. The McMichael is in a woodland setting in Kleinberg, about half an hour north of downtown Toronto by car. Head up the Don Valley Parkway, which runs between the QEW and the 401 and turns into Highway 404 after it crosses

the 401. Take Major Mackenzie Drive off the 404 and follow the signs. Admission is $6 for adults, $3 for students
and seniors, and $13 for families. Seniors get in free on
Wednesdays. Open hours are 10:00 a.m. to 5:00 p.m. daily
from April 1 to October 31 and 10:00 a.m. to 4:30 p.m.
Tuesday through Sunday the rest of the year. Phone
893-1121 for information.

Helpful Hints
There are all manner of festivals and events in Toronto
each year, but the most fun is **Caribana**, a two-week
blowout in late July during which Torontonians uncharac-
teristically let down their hair. Toronto's 300,000-strong
West Indian community includes immigrants from all 25
Caribbean islands, and the carnival-like Caribana festival
now draws more than a million visitors to the city each
summer. Its highlight is a parade, usually held on Aug. 1.

For more traditional family-style entertainment, consider
visiting the city during the last couple of weeks of August,
when the annual **Canadian National Exhibition** takes
place at the Canadian National Exhibition Grounds west of
downtown. Amusement-park rides are the major attraction, but there are also lots of exhibits.

KINGSTON, GANANOQUE, AND THE THOUSAND ISLANDS

The Thousand Islands, a necklace of islands scattered along 80 kilometers (50 miles) of the St. Lawrence River from Kingston to Brockville, make for one of the most scenic stretches in all of Ontario. Picturesque, historic Kingston is less than three hours from Toronto by road, and Gananoque, the Canadian gateway to the Thousand Islands, is about 20 minutes farther on. A visit to Fort Henry, lunch in Kingston, a drive along the Thousand Islands Parkway, and a cruise through the Thousand Islands fill out the day. Wierdly fascinating Boldt Castle can be visited during the cruise. An optional sidetrip takes you to see the murals of Athens.

Suggested Schedule

8:00 a.m.	Depart Toronto early.
11:00 a.m.	Arrive Kingston, visit Fort Henry, wander along the Kingston waterfront, or take a tram tour of town.
1:00 p.m.	Lunch.
2:00 p.m.	Cruise the Thousands Islands out of Kingston, Gananoque, Ivy Lea Village, or Brockville.
5:30 p.m.	Drive along the Thousand Islands Parkway, making a short sidetrip to Athens if there's time, and thence to Ottawa.

Driving Route: Toronto to Ottawa (450 km/270 miles)
Take Highway 401 East from Toronto and stay on it as far as Kingston. It's about 260 kilometers (158 miles), or two-and-a-half-hours of boring driving. To break it up, you might want to stop at the Big Apple, a wonderfully ticky-tacky souvenir shop-restaurant-petting zoo at Exit 497 off the 401, near Colborne, about midway between Toronto and Kingston. When I was last there, they had llamas and

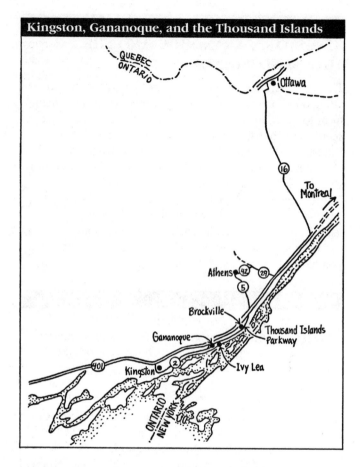

Kingston, Gananoque, and the Thousand Islands

goats in the petting zoo. You can't miss it; watch for the 10-meter-high (32 feet) "apple" from the highway.

In Kingston, take exit 623 and follow Highway 15 south to Fort Henry. If you're willing to forgo seeing Boldt Castle up close, you can take a Thousand Islands cruise from the Kingston waterfront. Otherwise, take Highway 2 from Kingston to Gananoque. Past Gananoque, at interchange 107, follow the signs for the Thousand Islands Parkway. This route winds for about 40 kilometers (24 miles) along the riverbank, and you'll see more of the islands. There are also cruises available from Ivy Lea Village, about 10 minutes east of Gananoque on the parkway, and from Brockville at the eastern end of the islands.

To see the Athens murals, turn off the Thousand Islands Parkway on the road towards Mallorytown (not Mallorytown Landing) and follow it past Mallorytown to Caintown to Athens. Coming back to the 401, take Highway 29, a shorter route. Ottawa is about an hour away.

Otherwise, follow the parkway to its end at exit 685 of the 401. Continue east on the 401 and just before Prescott, take Highway 16 north into Ottawa.

Sightseeing Highlights

▲▲▲**Kingston**—One-time capital of Canada and one of its oldest settlements, this attractive city on the banks of the St. Lawrence River is filled with 150-year-old buildings and cobblestone lanes that lead to cafés and restaurants. It has both a university—Queen's—and more penitentiaries than anywhere else in Canada. (Not normally something the tourism agencies like to talk about, but now the new Kingston Penitentiary Museum across from the brooding Kingston Penitentiary houses a collection of rare photographs, inmate hobbycrafts, homemade weapons, and escape paraphenalia.) The university presence makes for some good bookstores and a lively nightlife, and Kingston is well worth a few days if you have the time. If not, the best bet is to head for the central square on Ontario Street across from City Hall and take a Confederation Tour Train ride. The 50-minute trip, operating throughout the summer, takes in Queen's, Royal Military College, Fort Henry, the Marine Museum, and Bellevue House, an early home of Sir John A. Macdonald, Canada's first prime minister. If you have any questions, the tourist information center across from City Hall has all manner of information.

▲▲**Fort Henry**—The most famous landmark in Kingston is Fort Henry, the so-called Citadel of Upper Canada. It was constructed during the War of 1812 on a point of land overlooking the confluence of Lake Ontario and the St. Lawrence. Its guns have never fired a shot in anger. Nowadays the Fort Henry Guard recreates drills and marches for the public. The fort opens daily at 10:00 a.m., with the first tour departing at 10:15 a.m. There are tours from mid-May to mid-October, departing every 15 minutes at the height of the season. They last about an hour.

Admission is $9 for adults, $5 for seniors, $5.85 for students, and $3.80 for children aged 6 to 12.

▲▲▲**Thousand Islands**—There are, in fact, 1,865 islands—or at least that's one figure bandied about. To be classified as an island, a piece of land here must have two trees and six square feet of soil. Some—hundreds of them—are indeed that small, and many others are just large enough to hold a small house, a couple of trees and a dock. Still others, particularly along so-called Millionaire's Row, boast mansions or even castles. Most are privately owned. On a steamer from Kingston to Montreal in 1842, Charles Dickens described the scene as "a picture fraught with uncommon interest and pleasure." Indeed. The best way to see them is to take a cruise, offered from Kingston, Gananoque (pronounced ga-na-naw-quai), or Ivy Lea Village from May to October. The Canada-U.S. border cuts right through the Thousand Islands, so part of the time on the cruise you're in the U.S. Canadian and United States citizens need proper I.D., while citizens of other countries need passports and, if they're visiting Boldt Island, a U.S. visa.

From Kingston, **1000 Islands Cruises** offers three-hour trips from #1 Brock Street on the waterfront, opposite city hall. Rates are around $15.95 for adults and $5.60 for kids aged 4 to 12. Call (613) 549-5544 or 549-5545. These cruises do not go near Boldt Castle. If you want to see the castle, leave from Gananoque or Ivy Lea instead. From Gananoque, **Gananoque Boat Line** offers regular three-hour cruises at $15 for adults and $6 for children aged 7 to 12. Phone (613) 382-2146. These cruises feature an unlimited stop at Boldt Castle, allowing you to get off there, spend as long as you like and take the next boat back. From Ivy Lea Village, about 11 kilometers (seven miles) east of Gananoque, there are 90-minute cruises that also include stopovers at Boldt Castle. This cruise is the best bet if you're pressed for time. Phone **Ivy Lea 1000 Islands Boat Tours** at (613) 659-2293. From Brockville at the eastern end of the Thousand Islands, Upper Canada Steamboats offers a three-and-a-half-hour cruise that includes a view of Boldt castle. Call (613) 345-6454 or 1-800-267-8123 toll-free.

▲▲▲**Boldt Castle**—Boldt Castle, on Heart Island on the New York State side of the islands, is a massive monument to a monumental kind of love. In 1900, George Boldt, millionaire proprietor of the Waldorf Astoria hotel in New York City, decided to build a full-sized replica of a Rhineland Castle for his wife, Louise. He bought heart-shaped Hart Island and renamed it Heart Island. Work was well under way on 11 buildings, with over US$2.5 million invested in construction and furnishing costs, when Louise died suddenly in 1904. Grief-stricken, George Boldt ordered construction halted immediately, in mid-hammer-strike, and for decades thereafter the castle was left open to the elements and to any people who cared to stop at the island. Its interior walls and even some of the ceilings are covered with graffiti. In 1977, the Thousand Island Bridge Authority assumed ownership of the badly deteriorated castle, began charging visitors to see the place, using all net revenues to gradually restore the castle. The idea is not to make it what it would have been, but to bring it back to the point where it was when the construction workers laid down their tools. The exteriors of most of the buildings have been largely restored, and they look magnificent from the outside. Inside is another story, and it's the contrast that's so compelling. One of the most remarkable buildings is the Alster Tower, or the Play House, as the Boldts called it. They actually lived in this whimsical mini-castle for a time, and once it's fully restored, complete with furnishings, it promises to be an amazing place. The architecture is so eccentric it defies description; go in, wander around, and see for yourself. Admission to Boldt Castle, which is not included in cruise prices, is US$3.25 for adults and US$1.75 for children aged 6 to 12. Call 1-800-8-ISLAND for more information.

▲**Athens Murals**—Athens is a tiny town about 25 minutes north of Highway 401; if you have time, make this side trip. Scattered throughout Athens are a number of large, eye-catching murals. Just park on the main street and wander. One mural is of the main street in the last century, another of a park scene. Another—on the side of the fire-department building—depicts the worst thing that ever happened in Athens, which was a big fire that the new truck couldn't fight because the hose was too short. A local hero climbed down a well within yards of the flaming building and passed up buckets of water, saving the day. My personal favorite is the mural that includes a depiction of the artist painting it.

Lodging

At the high end of Ottawa's accommodations spectrum, room rates at several hotels begin around $120 a night for a double, but they also periodically offer specials or weekend rates. The **Chateau Laurier** at 1 Rideau Street, down a slope from Parliament Hill, is a landmark in itself; phone 241-1414 locally or 1-800-441-1414 toll-free. Other central hotels/include the luxury **Westin Hotel Ottawa** next to the Rideau Centre ($155 to $165, 560-7000 locally or 1-800-228-3000 toll-free); **Minto Place Suite Hotel** at 433 Laurier Avenue West (regular $120 and up, special rates $93 and up, 232-2200 locally, 1-800-267-3377 from Ontario and Quebec, 1-800-267-3377 from elsewhere in North America); **Quality Hotel** at 290 Rideau Street (from $69 a night, 789-7511 locally or 1-800-268-6116 toll-free); and **Holiday Inn Market Square** at 350 Dalhousie in the Byward Market ($125 a night, 241-1000 locally or 1-800-465-4329 toll-free). The grand old **Lord Elgin Hotel** at 100 Elgin Street has lately been renovated and offers room rates starting at $81; call (613) 235-3333 or 1-800-267-4298 toll-free.

The Doral Inn, at 486 Albert Street near Bay Street, is not right downtown but is central enough and, being both small and relatively inexpensive, worth checking out. Regular rates for two begin at $69, special rates at $65. Call 230-8055 locally or 1-800-26-DORAL toll-free.

For a rather eerie experience, try the **Ottawa International Hostel** at 75 Nicholas. It served as the Nicholas Street Jail for more than 100 years before being converted into a hostel. Accommodation is provided in the refurbished cells. Call (613) 235-2595 for reservations or just for a tour of the place.

The Visitor Information Centre at the National Arts Centre runs a free summertime booking service for hotels, motels, and bed & breakfasts; call (613) 237-5158 or 1-800-465-1867 toll-free. You can also reserve at selected hotels through Ontario's toll-free tourist information line, 1-800-ONTARIO.

The local B&B referral service, **Ottawa Bed and Breakfast**, is at 488 Cooper, Ottawa, Ont., Canada K1R 5H9, (613) 563-0161 or 1-800-461-7889 toll-free. Singles begin around $40 a night, doubles around $50.

The Ottawa Visitor Guide, put out by the Ottawa Tourism and Convention Authority and the National Capital Commission, has pages of listings of hotels, motels, B&Bs, inns, guesthouses and campgrounds.

Camping
Of four National Capital Commission campgrounds in the area, **Lac Philippe Family Campground** in Gatineau has the most facilities. The rate per site is $16. You can make reservations by mail from early April by writing to NCC Campgrounds, 161 Laurier Avenue West, Ottawa, Ont., Canada K1P 6J6, and by telephone after early June by calling (819) 456-3016.

Helpful Hints
The cruise from Ivy Lea is the best bet for seeing the most in the least amount of time, since it takes in Boldt Castle.

The Festival of the Islands is an annual event centered in Gananoque that runs for 10 days in the middle of August. Waterfront fireworks, sound-and-light shows, children's concerts, period costumes and displays and power boat races are just some of the dozens of activities offered.

Kingston, too, now has an annual festival of music, comedy, and drama that takes place at the Grand Theater almost nightly in July and August. To find out what's on, call (613) 546-4465.

For more information on the Thousand Islands, contact the Greater Kingston Tourist Information Office, 209 Ontario St., Kingston, Ont., Canada K7L 2Z1, (613) 548-4415; the Gananoque & Area Chamber of Commerce, 2 King Street East, Gananoque, Ont., Canada K7G 1E6, (613) 382-3250 or 1-800-561-1595 toll-free; or, for information on the entire area, call 1-800-567-EAST toll-free.

OTTAWA

Twenty years ago a federal cabinet minister was heard to declare that "the best thing about Ottawa is the train to Montreal." Some people may still feel that way, but in truth the city has changed for the better since then, with improved dining, shopping, and nightlife. Several new major attractions have opened in the last few years, notably the National Gallery of Canada and the Canadian Museum of Civilization. Also new to Ottawa is a National Hockey League team, the Senators.

Suggested Schedule

9:00 a.m.	Parliament Hill. Get in on the first tour of the day.
10:30 a.m.	The National Gallery of Canada.
12:30 p.m.	Lunch.
1:30 p.m.	Stop in at the Canadian Museum of Caricature and then stroll the Byward Market.
3:30 p.m.	Cross the river to the Civilization Museum in Hull.
5:30 p.m.	Back to Ottawa for a stroll or boat ride down the Rideau Canal before or after dinner.

Ottawa

Ottawa wasn't always a government town. After the first Europeans arrived in the area in 1613 in the form of French explorer Samuel de Champlain and his group, it became a trading center for whites and natives because of its location at the confluence of the Ottawa, Rideau, and Gatineau Rivers. By the 1800s Ottawa and Hull, the settlement across the river, were brawling lumber towns. In 1857, Queen Victoria named Ottawa the capital of the United Provinces of Canada, chiefly because it was centrally located and politically acceptable to both Canada

East and Canada West. Or, as Sir Edmund Head, then governor general, put it, "I believe that the least objectionable place is the city of Ottawa. Every city is jealous of every other city except Ottawa."

With its miles of bicycle paths, generous amounts of green space and the Rideau Canal snaking lazily through its heart, Ottawa is one of the prettiest capital cities anywhere. It reaches a picturesque peak during April and May, when millions of tulips burst into glorious blossom all over the capital region. During the Second World War, the Dutch royal family fled Holland and sought shelter in Ottawa. While there, then-Princess Juliana gave birth to Princess Margriet, but a problem arose because Dutch royalty must be born on Dutch soil, so the hospital room was declared to be part of the Netherlands. Every year since the end of the war, the grateful people of the Netherlands have shipped 10,000 tulip bulbs over to Ottawa.

It must also be noted that Ottawa is the coldest national capital in the Western world (Ulan Bator, Mongolia, holds the world record). The pain of making it through those snowy, subdued months is eased by Winterlude, an annual 10-day February fete that draws a million people a year. During Winterlude, locals and visitors alike throw themselves into winter sports, chief among them skating on the Rideau Canal, transformed each winter into the world's longest skating rink—7.8 kilometers (almost 5 miles) long.

Summer is deliciously warm, while autumn is the best time to check out Gatineau Park, a vast natural reserve of lakes and forests behind Hull.

Getting Around
With a population of 304,000, Ottawa boasts the prime advantage of a small city: the major hotels, most noteworthy sights and best shopping and dining are virtually all in the downtown area. Arriving from Ogdensburg, Highway 16 becomes Preston Street as you get into Ottawa. Follow it to Somerset and turn right. Follow Somerset all the way down to Elgin and turn left. A few blocks later you're at Confederation Square, the heart of the city. Confederation

Ottawa

① Parliament Hill
② National Gallery
③ War Museum
④ Royal Canadian Mint
⑤ Canadian Museum of Caricature
⑥ Canadian Museum of Contemporary Photography
⑦ National Arts Center
⑧ Nature Museum

Square is actually a triangular piece of land rimmed by Parliament Hill and the stately Chateau Laurier hotel, the National Arts Center, Ottawa's showcase for performing arts, and the Sparks Street Mall.

The Byward Market, a lively area of shops, bars and restaurants, and the Rideau Centre, Ottawa's largest shopping mall (with some 230 boutiques), lie below the Chateau Laurier, while the National Gallery of Canada is down Sussex Drive behind the hotel. Leave your car at the hotel and get around on foot or on city buses. Weekdays, riding OC Transpo buses costs $2.10 in the peak periods between 6:00 and 8:30 a.m. and 3:00 to 5:30 p.m. The rest of the time, a single fare is $1.60. For more information, contact the OC Transpo offices at 294 Albert Street, or phone (613) 741-4370.

Sightseeing Highlights

▲▲▲**Parliament Hill**—In Ottawa, the nation's capital, you simply must visit the Parliament buildings, which stand on a cliff overlooking the Ottawa River. In season, you should book same-day free tours through Infotent on Parliament Hill. It operates from 9:00 a.m. to 5:00 p.m. from May 17 to June 30; 9:00 a.m. to 9:00 p.m. weekdays, and 9:00 a.m. to 6:00 p.m. weekends from July 1 to 31; 9:00 a.m. to 8:30 p.m weekdays, and 9:00 a.m. to 6:00 p.m. weekends from August 1 to September 7. It's closed on July 1, Canada Day. The rest of the year, free tours are offered daily except on Christmas and New Year's. The tours begin at the main entrance and last from 30 to 45 minutes. After each tour except for the final one of the day, visitors are free to take the elevator to the observation deck of the Peace Tower, the central tower that rises 92 meters (300 feet) over Parliament Hill. When Parliament is in session, visitors may obtain tickets to sit in the public galleries of the Senate and the House of Commons to listen to debate. Call (613) 992-4793 for information about Commons sittings.

▲**Changing of the Guard**—If you're on Parliament Hill when it happens, fine. Otherwise don't sweat it. The Changing of the Guard takes place at 10:00 a.m. daily, weather permitting, from June 22 to August 30.

▲▲▲**The National Gallery of Canada**—A luminous structure of glass and granite, the National Gallery rises from a promotory about a mile downstream from the Parliament buildings. Prominent Canadian architect Moshe Safdie broke up the building by creating a series of smaller pavilions to house the various permanent collections and temporary exhibits, including what's billed as the world's most comprehensive collection of Canadian art. One standout permanent exhibit is the reconstructed interior of the Rideau Street Chapel, with its neo-gothic fan-vaulted ceiling. Public tours are offered daily, at 11:00 a.m. and 2:00 p.m. There are a bookstore, a gift shop, and two restaurants. Admission to the permanent collection is free. From May 1 until after Labor Day, hours are 10:00 a.m. to 8:00 p.m. on Thursdays and 10:00 a.m. to 6:00 p.m. the rest of the week. Winter hours are 10:00 a.m. to 5:00 p.m. except on Thursdays, when the art gallery stays open until 8:00 p.m., and Mondays, when it's closed. The National Gallery is at 380 Sussex Drive; phone (613) 990-1985 for more information.

▲**Canadian Museum of Caricature**—It has cartoons and caricatures spanning three centuries of Canadian history, but most of the exhibit dates from the 1950s to the present. It will (hopefully) make you laugh, and admission is free. It's open 10:00 a.m. to 6:00 p.m. Saturday to Tuesday and from 10:00 a.m. to 8:00 p.m. Wednesday to Friday. It's at 136 St. Patrick Street at Sussex Drive. Call (613) 995-3145.

▲▲▲**Byward Market**—This formerly seedy section of town is now a quirky combination of pricey boutiques and second-hand stores, food markets and Yuppie bistros. The Market, as locals call it, is the oldest part of Ottawa; the city's first houses and taverns went up there, in what was then called Lower Town, 150 years ago. Over the last 25 years the six-square-block area has been fully restored. But part of the Market has remained unchanged—there are still meat, fish, poultry, cheese and fresh produce shops there, and they still have the freshest food and best prices in town. In summer, farmers set up outdoor stalls selling fruit, vegetables, and flowers. Ottawans do their marketing there in droves on weekends. There are also pubs, wine bars, live-music bars, French bistros, health-food cafés, and restaurants. A takeout stand called Hooker's at the corner of William and York serves beaver tails—paddle-shaped yeasty dough, deep-fried. Sprinkle cinnamon and sugar on the puffy, soft confection and enjoy.

▲▲▲**The Canadian Museum of Civilization**—This massive complex houses a world of wonders, including a unique, convertible Imax-Omnimax theater and a History Hall featuring life-size buildings that represent historic Canadian scenes. For kids, there is a Children's Museum with hands-on activities designed to impart information about other cultures. Interactive computer terminals are located throughout the museum, allowing visitors to learn more about each exhibit. The museum is at 100 rue Laurier in Hull, housed in a futuristic, undulating building across the Ottawa River from Parliament Hill. Museum admission is $4.50 for adults, $3 for youths and seniors, and free for children 15 and under. Admission to the Imax-Omnimax theater, known as Cineplus, is $7 for adults and $5 for seniors, youths, and kids. Admission to both museum and theater is $11 for adults, $7 for youths and seniors, and $5 for children 15 and under. The museum is open daily except in winter, when it closes on Mondays. Hours are 9:00 a.m. to 8:00 p.m. on Thursdays and, depending on the season, 9:00 a.m. to 6:00 p.m. the rest of the week. Phone (819) 776-7000.

▲▲▲**Rideau Canal Promenade**—This is a particularly scenic walk in a city filled with scenic walkways. The canal was designed and built after the War of 1812 to provide a protected military supply route from Montreal to the Great Lakes. It runs for 202 kilometers (121 miles) between the Ottawa River and Lake Ontario at Kingston. The part that goes through Ottawa has a promenade running along nearly eight kilometers (five miles) through downtown and beyond. Start next to Confederation Square and wander at will, or take a boat ride. Call Paul's Boat Lines at (613) 225-6781 for information. Boat tours depart from near the National Arts Centre.

▲**The Canadian Museum of Contemporary Photography**—Canada's first photography museum opened in 1992 and houses an impressive collection of some 158,000 images (not all on display at one time!). It also has a boutique that should delight photo buffs. It's incredibly easy to find at 1 Rideau Canal, between the Parliament Buildings and the Chateau Laurier. In summer, open daily from 11:00 a.m. to 5:00 p.m., except Wednesday, when the hours are 4:00 to 8:00 p.m., and Thursday, when the hours are 11:00 a.m. to 8:00 p.m. Hours are shorter the rest of the year. Admission is free. Call 990-8257 for information.

▲**National Museum of Science and Technology**—This is a particularly good bet for children because of its hands-on exhibits. It's at 1867 St-Laurent Boulevard; take the Queensway to St-Laurent, exit south and follow your nose until you see a lighthouse on your left. Open 9:00 a.m. to 5:00 p.m. daily and 9:00 a.m. to 9:00 p.m. Thursday between May 1 and Sept. 6, and from 9:00 a.m. to 5:00 p.m. Tuesday through Sunday the rest of the year. Admission is $4.28 for adults, $3.50 for students and seniors and $1.50 for children aged 6 to 15. Call 991-3044 for information.

▲**Canadian Museum of Nature**—This venerable establishment on McLeod Street at Metcalfe displays everything from insects to dinosaurs. It's open 9:30 a.m. to 8:00 p.m. Sunday, Monday, and Thursday and 9:30 a.m. to 5:00 p.m. Tuesday, Wednesday, Friday, and Saturday. Admission is $5 for adults, $4 for students and seniors, $1.75 for children, and $10 for families. Call 996-3102 for information.

▲**National Aviation Museum**—Housed at Rockcliffe Airport, this museum boasts an impressive collection of vintage and modern planes and related artifacts. Open 9:00 a.m. to 5:00 p.m. daily and 9:00 a.m. to 9:00 p.m. Thursday from May 1 to Sept. 6, and 9:00 a.m. to 5:00 p.m. Tuesday to Sunday the rest of the year. Admission is $5 for adults, $4 for seniors and students, and $1.75 for children aged 6 to 15. Call 993-2010 for information.

▲**Canadian Ski Museum**—This is for ski buffs only. Located at 457A Sussex Drive, the museum features ski memorabilia, including a 5,000-year-old cave drawing of men on skis. Open Tuesday to Sunday year-round, 11:00 a.m. to 4:00 p.m. from May through September and 12:00 noon to 4:00 p.m. the rest of the year. Admission is $1 for adults and 50 cents for children aged 12 and up. Call 241-5832 for information.

▲**Currency Museum**—This small display in the Bank of Canada building at 235 Sparks Street depicts the history of money in Canada by showcasing various kinds of cash that have been used over the years, including $3, $6, $7, and $8 bills. Open year-round 10:30 a.m. to 5:00 p.m. Monday to Saturday and 1:00 p.m. to 5:00 p.m. Sunday. Admission is $2 for adults, $5 for families, and free for kids under 7. For information, call 782-8914.

▲**Royal Canadian Mint**—Speaking of currency, if you want to know how Canada makes its money, visit the Royal Canadian Mint at 320 Sussex Drive. Open 8:30 to 11:00 a.m. and 12:30 p.m. to 2:30 p.m. from May through August, weekdays only. Call 993-8990 to reserve space on a tour.

▲**Canadian War Museum**—Right next door to the National Gallery of Canada, the Canadian War Museum at 330 Sussex Drive houses a permanent collection of the history of the Canadian military. Open 9:30 a.m. to 5:00 p.m. daily and 9:30 a.m. to 8:00 p.m. on Thursday; closed Mondays in the off-season. Admission is $2.50 for adults, $1.25 for seniors and students, and free for kids under 16. Call 776-8600 for information.

▲**Gatineau Park**—Nature lovers will find Gatineau Park, across the river on the other side of Hull, well worth the 20-minute drive from Ottawa. The park, spread over hundreds of acres of the gently rolling Gatineau Hills, boasts endless kilometers of nature trails. Kingsmere, the country estate of the late, eccentric prime minister, Mackenzie King, is also located in the park and is open to visitors (King seemed rather a rather colorless man during his prime-ministership, which ran for a total of nearly 22 years at various times in the '20s, '30s, and '40s. It has since been revealed that he believed in spirits and communed regularly with the dead, chief among them his deceased mother). To get to Gatineau Park, follow Tache Boulevard west from Hull and turn north onto the Gatineau Parkway. Open year-round; free admission. For information on tours and activities, call the park's visitors center at (819) 827-2020.

Restaurants

The range and quality of restaurants in Ottawa has improved dramatically in recent years; following is a sampling of the best of what's available in various price ranges.

For designer pasta dishes, the **Ritz** chain of Italian restaurants are a good bet. They don't take reservations and are very busy around 7:00 p.m., which seems to be

Ottawa's peak dining hour, so try to arrive earlier or later
than that. The **Ritz Canal**, which provides a view of skating in winter and boating in summer, is at 375 Queen
Elizabeth Driveway. **Ritz Uptown** is at 226 Nepean. Other
Ritz restaurants are at 15 Clarence Street in the Market; at
1665 Bank Street; and at 274 Elgin Street. For affordable
fish, chicken and meat dishes plus gourmet pasta and
pizza, try the **Bay Street Bistro** (234-1111), an indoor-out-
door bistro-cafe at 160 Bay Street at the corner of Albert.

   Mexicali Rosa's is a chain that started out as a single
small establishment on Bank Street and has now spread
not just to other locations in Ottawa, but to a few other
Canadian cities. The reason for their success is the reasonably priced Mexican food and casual atmosphere. You'll
probably have to line up. A few addresses: 895 Bank
Street; 1001 Queen Elizabeth Drive; and 207 Rideau Street.

   In the Byward Market, check out **Zak's Diner**, a retro
kind of place with jukeboxes and formica at 14 Byward at
the corner of York. Zak's is a particularly good bet if
you're with kids or teenagers. **Memories** at 7 Clarence
Street in the Market is the local dessert place, while the
Blue Cactus Bar and Grill at 2 Byward on the corner of
Clarence serves Cajun, southwest, and Texan dishes.

   On Sundays, it often seems as if the entire city decides
to have brunch in the Market. Inevitably you'll have to
line up. Be smart—line up at the **Bohemian Café** at 89
Clarence Street, which serves good eggs benedict and
bottomless cups of café-au-lait.

   There's a Malaysian restaurant, **Chahaya Malaysia**, at
749 Bank St., that has a good reputation; call 237-4304.
For Thai food, try the **Thai Kitchen**, a small, unpreten-
tious place at 144 Maisonneuve Boulevard in Hull; call
595-3505. For traditional German fare, there's **Lindenhof**
at 965 Richmond Road; call 725-3481.

   When it comes to French dining, **Le Metro** is highly
recommended for both its ambience and its food. It's at
315 Somerset Street West; call 230-8123 for reservations.
Other noteworthy (and pricey) French restaurants include
the **Café Henry Burger** at 69 rue Laurier in Hull (777-

5646) and **Le Pied de Cochon** at 248 Montcalm in Hull. (Literally translated, "the pig's foot," but don't let that put you off; call 777-5805.)

At the National Arts Center, the canal-side **Le Café** serves Canadian fare like caribou and northern pike—all of it quite delicious. Call 594-5127.

Nightlife
There are several lively places in the Byward Market area and another clump of bars along Elgin Street, which runs up to the Parliament buildings. Wander through either area and take your pick. You'll know the trendy spots, which tend to change every few months, by the lineups. The Chateau Laurier's exquisitely restful lounge, **Zoe's**, overlooking Confederation Square, is one of the best places in town for a quiet drink at the end of a long after-noon of sightseeing. Because this is Ontario, the bars close at 1:00 a.m., but unlike most Ontario cities, Ottawa has the supreme advantage of being within a 10-minute drive of another province, in this case Quebec, where the bars shut at 3:00 a.m. All you have to do if you're still going strong at 1:00 a.m. is grab a taxi to Hull.

To find out what's on at the National Arts Centre, phone (613) 996-5051, ext. 375, or check the listings in *The Ottawa Citizen* or *The Ottawa Sun*.

Helpful Hints
Ottawa is the national capital, and 24 Sussex Drive is the Canadian version of 1600 Pennsylvania Avenue or 10 Downing Street. The prime minister's residence is set back from the street behind walls and shrubbery, and you can't see much of the house. It's a waste of time unless you happen to be out that way anyway. Nearby, however, is Rideau Hall, the governor-general's residence. Rideau Hall's lush grounds are open to the public is summer.

For more information on Ottawa, contact the Ottawa Tourism and Convention Authority, 2nd Floor, 111 Lisgar Street, Ottawa, Ont., Canada K2P 2L7, or phone (613) 237-5158.

There are visitor information centres in the National Arts Center at 65 Elgin Street and at 14 Metcalfe Street across from Parliament Hill; or call Canada's Capital Information Centre at (613) 239-5000 or 1-800-465-1867 toll-free. Or, for more information on other parts of eastern Ontario as well as Ottowa, call 1-800-567-EAST toll-free.

MONTREAL

Ah, Montreal. Paris of North America, *joie de vivre*, cosmopolitan, all that sort of thing—all true, especially the European-flavor part. I happened to wander through old Montreal recently, just a day after returning from Europe, and briefly felt confused as to which continent I was on. Montreal has much to offer—history, festivals, Old Montreal, drinking, and eating, all set against the background of a culture that's an odd hybrid of European and North American. It ought to be one of this continent's tourist meccas, but it's not. Go there and you can be smug in the knowledge that you're onto someplace a lot of travelers miss.

Suggested Schedule	
9:00 a.m.	Depart Ottawa.
11:00 a.m.	Arrive Montreal, check in at hotel.
12:00 noon	Mount Royal lookout.
1:00 p.m.	Back downtown for lunch.
2:00 p.m.	Explore downtown for the rest of the afternoon. Sherbrooke Street West has mansions and museums, Ste-Catherine Street West has shopping.

Driving Route: Ottawa to Montreal (200 km/120 miles)

Get onto the eastbound Queensway in Ottawa and follow the signs for Montreal and Highway 417, also the TransCanada. The 417 becomes Highway 40 just before you get onto Montreal Island. Coming into Montreal, take the Décarie expressway south and follow the signs for the Ville Marie autoroute, which takes you downtown. Exit at de la Montagne (Mountain Street) and you're in the downtown core. From downtown Ottawa to downtown Montreal is 200 kilometers (120 miles), about a two-hour drive.

Optional Route: If you want to see Upper Canada Village, a recreation of a mid-19th-century village that's quite famous in Canada, take Highway 16 or Highway 31 south from Ottawa to Morrisburg. Upper Canada Village, 11 kilometers (7 miles) east of Morrisburg, is an "outdoor historical museum" complete with some 40 buildings on 163 hectares (66 acres), plus costumed staff in the mills, bakery, cheese factory, printing office, general store, tavern, and homes who can explain all the workings to visitors. The major buildings are all in a fairly compact area, and village operators suggest either a one-hour tour and or two-hour tour. The village is open from May to mid-October. Admission is $9.50 for adults, $7.25 for seniors and students, and $4.25 for children aged 6 to 12. Call (613) 543-3704 for more information.

Afterwards, get onto Highway 401 heading east; Montreal is about an hour away. The 401 becomes Highway 20 as it crosses to Montreal Island and then, eventually, the Ville Marie autoroute. As above, exit at de la Montagne.

Montreal

In 1535 French explorer Jacques Cartier, searching for a passage to India, became the first known white man to set foot on the island that would become Montreal. It was then the site of Hochelaga, an Iroquois village. Cartier named the mountain Mount Royal. In 1611, another French explorer, Samuel de Champlain, founder of New France, arrived and set up a fortified settlement, Place Royale. In 1642 a small group of French colonists established a settlement called Ville Marie at the Pointe-à-Callière; later they moved to higher ground in the heart of what is now Old Montreal. Initially a mission to convert the natives, the settlement quickly became a busy trading center thanks to its location at the confluence of the St. Lawrence, Ottawa, and Richelieu rivers. In 1760, the British conquered New France. British soldiers and a handful of British colonists were left to build a British Canada among a French population of some 60,000. To do it sanely, Britain gradually confirmed the right of

French Canadians to retain their Roman Catholic faith, their language, and their legal code.

For some 200 years, the powerful English minority ran the province's economy. In the 1960s, a separatist movement began to grow among French Quebecers, and in 1976, the Parti Quebecois, whose main platform plank was independence, was voted into power. A provincial referendum on independence was narrowly defeated four years later, and the PQ themselves lost the next election to Robert Bourassa and his Liberals. But the sovereignty question remains unresolved. In October 1992, a national referendum was held on a new constitutional agreement that would have brought Quebec, the only province that had not signed a previous agreement, into the Canadian fold. The vote was a resounding no in most parts of the country—in Quebec because Quebecers thought they weren't getting enough and in some other provinces because people thought Quebec was getting too much. Then the Parti Quebecois returned to power in the September 1994 election, promising to hold another provincial referendum on independence within a year.

I have lived in Quebec most of my life and the debate has continued for as long as I can remember. My feeling is it might never end, but meanwhile life goes on much as usual. English-speaking Montrealers make up about 14 percent of the city's 3.1 million residents, and many francophones are bilingual, so visitors get the best of both worlds—a distinct French flavor, but with plenty of people around who can speak English.

The English-speaking minority has shrunk in size and power, and now makes up about 14 percent of Montreal's population of 3.1 million. Most Montreal anglophones, or anglos as they are colloquially known, are bilingual. But then again so are many francophones.

While in Montreal, you may hear references to not just anglophones and francophones, but "allophones." Allophones are basically "others"—residents whose mother tonque is neither French nor English. Altogether, more than a million of the province's seven million residents speak English or languages other than French at home.

Montreal has two international airports; Dorval is about 20 minutes from downtown, Mirabel an hour north of the city. Domestic and transborder flights come into Dorval, while huge Mirabel, widely known as a white elephant, serves international flights and is never busy. Via Rail trains come in to Central Station next to the Queen Elizabeth Hotel downtown, while intercity buses come in to the Voyageur bus station on Berri Street east of downtown.

We'll concentrate on three areas of the city: downtown, the Olympic Park in the east end and, of course, Old Montreal and the Old Port. For an overview of the whole city, the first thing to do is head up to one of the lookouts on Mount Royal, the mountain in the middle of the city.

Getting Around

Sherbooke Street is the major artery running east-west through Montreal. The next streets south are de Maisonneuve Boulevard, Ste-Catherine Street, and René-Lévesque Boulevard, in that order. North of Sherbrooke Street, at least in the downtown area, the slopes of Mount Royal begin. South of René-Lévesque, the major streets are St-Antoine, St-Jacques and Notre-Dame, while de la Commune fronts the St. Lawrence River. The major cross-streets from west to east are Atwater, Guy, Crescent, de la Montagne, Peel, and University. Eight blocks east of University, St. Lawrence Street, alias St-Laurent, alias The Main, divides the city into east and west.

Old Montreal is southeast of downtown, near the waterfront, spreading east from the corner of University and St-Jacques and south towards the river. The Olympic Stadium, the Biodome and the Botanical Gardens are in a clump in the east end, about 15 minutes by subway from downtown.

Parking downtown is hard to find, and driving in Montreal can be nervewracking for people who aren't accustomed to it. Drivers and pedestrians are constantly at war. Montrealers jaywalk all the time. Occasionally police decide to crack down and start handing out fines for jay-walking. It never lasts very long and nobody takes it seriously. Drivers aren't much better, frequently changing

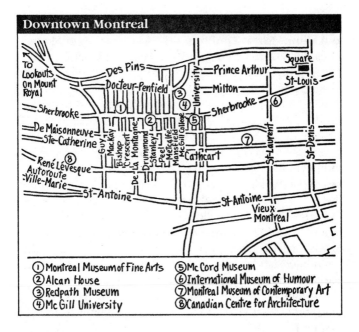

Downtown Montreal

① Montreal Museum of Fine Arts
② Alcan House
③ Redpath Museum
④ McGill University
⑤ McCord Museum
⑥ International Museum of Humour
⑦ Montreal Museum of Contemporary Art
⑧ Canadian Centre for Architecture

lanes without indicators, racing through yellow lights as they turn red and honking impatiently if the car in front doesn't move fast enough. So drive—and walk—defensively in Montreal.

Drive to the Mount Royal lookout, then abandon your car at the hotel and get around on the public transit system. In this case that means chiefly the clean, efficient and relatively crime-free subway, known in Montreal as the métro. One of the subway lines runs right along St. Catherine and out past the Olympic Stadium in the east end of the city; another goes past the edge of old Montreal. Single tickets for bus or métro cost $1.75, while a strip of six tickets costs $7. For information, call A.U.T.O.B.U.S. (288-6287).

The major tourist information center is Centre Infotouriste at 1001 Dorchester Square Street, in the block bordered by Ste-Catherine, René-Lévesque, Peel and Metcalfe streets (nearest métro stop is Peel). There is also an information kiosk at 174 Notre-Dame Street East on Place Jacques Cartier in Old Montreal.

Sightseeing Highlights
▲▲**Mount Royal Lookout**—The lower slopes of Mount
Royal are layered with mansions. Many now belong to
McGill University. When they were privately owned, they
formed part of the Golden Square Mile between
Sherbrooke, the mountain, Côte-des-Neiges and Avenue
du Parc. At the turn of the century it was estimated that 70
percent of Canada's wealth was controlled by about 100
people who lived in this area. The upper part of the
mountain has been preserved as a 200-hectare green
space overlooking the city. This is one area it's best to use
the car to see. Head north on Guy Street, which becomes
Côte-des-Neiges, and follow it until you see signs for
Mount Royal. There are two lookouts. From the Mount
Royal Chalet Lookout, you can see Westmount and downtown, the islands of Île Ste-Hélène and Île Notre-Dame in
the river and, beyond them, the hills of the Eastern
Townships. The other lookout, further along the same
road, provides a view of the Olympic Stadium and the
east end.
▲▲▲**Montreal Museum of Fine Arts**—Founded in
1860, the oldest art museum in Canada is now made up
of two buildings facing each other across Sherbrooke
Street. The original is a magnificent neoclassical structure
on the north side of the street; the new extension across
from it was designed by the busy Moshe Safdie, architect
of the National Gallery of Canada in Ottawa. Permanent
collections include prints, drawings, sculpture, paintings
by both old masters and contemporary artists, furniture,
and silver. There's a gift shop too. The museum also usually brings some sort of blockbuster show to Montreal
each summer. Open Tuesday to Sunday from 11:00 a.m.
to 6:00 p.m., Saturday 11:00 a.m. to 9:00 p.m. Admission
to the permanent collection is $9.50 for adults, $4.75 for
students, $4.50 for seniors, $2 for children 12 and under,
and $19 for a family. Entrance to temporary exhibtions
generally costs more and includes entrance to permanent
exhibits. The address is 1379-80 Sherbrooke Street West;
phone 285-1600.

▲**Alcan House**—Stop in at the Maison Alcan, on the south side of Sherbrooke Street at the corner of Stanley Street, just to look around. The pleasing modern architecture artfully combines old building facades and airy spaces to attractive effect. A restaurant in the building, La Tulipe Noire, serves incredible chocolate desserts and sells divine chocolates at the counter.

▲**McGill University**—The gates to the university are on Sherbrooke at the top of McGill College Avenue. Founded in 1821, the university grounds contain imposing old buildings and the Redpath Museum of animal groups, fossils, Egyptian antiquities, gems, crystals, and rocks. Temporary exhibits often have an ecological theme. The address is 859 Sherbrooke Street West, and the phone number 398-4086. Open Monday to Thursday from June to September and Monday to Friday the rest of the year. Free admission. Afterwards, take time to stroll down McGill College Avenue and check out an intriguing sculpture called *Illuminated Crowd* outside the BNP headquarters. You can't miss it; it portrays a crowd of people gawking off into the distance.

▲▲**McCord Museum of Canadian History**—Re-opened in 1992 after three years of expansion and renovation, the McCord, one of Canada's leading history museums, now has more than twice its former space, with exhibits dating back to the 17th century that bring Canadian social history vividly to life. The main collections include photographic archives, decorative arts and paintings, prints and drawings, costumes and textiles, and ethnology and archeology. The museum has a gift shop and tea room. Open Tuesday, Wednesday and Friday, 10:00 a.m. to 6:00 p.m., Thursday 10:00 a.m. to 9:00 p.m., Saturday and Sunday 10:00 a.m. to 5:00 a.m. Closed Mondays except on statutory holidays. Admission is $5 for adults, $2 for students, $3 for seniors, $8 for families. The McCord is at 690 Sherbrooke Street West; phone 398-7100.

▲▲**Montreal Museum of Contemporary Art**—Newly housed in Place des Arts, the museum has a permanent collection of 3,000 works by Quebec, Canadian, and international artists, from Jean-Paul Riopelle to Andy Warhol. Open Tuesday to Sunday, 11:00 a.m. to 6:00 p.m. Admission is $5 for adults, $4 for seniors, $3 for students age 12 and up, and $12 for families; 185 Ste-Catherine Street W., 847-6226.

▲**The International Museum of Humor**—The permanent exhibition in this one-of-a-kind museum is titled *Laughing Matters—Humor Through the Ages*. There are also a documentation center, a hall of fame, a cabaret-theater, a restaurant, and a boutique. The museum is open from 1:00 p.m. to 8:00 p.m., Tuesday to Sunday. The address is 2111 St-Laurent Boulevard and admission is $5. Call 845-4000 for current information.

▲▲**The Canadian Center for Artchitecture**—Opened in 1989, the CCA, devoted to architecture and its history, incorporates the landmark Shaughnessy House into its striking modern structure. The center was funded almost entirely by Phyllis Lambert, an architect who also happens to be one of the millionaire Bronfmans. The unique collection includes thousands of drawings and print, books, and photographs. The CAA is a must for any architectural tour or aficionado. The building fronts René Lévesque Boulevard, but the entrance is on the other side at 1920 Baile Street. Open Wednesday and Friday 11:00 a.m. to 6:00 p.m., Thursday 11:00 a.m. to 8:00 p.m., Saturday and Sunday 11:00 a.m. to 5:00 p.m. Closed Monday and Tuesday. Adults $5, students $3, free for children aged 12 and under. Phone 939-7000 for more information.

Lodging

If money is no object, try the **Ritz-Carlton** ($160 to $250 depending on the season; 1228 Sherbrooke Street West, 842-4212 locally, 1-800-363-0366 toll-free from Canada, 1-800-426-3135 from U.S.), next-door to the tony Holt Renfrew department store and just up the street from the Montreal Museum of Fine Arts; the **Westin Mount-Royall** ($155 to $245; 1050 Sherbrooke Street West, 284-1110), which bills itself as the only five-diamond hotel in the city, as selected by the American Automobile Association; the

Inter-Continental ($119 and up; 360 St-Antoine West, 987-9900 or 1-800-361-3600 toll-free), part of the new World Trade Centre complex at the edge of Old Montreal; or **Hotel Vogue** ($175 to $235; 1425 de la Montagne, 285-5555 or 1-800-465-6654 toll-free), a relatively small, "European-style" establishment that features a "designer floor" with futuristic, black-and-grey furnishings.

The venerable old **Queen Elizabeth Hotel** was recently renovated. People still sometimes leave flowers at the door of suite 1742, where John Lennon and Yoko Ono held a bed-in in 1969 ($110 to $220; 900 René Lévesque Boulevard West, 861-3511 locally, 1-800-441-1414 toll-free). Other central hotels include **Bonaventure Hilton** ($125 to $213; 1 Place Bonaventure, 878-2332 or 1-800-HILTONS), which has a heated outdoor pool on its rooftop; **Hotel du Fort** ($89 to $130; 1390 du Fort Street, 938-8333 or 1-800-565-6333), another "boutique" hotel; the **Holiday Inn Sinomonde Garden** ($105 to $115; 99 Viger Street West, 878-9888 or 1-800-HOLIDAY), a new hotel at the edge of Chinatown and Old Montreal; the **Radisson Gouverneurs Montreal** ($115 to $165; 777 University Street, 879-1370 or 1-800-333-3333), midway between downtown and Old Montreal; and **Château Versailles**, in a beautiful old building on Sherbrooke Street West near the corner of Guy ($80 to $155; 1659 Sherbrooke Street West, 933-3611 or 1-800-361-7199).

More moderately, the downtown **Quality Hotel** at 3440 Park Avenue (avenue du Parc) offers rooms priced between $87 and $105 (849-1413 or 1-800-268-6116 toll-free), while rooms at the no-frills **Hotel Arcade** (50 René-Lévesque Boulevard West, 874-9090 or 1-800-363-6535 toll-free) range from $60 to $72.

For B&Bs (*gîtes* in French), the largest networks include **Bed & Breakfast Downtown Network** (write to Bob Finkelstein, 3458 Laval Avenue, Montreal, Que., Canada H2X 3C8, or phone (514) 289-9749); **Bed & Breakfast a Montreal** (C.P. 575, succ. Snowdon, Montreal, Que., Canada H3X 3T8, (514) 738-9410); **Bed & Breakfast Mont-Royal** (C.P. Jeanne-Mance 42002,

Montreal, Que., Canada H2W 2T3, (514) 289-9749); and
Network Hospitality Montreal Relay (3977 Laval Avenue,
Montreal, Que., Canada H2W 2H9, (514) 287-9635).

Camping

There are several campgrounds within an hour of
Montreal on the South Shore, across the St. Lawrence
River. All have sites with water sewage disposal and elec-
tricity, at prices running around $20. Other sites cost from
$12 to $15 nightly. **Camp Alouette** in Beloeil is at (514)
464-1661; **Camping Pointe-des-Cascades** in Pointe-des-
Cascades is at (514) 455-2501; in St-Philippe, **Camping
Bon Air** is at (514) 659-8868, and **Camping KOA
Montreal Sud** is at (514) 659-8626; and **Camping Daoust**
in Vaudreuil is at (514) 458-7301.

Restaurants

On a summer night, one of the best things to do is try any
of the restaurants along Prince Arthur or Duluth streets.
Prince Arthur, a lively three-block pedestrian mall of bars,
cafés, and restaurants off St-Laurant a few blocks north of
Sherbrooke, is a great place to eat, linger, people-watch,
and party in the summer. Duluth Street, several blocks
north of Prince Arthur, is not a pedestrian mall and so not
as lively, but it has some good restaurants. For example,
the **Jardin de Panos**, a Greek restaurant at 529 Duluth
Street East, has a wonderful open-air terrace out back that
seats 350 and is usually crowded; the phone number is
521-4206.

The wonderful thing about the restaurants on Prince
Arthur and Duluth is that most are bring-your-own-wine
establishments. You have to remember to buy a bottle
before getting there, but this one small factor makes eating out markedly cheaper. Most of the restaurants on both
streets are crowded most evenings, and most don't take
reservations, so you may have to line up.

There are a zillion other restaurants in Montreal.
Personal favorites include **La Rôtisserie Italienne**, serving good food cafeteria-style at ridiculously low prices at
1933 Ste-Catherine Street West; **Fiestas Tapas**, a Spanish

restaurant at 479 St-Alexis (at the corner of Notre-Dame West) in Old Montreal that serves a wide selection of the tasty little dishes called *tapas* (844-5700); **Biddles**, which serves up ribs and live jazz at 2060 Aylmer (842-8656); **L'Express** at 3927 St-Denis, a French bistro-style place with affordable prices that remains steadfastly trendy and popular (845-5333); **Cajun House**, with delicious Cajun food but fairly expensive, at 1219 Mackay Street (871-3898); **Chao Phraya**, a fine Thai restaurant at 50 Laurier Boulevard West (272-5339); and **Curry House**, one of the best Indian restaurants in town and very reasonably priced, at 1433 Bishop Street (845-0326).

Several places around town tend to attract lots of tourists. The **Bar-B-Barn** at 1201 Guy Street (931-3811) features excellent ribs but serves you so quickly and hustles you out of there so fast it becomes an eat-and-run experience. For a not-bad deal in touristy Old Montreal, try **Le Jardin Nelson** on Place Jacques Cartier, which offers crepes, sandwiches and salads on its courtyard terrace.

At the high end are **Les Halles** at 1450 Crescent (844-2328), a French restaurant that is one of the most expensive establishments in town and worth it; the **Katsura** at 2170 de la Montagne (849-1172), among the best Japanese restaurants in town; and the **Pavilion de l'Atlantique** at the corner of Sherbrooke and Stanley streets (285-1636) for expensive seafood in the Maison Alcan.

In the cheap-but-lots-of-atmosphere category, there are **Ben's Delicatessen**, a landmark establishment at 990 de Maisonneuve West at the corner of Mackay, right downtown, and **Schwartz's**, at 3895 St-Laurent. The latter is pretty small and often has long lines. Both establishments are known for smoked-meat sandwiches.

Many restaurants throughout the city offer Sunday brunch. Two of my favorites are **Beauty's** at 93 Mount-Royal Avenue and **Dusty's** at 4510 Park Avenue.

Some Montrealers who would argue that Montreal bagels are better than New York bagels. Find out for yourself at either of two well-known bakeries where you can watch the bagels being cooked in huge wood-burning

ovens—the **Fairmount Bagel Bakery** at 74 Fairmount
Street West or the **St-Viateur Bagel Shop** at 263 St-Viateur
West.

Finally, there is one place in Montreal where afternoon
tea is still a grand tradition—the **Jardin du Ritz**, an
exquisite garden cafe in a courtyard of the Ritz-Carlton.
Open only in summer, at 1228 Sherbrooke Street West
(842-4212).

Nightlife

There's lots of it. Try the aforementioned Prince Arthur
Street; St-Laurent, mainly north of Prince Arthur; Crescent
Street, still famous after all these years and still something
of an English enclave, or neighboring Bishop Street; or St-
Denis Street, the so-called Latin quarter and the east-end
equivalent of Crescent Street, much more French.

Also, Montreal now has a casino. Run by Loto-Quebec,
the provincial government's lottery corporation, it opened
in 1993 on Île Notre-Dame, which with Île Ste-Helene was
home to Expo '67. The casino, in fact, is in the former
French pavilion. The casino was an immediate hit and is
always crowded during its opening hours of 11:00 a.m. to
3:00 a.m. Admission is free and so is parking, but since
the parking lots fill up rapidly, it's best to get there by taxi
(5 minutes from downtown) or subway and bus (Île Notre
Dame Subway stop, bus 167 to the casino). Children are
not admitted; you must be 18 or over to enter. Dress is
generally casual, but no T-shirts, jeans, or sneakers are
allowed. For more information, phone 392-2746 locally or
1-800-665-2274 toll-free from elsewhere.

The city has a handful of English-language theaters,
namely the Centaur (453 St-Francois-Xavier Street, 288-
3161), the Saidye Bronfman Centre (5170 Cote-Ste-
Catherine Road, 739-7944 or 739-4816), Theatre 1774
(3964 St-Laurent Boulevard, 987-1774; plays are bilingual);
and Bulldog Productions, 5723 Park Ave., 272-4290 (tickets), 933-6292 (information).

In summer, there are Shakespeare-in-the-park performances at several parks around town. Check *The Gazette*,
the city's only English-language daily, for dates and times.

Take a blanket or folding chair if you go to one of the performances.

For up-to-date entertainment listings, check *The Gazette* or pick up copies of the *Mirror* or the *Hour*, weekly independent newspapers that are distributed free.

Shopping

The best shopping is downtown. The main shopping strip runs along Ste-Catherine Street from **Faubourg Ste-Catherine**, a trendy market-like shopping center on the south side of the street at the corner of Guy (nearest metro stop is Guy-Concordia), all the way east to St-Laurent. In between are **Ogilvy** (Guy métro stop), an upscale department store complex at the corner of de la Montagne Street; **Les Cours Mont-Royal**, an enclave of pricey designer boutiques half a block north of Ste-Catherine on Peel Street (Peel métro stop); the **Eaton Centre**; **Place Montreal Trust** and **Les Promenades de la Cathedrale**, with some 220 boutiques between them (McGill métro stop); **The Bay** department store (McGill); and **Complexe Desjardins**, yet another big mall of boutiques (Place des Arts métro). Other shopping points downtown include **Holt-Renfrew**, an exclusive department store on Sherbrooke at the corner of de la Montagne; **Place Ville Marie**, more boutiques at René-Lévesque Boulevard and University Street; and **Place Bonaventure**, a shopping promenade beneath the Bonaventure Hilton.

Most of these shopping areas are part of the underground city, so if the weather's bad you can thread your way underground from one to the other. It's possible, for example, to walk from Les Cours Mont Royal to The Bay (or *La Baie*) underground.

The Underground City

Some visitors are disappointed by Montreal's vaunted underground city. In fact, it's a whole lot of corridors lined with shops, restaurants and movie theaters. There are 29 kilometers (18 miles) of corridors. Even if it doesn't look impressive, it sure makes life easier on blustery winter

days. It's possible to stay at downtown hotels that connect
with the underground city and eat, shop, and party for
days at a time—without ever stepping outside.

Festivals

Summer in Montreal means almost wall-to-wall festivals.
The season gets off to an explosive start in June with the
International Fireworks Competition, wherein countries show off their pyrotechnic prowess in the skies over
La Ronde, the amusement park on Île Ste-Hélène. The
shows are normally twice a week for three weeks, but
then again sometimes they're once a week over two
months. Next up is the **Montreal International Jazz
Festival**, in many ways the funkiest revel of the summer
because it includes dozens of free concerts staged outdoors in an area around Place des Arts, Montreal's pre-
miere concert hall. The "jazz village" is bordered by Ste-
Catherine Street, Jeanne-Mance Street, de Maisonneuve
Boulevard and St-Urbain Street. A few days after the 10-day
jazz fest winds up around the end of the first week of
July, the **Just for Laughs** international comedy festival
begins. It started out as a tiny, French-only affair in the
mid-1980s but is now big and bilingual, with an English
gala and a French gala plus dozens of shows in both languages by comedians from Quebec, Canada, and around
the world. After that there's a pause until late August,
when the glamorous and gaudy **Montreal World Film
Festival** begins. In between are myriad less-known events
and art exhibits; Infotouriste can supply information.

Helpful Hints

Museum lovers should note that a Montreal Museum Pass
is now available, providing entrance to 17 museums
around the city. A one-day pass costs $12 for adults or $24
for families, while a three-day pass costs $25 for adults
and $50 for families. The passes are on sale at participat-
ing museums, Infotouriste, and numerous hotels.

Drop in at the Centre Infotouriste at 1001 Dorchester
Square Street between Peel and Metcalfe. Infotouriste is

open daily from 8:30 a.m. to 7:30 p.m. from May to October and 9:00 a.m. to 6:00 p.m. the rest of the year.

There is also an information kiosk at 174 Notre-Dame Street East on Place Jacques Cartier in Old Montreal.

Otherwise, call (514) 873-2015 locally or 1-800-363-7777 toll-free from elsewhere for more information on Montreal and the province.

MONTREAL

Enjoy Olympic Park, including the Biodome environmental museum, and then head for Old Montreal. Also known as *Vieux-Montréal*, its narrow cobblestoned streets are lined with old stone buildings housing boutiques, cafés, and fine restaurants. Take a *caleche* (horse-and-buggy) tour through Old Montreal or just wander.

Suggested Schedule

9:00 a.m.	Head for the Olympic Stadium for a view from its observation deck.
10:00 a.m.	Visit the Biodome.
11:30 a.m.	Take the shuttle bus to the botanical gardens.
1:00 p.m.	Take the subway to Old Montreal and have lunch.
2:00 p.m.	Wander around Old Montreal.
4:00 p.m.	Explore the Old Port.

Getting Around
To get to Olympic Park from downtown, take the green métro line, Honoré-Beaugrand direction, and get off at Viau. To get to Old Montreal from Olympic Park, take the green line, Angrignon direction, get off at Berri-UQAM, transfer to the orange line, direction Côte-Vertu, and get off at either the next stop, Champ-de-Mars, or at Place d'Armes, the one after that, if you plan to visit Notre-Dame Basilica first.

Sightseeing Highlights
▲▲**Olympic Stadium**—It's not so much the stadium that makes this place worth visiting; it's the tower. The $1.2 billion stadium was built for the 1976 Summer Olympic Games at monstrous cost overruns, hence its nickname, The Big Owe. Its landmark tower wasn't completed, nor its retractible roof installed and made workable, until nearly 15 years later. Now, finally, it boasts the

world's tallest inclined tower, the top of which provides a panorama of the city and Mount Royal. Guided tours of the stadium complex are available. The address is 4141 Pierre de Coubertin Avenue. Open September to April from 10:00 a.m. to 6:00 p.m. daily and May to August from 10:00 a.m. to 11:00 p.m. daily, closed from mid-January to mid-February. Admission to the tower is $7 for adults, $6 for seniors, and $5.50 for children. The nearest métro station is Viau. Call (514) 252-TOUR. In summer there is a free shuttle among Viau station, the Olympic Park (with the stadium and the Biodome) and the botanical gardens across Sherbrooke Street from the stadium.

▲▲▲**Biodome**—The Biodome, a strange combination of zoo, aquarium, botanical garden, and museum, became one of Montreal's most-visited tourist attractions as soon as it opened in 1992. Housed next to the stadium in the former Velodrome, it's quite simply a smash hit. The display of four different ecosystems is aimed at making visitors more aware of the planet's fragility. The environments, spread over 10,000 square meters, are a tropical rain forest, Quebec's Laurentian forestlands, the St. Lawrence River's marine world, and the polar worlds of the Arctic and Antarctic. Re-created with both authentic and artificial flora and fauna, the rain forest area is filled with suffocating heat, screeching birds, and chattering monkeys. The Laurentian woodland surrounds a huge beaver dam, while the centerpiece of the St. Lawrence River exhibit is a massive tank filled with cod, halibut, striped bass, even sharks, with northern gannets swimming on the surface. The polar region features waddling polar penguins. Because of the distinct temperature changes as you move from ecosystem to ecosystem through laser-prompted glass doors, officials recommend you wear something lightweight but carry a sweater or coat. Admission is $8.50 for adults, $4.25 for children aged 6 to 17, $6 for seniors, and free for children under 6. Joint tickets to the Biodome and the nearby Botanical Gardens are also available. Open daily year-round, 9:00 a.m. to 6:00 p.m. and 8:00 p.m. in summer. The Biodome is at 4777 Pierre-de-Coubertin Avenue, the phone number is 868-3000. The nearest subway station is Viau.

▲▲**Montreal Botanical Gardens**—The second-largest in the world, the botanical gardens contain some 10 greenhouses and 30 theme gardens, including Chinese and Japanese gardens and their pavilions. Also on the grounds is the Insectarium, with everything from butterflies to beetles, some live, some mounted. Housed in a building that looks like a stylized bug, the insectarium is billed as unique in North America. The botanical gardens may be a place to avoid on weekends, when wedding parties galore are having photographs taken. Open daily from 9:00 a.m. to 6:00 p.m. Between mid-May and mid-October, admission to the gardens, greenhouses, the insectarium is $7 for adults, $5 for seniors, $3.50 for

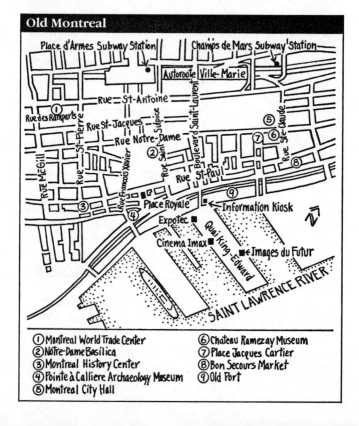

Old Montreal

① Montreal World Trade Center
② Notre-Dame Basilica
③ Montreal History Center
④ Pointe à Calliere Archaeology Museum
⑤ Montreal City Hall
⑥ Chateau Ramezay Museum
⑦ Place Jacques Cartier
⑧ Bon Secours Market
⑨ Old Port

students, and children under 6 get in free. Admission fees are slightly lower in the off-season. 4101 Sherbrooke Street East, Pix-IX metro stop; (514) 872-1400.

▲▲▲**Old Montreal**—Steeped in history, Old Montreal encompasses everything from narrow cobblestone streets and the towering Notre Dame Basilica to jazz bars and tacky souvenir shops. It's very much a tourist area, so prices run high. The renovated Old Port (the New Old Port, its promoters call it) just below Old Montreal has a 2-kilometer (1.2-mile) esplanade, exhibit halls, and an Imax theater.

At Infotouriste, pick up the 30-page *Old Montreal—A Walking Tour*, produced by Heritage Montreal, and the city's 28-page *Montreal—A Walking Tour of Vieux Montreal*. For great people-watching, get a seat at one of the outdoor cafes lining Place Jacques Cartier, the major square in Old Montreal.

▲▲▲**Notre-Dame Basilica**—One of the largest and most beautiful churches in North America, the basilica is ornate and quite magnificent. Its huge, 7,000-pipe organ has to be seen to be believed. Wander in and look around. Contrary to popular belief, the basilica design was not inspired by the cathedral of the same name in Paris but by two churches in London, Westminster Abbey and St. Martin's-in-the-Fields. It's at 110 Notre-Dame Street West on Place d'Armes. If it's your first stop in Old Montreal, use the Place d'Armes métro stop instead of Champs-de-Mars.

▲**Montreal World Trade Centre**—In Old Montreal, even the newest buildings find a way to incorporate history. The atrium of the World Trade Centre runs along the old Ruelle des Fortifications where city walls used to stand, between St-Jacques and St-Antoine streets. Beneath soaring glass, a suspended walkway connects the turreted tower of the Inter-Continental Hotel to the Nordheimer, an 1888 building at 363 St-Jacques West that has been richly restored to its original Victorian grandeur and contains the hotel's meeting rooms. Beneath the Nordheimer lie 200-year-old stone vaults that may once have been used to store ammunition but now house an oyster bar and a wine bar.

▲▲▲**Pointe-à-Callière, Museum of Archeology and History**—Unique and entertaining, this museum opened to rave reviews in 1992, on the same spot where the city was founded 350 years earlier. The modern building houses vestiges of Montreal's past discovered in archeological digs begun in 1980 at Place Royale and Pointe-à-Callière. The complex has three sites—the Eperon building, with archeological artifacts and the remains of Montreal's first cemetery; the archeological crypt beneath Place Royale, containing old stone foundations and artifacts; and the Old Customs House. To visit this museum is to take a walk through the city's foundations, in all senses. There is also a multiscreen film about the history of the city, plus computer-activated holograms. Open 10:00 a.m. to 5:00 p.m., Wednesdays until 8:00 p.m.; closed Mondays. Admission is $8 for adults, $5 for seniors, $4 for students, $2 for children aged 6 to 12, and free for children under 6. Free entry for all after 5:00 p.m. Wed-nesdays. 350 Place Royale; phone 872-9150 for information.

▲▲▲**Place Jacques Cartier**—In the very heart of Old Montreal, this cobblestoned square is where you'll find lively cafés, bars and restaurants and, on summer days, live entertainment by buskers. The imposing white building across the street from the top of the square is City Hall.

▲▲▲**The Old Port**—The waterfront area just south of Old Montreal has recently received a multi-million-dollar facelift after years of mouldering. Wander the esplanade that runs along de la Commune Street and check out historic buildings that now house various exhibitions, an Imax theater, and a flea market. The Imax-Expotec complex on the King Edward Pier at the base of St-Laurent Street houses the theater with its seven-story screen (call 496-4629 to find out what's playing) and Expotec, an interactive exhibit whose themes change from season to season. Images du Futur, one of the oldest exhibitions in the Old Port, boasts holograms, computer animations, virtual reality-style interactive exhibits, and assorted other mind-boggling audio-visual displays. It's tucked away at the end of King Edward Pier. The Cirque du Soleil,

Montreal's magically theatrical circus troupe, moved into its new permanent home in the Old Port in 1994; the big blue-and-yellow structure is impossible to miss. (If they're in town, get tickets. It's a must, no matter what your age.) The Old Port also features boat shuttles, picnicking, organized activities for children, live performances, cruises, excursions and a yacht harbor. You can rent pedal boats; ride a replica of an 18th-century Mississipi steamboat on a lunch or dinner cruise (842-7655); take a 90-minute cruise on the Bateau-Mouche, a climate-controlled boat with a glassed-in observation deck (849-9952); ride the Amphibus, a bizarre half-boat, half-bus vehicle that takes you on a cruise and a drive of the Old Port area; ride the Lachine Rapids on a jet-boat (284-9607); or tour the Pelican, a replica of the flagship commanded by Pierre de Moyne d'Iberville during the battle for Fort Nelson (Husdon Bay) in 1697 (842-6077). For information on port activities in general, call 496-PORT.

▲**Parc des Îles**—The one-time Expo islands in the St. Lawrence River between Montreal and the south shore Île Notre-Dame has a floral park that's open from mid-June to September, as well as the city's only beach and the casino. Neighboring Île Ste-Hélène is home to La Ronde, the amusement park left over from Expo 67. Admission is $20.50 for adults, $10.25 for children under 12, or $47.60 for families. A cheaper version for $9.50 provides access to the grounds and four rides only; call 872-7300 for information. La Ronde is also a good vantage point from which to watch the fireworks during the fireworks festival. Both islands have lots of green space and make for enjoyable strolling or cycling. The subway stop is Île Ste-Hélène.

▲**St-Joseph's Oratory**—This massively imposing basilica on a Mount Royal slope above Queen Mary Road is a renowned pilgrimmage site, and in fact you may see a few people making their way on their knees up the impossibly long flight of outside stairs. Brother André, one of Quebec's most popular religious figures of this century, founded the oratory. He was a functionally illiterate man who never advanced beyond lowly positions within his religious order, but he was also a faith healer, with St-Joseph as his patron. Although his work scandalized much of the established church, thousands of people attributed their miraculous healings to him, and in 1904 some of his fans helped him build a small oratory in honor of Joseph on the slopes of Mount Royal. Eventually the church got involved and a basilica was built on the site. The *Oratoire* also provides a lookout over the city. The nearest subway stop is Côte-des-Neiges.

▲**The Montreal History Centre**—Housed in restored Fire Station 1 at 335 Place d'Youville in Old Montreal, the history centre offers a montage that retraces the major historical events in Montreal. Open Tuesday to Sunday 10:00 a.m. to 5:00 p.m. late September to May; daily from 9:00 a.m. to 5:00 p.m. May to early July; daily from 10:00 a.m. to 6:00 p.m. July to September. Closed the last two weeks of December. Admission is $4.50 for adults, $3 for students and seniors. 872-3207. The nearest subway is Square-Victoria.

▲**The Château Ramezay Museum**—This mansion is a prime example of 18th-century architecture and now houses period furniture, engravings, paintings and costumes typical of the French Regime. Open Tuesday to Sunday from 10:00 a.m. to 4:30 p.m. Admission is $5 for adults, $3 for students and seniors, and $10 for families. 280 Notre-Dame Street East in Old Montreal, 861-3708.

▲**Marché Bonsecours**—An elegant 19th-century building on St-Paul Street in Old Montreal, Bonsecours Market was closed to the public for 30 years before being completely renovated in time for the city's 350th anniversary in 1992. It houses major exhibitions on the past, present, and future.

Helpful Hints
The skating rink on the ground floor of Le 1000 de la Gauchetiere building downtown, between the Bonaventure and Chateau Champlain hotels, is called the Amphitheatre Bell, and you can go skating there year-round. Skate rentals are available. For information, call 395-0555.

If you're in Montreal in the spring, try to find time to attend that great Quebec tradition, a "sugaring off." From mid-March to mid-April, sugar shacks in the countryside around Montreal convert the sap from maple trees into Quebec's fabled maple syrup, and many establishments open to the public in this period. You can watch the process by which the sap becomes maple syrup and then sit down for a huge meal of Quebecois fare like baked beans, *tourtière* (meat pie), and pancakes, all smothered in maple syrup. Ask for the names of some *établières* (sugar shacks) at Infotouriste.

Speaking of the country, Montreal is within an hour or so of two scenic areas, the Laurentians northwest of the city and the Eastern Townships (*Estrie*) to the southeast. Both are dotted with attractive towns and villages set amidst rolling hills. The Townships, particularly Knowlton (also known as Lac Brome) and Sutton, still have substantial English populations. Infotouriste can supply information booklets on each area.

QUEBEC CITY

Old Quebec (*Vieux-Québec*) is on UNESCO's World Heritage List, and deservedly so. With a population of 645,000, greater Quebec City sprawls over a sizeable area, but the most interesting part for visitors is definitely Old Quebec, a section of the city perched above the edge of the St. Lawrence River. It's like Old Montreal, only more so because the setting is so spectacular.

Suggested Schedule

8:30 a.m.	Depart Montreal
11:30 p.m.	Arrive Quebec City, check into hotel, have lunch.
1:00 p.m.	Plains of Abraham and the Quebec Museum.
3:00 p.m.	The Citadel.
5:00 p.m.	Promenade des Gouverneurs to Dufferin Terrace.

Driving Route: Montreal to Quebec City (233 km/140 miles)

To take the north shore route, get onto Highway 40 in Montreal, known as Metropolitan Boulevard in the city and running east-west north of the mountain, and head east. Coming into Quebec City, take exit 305 to the 540 south and follow it right into town. It becomes Laurier Boulevard, then Chemin St-Louis, then Grand-Allée, the heart of the city.

Or, to take the south-shore route, cross the Champlain or Victoria bridge from Montreal and take Highway 20 east, the TransCanada. Across the river from Quebec City, take Highway 73 north, which leads over the Pierre Laporte Bridge, and thence onto the 175 east (Laurier Boulevard) and into town. Either way, Quebec City is a 2½ to 3-hour drive from Montreal. The north shore route, which lies closer to the river, is the more scenic and slightly shorter of the two, but it's a little slower than the south shore route because it does not bypass Trois-Rivières, the largest city between Montreal and Quebec. The south shore route bypasses all towns.

The Quebec City Airport is in suburban Ancienne-Lorette, northwest of the city. The bus terminal is at 225 Charest Boulevard East in the centre of the city, while the railway station, Gare du Palais, is at 450 rue de la Gare-du-Palais in Lower Town.

Quebec City

The first known European to land in the area was French explorer Jacques Cartier, who arrived in the Algonquin village of Stadacona, high on a cape above the river, in 1534. Samuel de Champlain, founder of New France, settled in "Kebec" ("where the rivers meet" in the Algonquin language) in 1608, but because the area was considered the gateway to the continent, the English kept trying to conquer it without success. Then in 1759, as British armies marched on Montreal, a seaborn invasion sailed up the St. Lawrence to deliver General James Wolfe's army to the gates of Quebec. General Louis-Joseph de Montcalm and his men kept Wolfe from climbing the cliffs all summer long; Wolfe's army had to content itself with shelling from across the river. In the end, Wolfe finally got his men over the cliff by sending them up a narrow path under cover of darkness. Both generals were fatally wounded in the subsequent Battle of the Plains of Abraham, from which the British emerged victorious. In 1774, the Quebec Act allowed French Canadians to retain their right to practice their Roman Catholic religion (then banned in England) and to preserve their language and customs. In 1775, American rebels, trying to get all of British North America to join their movement, stormed the city but were badly defeated. That was the last battle at Quebec City, although the British later completed the fortifications that make Old Quebec one of the few walled cities in the world.

After arriving from Montreal, spend the afternoon exploring Upper Town, where the Citadel, the Plains of

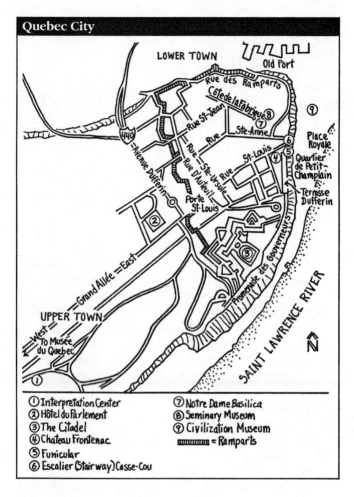

Quebec City

1. Interpretation Center
2. Hôtel du Parlement
3. The Citadel
4. Château Frontenac
5. Funicular
6. Escalier (Stairway) Casse-Cou
7. Notre Dame Basilica
8. Seminary Museum
9. Civilization Museum
▭▭▭▭ = Ramparts

Abraham and other historic and scenic must-sees are located. Tomorrow, the highlights include the quaint Petit-Champlain neighborhood and the Old Port.

Getting Around
Grande-Allée runs straight up to *Porte St-Louis* (St-Louis Gate), an entrance to the walled part of the city, after which it becomes St-Louis Street. Follow St-Louis a few blocks and you're at the Château Frontenac, set on a cliff

above Lower Town and Quartier du Petit-Champlain, the oldest commercial quarter in North America. You can take a funicular from the Château Frontenac down into Petit-Champlain, whose narrow, sloped streets are lined with boutiques, art galleries, bistros, and restaurants. Or you can walk down the steep set of stairs. Dufferin Terrace behind the hotel becomes *Promenade des Gouverneurs* and runs along the clifftop past the Citadel (or *Citadelle*). It provides a magnificent view of the harbor and the St. Lawrence River. Old Quebec is made up of Lower Town, which runs along the riverfront and includes the Old Port and Quartier Petit-Champlain, and Upper Town atop Cape Diamond. Upper Town includes the Plains of Abraham, also known as *Parc des Champs de Batailles* (Battlefields Park), the provincial legislature, Grande-Allée and the walled part of the city.

The city's tourist information bureau is at 60 D'Auteuil St.; turn left onto D'Auteuil, the first street you come to after entering the walled city through the Porte St-Louis. From early June to Labor Day, the bureau is open daily from 8:30 a.m. to 8:00 p.m. The provincial tourism bureau is at 12 Ste-Anne Street, across from the Chateau Frontenac, open from 8:30 a.m. to 7:30 p.m., June through Labor Day.

Walking is the best way to get around Quebec City. However, for information on city buses, call the municipal bus information line at (418) 627-2511. Daily passes are available.

Sightseeing Highlights
▲▲**Quebec Museum**—The *Musée du Québec* is in the middle of the Plains of Abraham, a historic battlefield that's now a broad expanse of greenery and gardens. The museum features Quebec art dating from earliest European life in the province to the present. A museum annex houses the National Battlefields Park Interpretation Center, a high-tech presentation about the history of the Plains of Abraham, 250 acres of woodlands and gardens. The museum is at 1 Wolfe-Montcalm Avenue and is open

10:00 a.m to 5:45 p.m. Thursday to Tuesday, and until
9:45 p.m. Wednesday, from May 24 to Labor Day; closed
Mondays the rest of the year. Admission is $4.75 for
adults, $3.75 for seniors, students 16 and up $2.75, and
free for children under 16. Free admission on Wednesdays.
Admission to the interpretation center is free. Phone (418)
643-2150 for more information.

▲▲**The Citadel**—A star-shaped fortress with more than
two dozen buildings, this is the largest fortified group of
buildings in North America still occupied by troops—the
Royal 22nd Regiment, or the Van-Doos (from *vingt-deux*,
or 22 in French) as they are known in Quebec. Buildings
include the Governor General's residence, the officers'
mess, and the Royal 22nd Regiment Museum. Guided
tours last 55 minutes, but military history buffs could
probably happily spend all day here. Admission is $4 for
adults, $2 for children aged 7 to 17, and free for children
under 7. From mid-June to Labor Day there is a daily
changing-of-the-guard at 10:00 a.m., weather permitting.
For information, call (418) 648-3563.

▲▲▲**Promenade des Gouverneurs and Dufferin
Terrace**—*Promendade des Gouverneurs* (Governors'
Walk) begins near the southwest corner of The Citadel
and leads along the clifftops to Dufferin Terrace behind
the Château Frontenac. A stroll along here provides a
magnificent panorama of Lower Town, the Old Port,
and the river.

▲**Hôtel du Parlement**—This imposing Renaissance-style
building off Grande-Allée East at Dufferin Avenue houses
Quebec's legislature, known as the National Assembly.
Free guided tours are available. Opposite Hôtel du
Parliament on Grande Allée, you'll notice a rather ugly
concrete complex that houses the premier's offices and is
known affectionately as The Bunker.

Lodging
Everything from B&Bs through small inns to luxury high-
rise hotels is available, but in Old Quebec the emphasis is
on inns (or *auberges*). The major exception is the magnificent **Château Frontenac**, which sits atop a cliff in the

heart of Old Quebec, overlooking the old town below and the river beyond. It's a tourist attraction as well as a hotel. Even if you don't stay there, it's the place to start a walking tour, take the funicular down the cliff, or wander along Dufferin Terrace. A hundred years old in 1993, the landmark, copper-roofed hotel has recently undergone major renovations and is one of the most photographed hotels in Canada. With room rates beginning around $125, it's also more expensive than most other establishments in the area. Call 692-3861 locally or 1-800-441-1414 toll-free.

Loews Le Concorde, another big luxury hotel ($135-$195), has the only rooftop revolving restaurant in the city. The hotel is at 1225 Place Montcalm, off Grande Allée; call 647-2222 locally or 1-800-223-0888 toll-free from the U.S.

The inns scattered around Old Quebec offer both moderate rates and lots of atmosphere. Try **Auberge Louis Hébert** at 668 Grande-Allee East, (418) 525-7812; **Auberge St-Louis** at 48 St-Louis, 692-2424 locally or 1-800-663-7878 toll-free; **Auberge de la Place d'Armes** ($60-$100) at 24 Ste-Anne, (418) 694-9485; **Hôtel Manoir Lafayette** ($60-$125) at 665 Grande-Allee East, 1-800-363-8203 toll-free; or **Hotel Château Bellevue** ($54-$94) at 16 Laporte Street, 1-800-463-2617 toll-free.

For bed and breakfasts, try **Bed and Breakfast Bonjour Québec**, which represents 11 homes within a few minutes' drive of Old Quebec. Write to Denise and Raymond Blanchet, 3765 Monaco Boulevard, Quebec, Que. G1P 3J3, or phone (418) 527-1465. Another B&B reservation service, run by Therese Tellier and representing more than 30 homes in the city and surrounding area, is **Gîte Québec Bed & Breakfast**, 3729 avenue Le Corbusier, Ste-Foy, Que. G1W 4R8, (418) 651-1860.

There is a motel strip along Laurier Boulevard just after you come off the highway or bridge into the city, but rooms aren't generally much cheaper here than in Old Quebec.

Camping
As to campgrounds, there are more than two dozen in the area around the city. They're all listed in the Greater

Quebec Area Tourist Guide, available for free from either the municipal or the provincial tourist boards. The most conveniently located is in Ste-Foy, the area of town immediately after you come off the bridge. **Camping Aéroport** has 145 sites and extensive facilities, including a restaurant. Rates are $21 and up. The campground is on Route 138 off Highway 73. Phone (418) 871-1574.

Restaurants

For memorable French dining, try **Restaurant Le Louis Hébert** at 668 Grande-Allée East (*Grande-Allée est*), (418) 525-7812. The food is wonderful, and you can eat it in the Sun Room abutting the main restaurant. The Sun Room is filled with natural light, wicker furniture, and plants, making for a summery setting even during Quebec City's severe winters. The inn is upstairs.

Another favorite French restaurant is **L'Échaudé** (literally translated, scalded person) at 73 Sault-au-Matelot, a narrow street in Lower Town. Call (418) 692-1299. **Aux Anciens Canadiens**, at 34 St-Louis a block from the Château Frontenac, serves Quebec specialties such as smoked sturgeon, Lac-St-Jean meat pie, hare civet and maple syrup pie. Call (418) 692-1627. At **Au Café Suisse** at 32 Ste-Anne (also a block from the Chateau Frontenac), fondues and raclettes are the specialties of the house. Call (418) 694-1320. For a pub-style atmosphere, try **Le D'Orsay** at 65 Buade Street, another street near the Chateau Frontenac, (418) 694-1582.

For a more complete listing of restaurants to suit every mood and budget, pick up a copy of the restaurant guide published by the Greater Quebec Area Tourism and Convention Bureau.

Nightlife

The nightlife is chiefly along Grande-Allée East between the Loews Le Concorde hotel and Place George V. In summer, particularly, this area is jammed with people because most of the restaurants and bars have street-side terraces. The tourism agencies like to refer to Grande-Allée as the Champs Elysée of Quebec City, although it's nowhere near as long or wide as the real thing.

Shopping

A two-block section at the eastern end of St-Paul Street in Lower Town is home to virtually all the city's antique shops and makes for a fine area to browse. As it happens, St-Paul and Sault-au-Matelot streets also have enticing neighborhood cafés, bistros, and restaurants, most of them budget-priced.

Festivals

The annual Quebec International Summer Festival, usually running the second and third week of July, offers a vast assortment of entertainment in the streets and parks of the city, especially Old Quebec. It's billed as the biggest French-language cultural festival in North America.

In winter—and Quebec City winters are brutally cold—locals and visitors warm up with a winter carnival (called *Carnaval*) that's billed as the largest winter festival in the world. The 10-day blowout in January or February is centered around a massive ice palace that is a glittering wonder to behold. The other star attraction is *Bonhomme Carnaval*, the jolly snowman-like festival mascot. During *Carnaval*, tradition calls for drinking a strong alcoholic concoction called Caribou out of hollow, plastic canes.

Helpful Hint

For more information on Quebec City, contact the Greater Quebec Area Tourism and Convention Bureau, 60, rue D'Auteuil, Quebec, Que., Canada G1R 4C4, or phone (418) 692-2471 or (418) 651-2882. The offices are open daily from 8:30 a.m. to 8:00 p.m. between early June and Labor Day; from 8:30 a.m. to 5:30 p.m. daily between Labor Day and mid-October; Monday to Friday, 9:00 a.m. to 5:00 p.m., from mid-October to mid-April; and 8:30 a.m to 5:30 p.m., Monday through Friday, from mid-April to early June. For information on Quebec City and the rest of the province, contact Tourisme Quebec toll-free at 1-800-363-7777 or drop by the information center at 12 Ste-Anne Street in Quebec City, across from the Chateau Frontenac.

QUEBEC CITY TO TADOUSSAC

After exploring more of Old Quebec this morning, hit the road for Tadoussac, a summer resort town where the Saguenay River meets the St. Lawrence River and where whale-watching and cruising the Saguenay fjords are the major attractions. Most of the drive is through Charlevoix County, the area where the Laurentian hills slope down to the north shore of the St. Lawrence. The Laurentians are part of the vast Canadian Shield, a continental crust so old that its "mountains" are now little more than round, gently sloping hills. Repeated advances and retreats of ice sheets have also left the shield strewn with countless lakes, rivers and ponds. It is said that in Quebec alone, there are six million lakes, but nobody knows for sure; they've never all been counted. Charlevoix has such starkly arresting scenery that it has been attracting tourists since holiday-making began in Canada in the late 18th century. If you have more than a day to spend here, many of the towns and villages that dot the riverside route boast attractive country inns and B&Bs. Along Highway 138, skirting the north shore of the St. Lawrence, possible sightseeing stops include the shrine at Ste-Anne-de-Beaupré and La Malbaie, formerly Murray Bay.

Suggested Schedule	
9:00 a.m.	Explore Lower Town and the Old Port, pause for lunch, explore some more.
1:30 p.m.	Depart Quebec City.
2:30 p.m.	Take a break in the artists' colony of Baie-St-Paul.
3:30 p.m.	Pointe-au-Pic and neighboring La Malbaie.
5:00 p.m.	Ferry across the Saguenay to Tadoussac.

Sightseeing Highlights in Quebec City
▲▲▲Quartier du Petit-Champlain—The funicular, whose entrance is on Dufferin Terrace at the Château Frontenac, takes you to the foot of the cliff to the Petit-

Champlain neighborhood, the oldest commercial quarter in North America. Its narrow, sloped streets are lined with boutiques, art galleries, bistros, bars, and restaurants, housed in restored 17th- and 18th-century buildings. This is an area to wander at will.

▲▲**Place Royale**—A charming cobblestone square near the waterfront, Place Royale is where the first French settlers landed. There are an interpretation center about its development (entrance is free), an exhibition that traces the history of Place Royale and Lower Town (also free), and an information center that is also the departure point for guided tours. In summer, Place Royale is the scene of an array of outdoor plays and shows.

▲▲▲**Old Port of Quebec**—Le Vieux-Port has a market, an amphitheater, and the Old Port of Quebec National Historic Site, an interpretation center that explains the shipbuilding and lumber industries, historically the main industries centered on the port. Open from June 24 to Labor Day, 1:00 to 5:00 p.m. on Mondays and 10:00 a.m. to 5:00 p.m. Tuesday through Sunday; hours are shorter the rest of the year, varying seasonally. Phone 648-3300 for current information. Admission to the interpretive center is $2.25 for adults, $1.50 for seniors, and $1 for children aged 5 to 15.

▲▲▲**Civilization Museum**—This imaginative museum houses assorted interactive, multimedia, and more traditional exhibits based on themes including language, natural resources, society, and the human body. Anything from clothing to sculptures might be on display at any given time. The museum, a blend of historic and new structures that was designed by the ubiquitous architect Moshe Safdie, is at 85 Dalhousie Road in the heart of the Old Port, near Place Royale. Open daily from 10:00 a.m. to 7:00 p.m. from June 24 to Labor Day and 10:00 a.m. to 5:00 p.m. Tuesday to Sunday the rest of the year. Admission is $5 for adults, $3 for students, $4 for seniors and free for children under age 16. Free admission on Tuesdays. Phone 643-2158.

▲**Basilique-cathédrale Notre-Dame-de-Québec**—First opened in 1650 and the oldest parish on the continent north of Mexico, this richly ornate edifice is replete with stained-glass windows, assorted artwork, a throned dais, a majestic organ and a lamp that was a gift from Louis XIV. Assorted Quebec bishops and governors of New France are buried in the crypt. The address is 16 Buade Street, a couple of blocks from the Château Frontenac.

▲**Seminary Museum**—The *Musée de Seminaire*, a history museum with a vast collection that focuses mainly on French North America, is at 9 University Street, a block or two from Notre-Dame Basilica. It houses everything from an Egyptian mummy to paintings by Canadian and European artists. Open daily from 10:00 a.m. to 5:30 p.m. from June 1 to September 30, closed Mondays the rest of the year. Admission $3 for adults, $2 for seniors, $1.50 for students, $1 for children 16 and under, or $6 for families. Phone 692-2843.

Driving Route: Quebec City to Tadoussac (206 km/123 miles)

From Grande-Allée, take Dufferin Avenue and follow the signs for the Dufferin-Montmorency Autoroute, or Highway 440, which veers east along the river. The Montmorency Falls are about 10 kilometers (six miles) outside the city. After that the highway turns into Ste-Anne Boulevard, or Highway 138. Ste-Anne-de-Beaupré is about 20 kilometers (12 miles) past the falls. Baie-St-Paul, in a lovely riverside valley and long known as an artists' colony, is 91 kilometers (55 miles) from Quebec City, while the resort town of La Malbaie lies 139 kilometers (83 miles) from Quebec City. From Baie-Ste-Catherine, the car ferry to Tadoussac across the mouth of the Saguenay takes 10 minutes. In season, it's best to reserve (see Helpful Hints).

With no stops, the drive would take between two and three hours; with stops here and there, make it about four hours.

Sightseeing Highlights

▲**Montmorency Falls**—The falls lie just east of Quebec, off the highway. At 83 meters (270 feet), Montmorency is one and one-half times higher than Niagara Falls, although

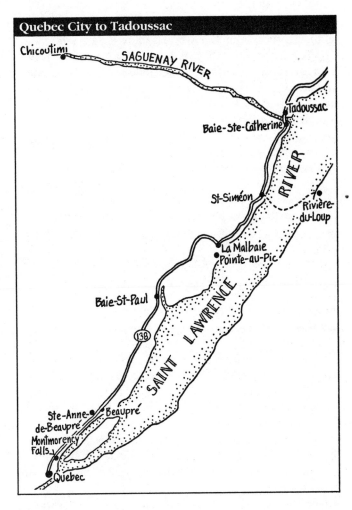

Quebec City to Tadoussac

nowhere near as wide and so somehow not as impressive. An information center, lookouts, picnic tables, trails, and a vast parking area are all open to the public in-season, with access clearly marked from the highway. If you're not taking time to stop, the falls are clearly visible from the highway.

▲**Ste-Anne-de-Beaupré**—More than 1.5 million pilgrims a year make their way to the famous Catholic shrine in

Ste-Anne-de-Beaupré. Legend has it that Ste. Anne, the mother of the Virgin Mary, saved shipwrecked sailors off Cap Tourmante after they prayed to her, and modern pilgrims similarly hope for miracles by coming to Ste-Anne-de-Beaupré. The original wooden chapel dedicated to the saint was built in 1658 and later replaced by a stone church, in turn destroyed by fire in 1922. The present-day stone basilica, a massive structure visible from far down the highway, went up in 1923. Admission is free.

▲**Baie-St-Paul**—Nestled in a scenic valley, the town of Baie-St-Paul has become known as an artists' colony. Over the years it has drawn not just painters but performers. Street performers in Baie-St-Paul in the 1970s formed a loose group that later became the Cirque du Soleil, the acclaimed Montreal-based circus. Baie-St-Paul's narrow streets are lined with boutiques, outdoor cafés, and, naturally, art galleries. Visit the Centre d'Art at 4 Ambroise-Fafard Street for a taste of local art. There is also a tourist information counter at the art center.

▲**Pointe-au-Pic**—The tourism people claim this village was the birthplace of tourism in Canada. Traditionally it drew the affluent from Montreal, Quebec, and even New York City, but these days it is more democratic. To get a taste of how the other half lived, though, stop off at the Manoir Richelieu, a grand old hotel on a bluff overlooking the river.

There is also a new casino at the Manoir Richelieu. Like the Montreal casino, it is operated by Loto Quebec and has the same policies and dress code—no T-shirts, jeans, or sneakers, please.

▲**La Malbaie**—The administrative center of the Charlevoix region, La Malbaie stands at the base of a lovely bay, so named because Samuel de Champlain's ship ran aground here back in 1608 and Champlain reportedly described it in French as "*la malbaie*"—bad bay. A promenade runs along the waterfront.

Tadoussac

A small but busy summer resort on the north shore of the Saguenay where it meets the St. Lawrence, Tadoussac has for decades attracted vacationers aiming to savor the wild beauty of the Saguenay River. Village-sized Tadoussac has a beach and a marina, overlooked by the famous old Hotel Tadoussac.

Tadoussac is surrounded by Saguenay Park (*Parc du Saguenay*), and several nature-study paths lead from the middle of the village to nearby points. They're no more than about two kilometers (just over a mile) round-trip, so a before- or after-dinner stroll may be in order. One trail leads to Colline de l'Anse a l'Eau, a good vantage point from whence to see the majestic Saguenay fjords, the St. Lawrence, and the village; the path skirting Pointe de l'Islet offers two lookouts towards the St. Lawrence; and two new trails, the Fjord Trail and the Anse à la Barque trail, lead toward the cliffs of the Saguenay.

At 108 de la Cale-Sèche Street in the village there is a marine interpretation center where you can learn all about St. Lawrence whales (*baleines* in French). Unlike most interpretation centers, which use photographs and displays, this one is filled with interactive displays that test your knowledge of whales and let you listen to their songs. Kids can play a video game in which the aim is to help Delphi the beluga whale hunt her daily ration of 12 kilograms (26 pounds) of food. The *Centre d'interpretation des mammifères marins* is open daily from 10:00 a.m. to 8:00 p.m. from mid-May through mid-October. Admission is $4.50 for adults, $2.50 for children ages 6 to 11, $3.50 for seniors, and $12 for families.

Lodging

The historic (c. 1864) **Hotel Tadoussac** is a prime place to stay if there's room and you can afford it. Rates for two people run from $129 to $228 per room. That includes breakfast. Call 235-4421 locally or 1-800-361-6162 toll-free from Quebec, or 1-800-463-5250 toll-free from Quebec, Ontario, the Maritimes and the United States.

There are plenty of inns, motels, and B&Bs. In season it's best to reserve well ahead. Some contact numbers: **Hôtel-Motel Georges**, from $45 to $85 depending on the season, (418) 235-4393; **Auberge du Lac**, from $50 to $85 depending on the season, (418) 235-4784; **Motel Chantmartin**, about $70 for two, (418) 235-4242; **Le Pionnier**, about $90 for two, (418) 235-4666; **Maison Clauphi Motel**, from $41 to $78, (418) 235-4303; and **Hôtel-Motel Le Beluga**, about $75 for two, (418) 235-4326

Camping

Try **Camping Tadoussac** at (418) 235-4501. It's on Highway 138, also known as rue du Bateau-Passeur, at the edge of town. Rates are $18 for fully serviced sites and $11 for tenters.

Restaurants

As to dining, there are restaurants to suit most tastes and budgets. Ask at the hotel or motel for recommendations, or just wander the streets until you find something that looks interesting. **Le Bateau**, at 246 rue des Forgerons (235-4427) serves up regional specialties such as meat stew and features a panoramic view of the two rivers. The large **Café du Fjord** at 154 rue du Bateau-Passeur (235-4626) offers a seafood buffet.

Helpful Hints

The car ferry between Baie-Ste-Catherine and Tadoussac runs year-round. In summer, the service is every 20 minutes between 8:00 a.m. and 8:00 p.m., every 40 minutes between 8:00 p.m. and 12:00 midnight and once an hour between midnight and 8:00 a.m. Remember that in season the area gets so busy it's best to reserve; call (418) 235-4395.

Most of today's route is covered in Tourisme Quebec's Charlevoix tourist guide, while information on Tadoussac is in the Manicouagan tourist guide. Call Tourisme Quebec at 1-800-363-7777 toll-free and ask for both guides. There are tourist information offices open year-round at 4 Ambroise-Fafard Street in Baie-St-Paul and at 166 de Comporte Boulevard in La Malbaie. In Tadoussac, the tourist information office at 196 des Pionniers Street is open in-season from 8:00 a.m. to 8:00 p.m. daily.

THE SAGUENAY RIVER AND THE GASPÉ PENINSULA

Set aside the morning for one of Tadoussac's must-do activities, a whale-watching cruise or a cruise up the Saguenay River. Take your choice; or, if you have extra time, by all means stay longer in Tadoussac and fit both in. After the cruise, take a ferry across the St. Lawrence and drive along the river's south shore (also known as *Le Bas St-Laurent*, or the Lower St. Lawrence) to the Gaspé Peninsula. Life along the Bas St-Laurent coast revolves around the river, which in part means tourism. There are inns, hotels, and summer cottages aplenty along the shore, and you may see whales in the river.

Suggested Schedule

9:00 a.m.	Cruise begins. Eat lunch on board if possible.
12:00 noon	Drive to either Les Escoumins or St-Siméon to catch the ferry.
2:00 p.m.	Begin driving along the coast and onto the Gaspé Peninsula.

The Gaspé Peninsula

The Bas St-Laurent melts into the Gaspé Peninsula, one of the most scenic regions in the province. The coast road is a panoply of rolling hills, craggy cliffs and picturesque villages with whimsical names. *Cap-Chat?* Cape Cat was reportedly so named because of a rock near the light-house that resembles a crouching cat. *Anse-Pleureuse?* The winds in Crying Cove sound like people wailing. *Cap-aux-Os?* Cape Bones was named after the whale bones people used to find there.

The Gaspé peninsula is one of the oldest land masses on earth, but it was one of the last to be inhabited by humans and is still only sparsely populated (235,000 residents on the whole peninsula, the vast majority living along the coast). Thankfully, its wild beauty remains largely unspoiled despite its popularity as a tourist destination.

The Micmacs (or Mi'Kmaq, as it's also spelled), or "Indians of the Sea," have lived in the Gaspé for more than 2,500 years. In fact, the name Gaspé probably comes from a Micmac word meaning "land's end." Over the years, myriad European ethnic groups and Loyalists (refugees from the American Revolution) also settled on the peninsula, making for a multicultural mix that continues to this day.

The major industries in the Gaspé are fishing and forestry, and—increasingly—tourism. The area suffers from chronic economic problems, so not only will you see superb scenery, you'll be providing a badly needed shot in the arm for the local economy.

Driving Route: Tadoussac to Forillon National Park (490 km/294 miles)

There are car ferries across the St. Lawrence from St-Siméon, 33 kilometers (20 miles) southwest of Baie-Ste-Catherine on Highway 138, or from Les Escoumins, 39 kilometers (23 miles) northeast of Tadoussac on Highway 138. In the interest of time, it may be better to depart from Les Escoumins because the ferry from there crosses to Trois-Pistoles, thereby saving about 50 kilometers of driving once you're across the river. From St-Siméon, the ferry crosses to Rivière-du-Loup. Either crossing takes an hour and 15 minutes. The St-Siméon ferry begins running in April; find out exact crossing times and make a reservation by calling (418) 862-5094. The ferry between Les Escoumins and Trois-Pistoles runs from June 1 to October 31; for information and reservations, phone (418) 233-2202 in Les Escoumins or (418) 851-4676 in Trois-Pistoles.

From Rivière-du-Loup, take Highway 20 East, which becomes Highway 132. From Trois-Pistoles, get directly onto the 132 east. Follow the 132 all the way around to Forillon National Park, where the peninsula's natural beauty reaches an apex. This is a lot of driving—some 450 kilometers (about 270 miles) from Trois-Pistoles to

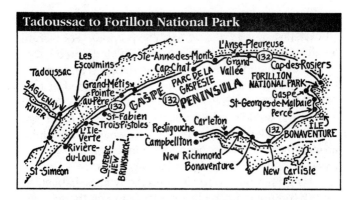

Tadoussac to Forillon National Park

Forillon, or about five hours if you make only washroom stops. The highway winds along the shore of the St. Lawrence the whole way, and if it's summer and light until 9:00 p.m., you'll be able to do the whole thing in daylight.

Alternatively, start out as above but turn south from Route 132 onto Route 198 at Anse-Pleureuse. Route 198 cuts across the peninsula to the town of Gaspé, near Forillon National Park, but going this way actually shaves only about 10 kilometers from the total distance.

Highway 132 goes all the way around the peninsula; the idea is to divide it into two segments, with an overnight stay en route. Aim to stop for the night somewhere between Grande Vallée and Forillon.

Sightseeing Highlights

▲▲▲**The Saguenay Fjord**—The majestic, stark beauty of the glacier-carved Saguenay River is compelling by anyone's standards, except maybe for people who live on the fjords of Norway. The river, which issues from Lac-St-Jean in the Laurentian highlands, is lined with soaring cliffs averaging 300 meters (980 feet) in height, accentuated by coves and bays. For most of its length the water runs deep and swift and never really warms up, even at the height of summer, but the waters where the fresh-water Saguenay joins the salt-water St. Lawrence are shallow, with an abundance of aquatic flora and fauna—and hence a rich feeding ground for whales.

The Saguenay estuary has a resident population of beluga whales, a variety of white arctic porpoise. For assorted reasons, most having to do with humankind's greed, the beluga population is today severely depleted and has been declared endangered. One study concluded that the 500 belugas living in the heavily polluted St. Lawrence are among the world's sickest whales, in the sense that more than half of all the tumors reported in whales and dolphins around the world have been found in the St. Lawrence belugas. The federal and provincial governments are spending $110 million to clean up the whales' habitat, so there's still hope for the belugas. In summer, the feeding grounds at the mouth of the river may also attract blue whales, humpbacks, fin-backs, and assorted other species of whales.

From Tadoussac or Baie Ste-Catherine, whale-watching cruises and boat rides on the Saguenay are available from about mid-May through September, on everything from four-passenger Zodiacs to ships that carry 300 people, lasting anywhere from 90 minutes to four hours. They average between $10 and $15 per hour for adults and half that for kids. These cruises are popular; try to make reservations ahead of time. It's a good idea to take warm clothing to wear on board. Companies offering whale-watching cruises from Tadoussac and-or Baie Ste-Catherine include **Croisière Navimenx,** offering 3-hour whale-watching cruises ($30 to $40 for adults and $15 to $20 for children, depending on the cruise); call (418) 237-4274 in season in Baie-Ste-Catherine or (418) 692-4643 in Quebec City the rest of the year; **Compagnie de la Baie de Tadoussac,** charging $30 per adult and $15 per child for a 3-hour whale-watching trip; call (418) 235-4548 in Tadoussac; and **Croisière Express**, offering 3-hour cruises in 12-passenger boats at $30 for adults and $15 for children; call (418) 235-4770 in summer and (418) 235-4283 in winter.

Hotel Tadoussac also runs three-hour cruises both up the river and to whale-watch; prices are $30 for adults and $15 for kids. Call 827-5711 in Tadoussac, 1-800-361-6162

toll-free from Quebec, or 1-800-463-5250 toll-free from Quebec, Ontario, the Maritimes and the United States.
▲**Rivière-du-Loup**—Literally translated as "river of the wolf," Rivière-du-Loup is the Bas St-Laurent's commercial center. Here, the St. Lawrence widens to 20 kilometers (12 miles) and becomes known as "the sea." The one thing worth stopping for may be the waterfalls in the center of the city. Take either Frontenac or de la Chute Street, climb the stairs, and follow the fence to the lookout. The waterfalls are 30 meters (98 feet) high.
▲**Île Verte**—"Green Island" is the only one in the region inhabited year-round. Forty people live there. There's a ferry service from L'Île-Verte on the mainland. The bucolic island also boasts the oldest lighthouse on the river. Built in 1809, the lighthouse provides a good vantage point for whale-watching.
▲**St-Fabien**—More beaches and summer cottages, along with the only octagonal barn in the region. The barn, built in 1888, is in the center of the village.
▲**Pointe-au-Père**—If you want to know more about the social history of the area, take Père Nouvel St. towards the river to the *Musée de la mer et lieu historique national de Pointe-au-Père*. This national historic site contains exhibitions and interpretations of regional history and marine life, plus a lighthouse. Admission is $3 for adults, $2.50 for students and seniors, and $1.25 for children aged 6 and up.
▲▲**Grand-Métis**—Having passed through Ste-Flavie, the "gateway to the Gaspé," consider a stop in Grand-Métis to see the enchanting *Jardins de Métis* (Metis Gardens), featuring six different ornamental gardens surrounding a luxurious villa. Now owned by the Quebec government, the estate used to belong the niece of Lord Mount Stephen, the first president of Canadian Pacific Railroad. The niece, Elsie Reford, who moved in in the 1920s, was an avid gardener. The mansion now houses a museum, a restaurant, and a crafts shop. The Jardins de Métis are open from June to September, from 8:30 a.m. to 8:00 p.m. daily. Admission is $4.25 for adults, 50 cents for kids aged 8 to 14, $3 for seniors, and free for children under age 8.

▲**Cap-Chat**—Cap-Chat is where the St. Lawrence River officially becomes the Gulf of St. Lawrence. Cap-Chat also boasts the biggest and most powerful vertical-axis wind-tower in the world, three kilometers west of the Cap-Chat bridge. There is a bilingual, multimedia show about the windtower and life in the region at the *Centre d'interpre-tation du vent et de la mer* (wind and sea interpretation center).

▲▲**Parc de la Gaspésie**—This sidetrip is worth it if you have the time. At Ste-Anne-des-Monts, turn south on Highway 299; the park entrance is 15 kilometers down the 299. The mountainous park is the only place in the province where moose, wood caribou, and Virginia deer all live in the same territory. The park's Chic-Chocs are the highest mountains in eastern Canada, with Mont Jacques-Cartier the loftiest at 1,268 meters (4,145 feet). The summit of another mountain, Mont Albert, is a 30-square-kilometer plateau boasting mosses, lichens, and shrubs that are nor-mally found only in the far north. There are several lodg-ing facilities in the park, which also features some 120 kilometers of hiking trails. The reception center is open from early June until Labor Day.

▲**Anse-Pleureuse**—Back on Highway 132, the route passes through several scenic coastal villages and then to Anse-Pleureuse. Get out of the car to listen to the wind in the trees, a haunting sound that according to local legend is the moans of the ghosts of two little girls, the sobs of a man who was murdered and/or the cries of shipwrecked ghosts.

▲**Grande-Vallée**—Outside Grande-Vallée (big valley), there is a roadside rest area that offers a magnificent view of the village and valley. A covered bridge in the middle of the village adds a nice touch to the quaint, peaceful nature of the scene.

▲**Cap-des-Rosiers**—Named by Samuel de Champlain for the wild roses that grow on its cliffs, Cap-des-Rosiers fea-tures a lighthouse atop a 37-meter (120-foot) cliff, making it the highest site for a Canadian lighthouse. The village is also considered the gateway to Forillon National Park.

Lodging

There are numerous hotels, motels, and inns in many of the villages and towns along Highway 132. Possibilities in the Forillon National Park vicinity include **Châlets au Gaspésien** ($35-$50) at 58 des Touristes in l'Anse-à-Valleau, (418) 269-3191. In Rivière-au-Renard just outside the park, try **Auberge Motel Caribou** ($65-$70) at 82 Renard Boulevard West, (418) 269-3237. Other establishments within shouting distance of the park include **Motel Atlantique** ($40-$65) at 1334 Highway 132 in Cap-des-Rosiers, (418) 892-5533; **Le Pharillon** ($45-$70), also on Highway 132 in Cap-des-Rosiers, (418) 892-5200; and **Motel Le Noroit** ($45-$55) at 589 Griffon Boulevard in l'Anse-au-Griffon, (418) 892-5531.

There are two B&Bs in Cap-aux-Os (follow Highway 132 around the bottom of the park to get to Cap-aux-Os), both right on the route. Write to **Gîte du Parc**, Solange and Claude Cassivi, 2045 Highway 132, Cap-aux-Os, Forillon, Que. G0E 1J0, or phone (418) 892-5864; or **Gîte du Levant**, W. Zomer and G. Ouellet, 1626 Forillon Blvd., Cap-aux-Os, Forillon, Que. G0E 1J0, (418) 892-5814. Gîte du Levant is a non-smoking establishment.

Camping

There are several campgrounds inside Forillon National Park. They include **Camping Cap Bon-Ami** (Cape Good Friend Campground) and **Camping des Rosiers** (Rosebush Campground), both at (418) 892-5100, and **Camping Petit Gaspé** (Little Gaspé Campground) at (418) 892-5911. Or try **Camping au Soleil Couchant** (Setting Sun Campground) at 73 Highway 132 in Grand-Vallee, (418) 393-2646, or **Camping Griffon** at 419 Griffon Boulevard in L'Anse-au-Griffon, (418) 892-5938. Rates run from $10 to $20 at all of these campgrounds.

Restaurants

Any restaurant serving seafood should be fine; the seafood should be as fresh as the catch of the day. In nearby Gaspé, try the **Bistro-Bar Brise Bize** for moderately

priced fare. It's at 2 Côte Charter (368-1456). The food is
fancier and the prices higher at the **Café-Restaurant La
Belle Hélène**, one of the region's best restaurants, at
135-A rue de la Reine (368-1455).

Helpful Hints

Via Rail offers an overnight train, the Chaleur, between
Montreal and the town of Gaspé. The train runs along the
south shore from Montreal to Levis, Rivière du Loup,
Rimouski, and Mont Joli, then down the Matapedia Valley
to Matapedia, east along the south Gaspé coast through
New Carlisle and Percé and finally to Gaspé. It takes 17
hours, and in both directions the trip sector between
Matapedia and Gaspé is in daylight (at least in summer),
allowing passengers to take in the spectacular scenery
along the south Gaspé coast. If you're tired of driving,
consider this trip instead. The Chaleur was renovated in
1992 and has comfortable coach cars, a dining car complete with a bar lounge, and sleeper cars with showers. If
you're traveling in summer, reserve well ahead. For information, contact Via or see a travel agent.

For more information on the places along today's route,
use Tourisme Quebec's Bas St-Laurent and Gaspésie booklets. Call 1-800-363-7777 toll-free. For still more information,
contact the Association Touristique du Bas-St-Laurent at
189, rue Hôtel-de-Ville, Rivière-du-Loup, Que., Canada
G5R 4C3, (418) 867-3015; and the Association Touristique
de la Gaspésie, 357 route de la Mer, Sainte-Flavie, Que.,
Canada G0J 2L0, (418) 775-2223. In person, drop in to the
Ste-Flavie office, open year-round. Ste-Flavie, between
Pointe-au-Père and Grand-Métis, is the so-called gateway
to the Gaspé Peninsula. There are also seasonal tourist
information offices in 12 different towns and villages
along Highway 132, including Rivière-au-Renard.

GASPÉ PENINSULA

Continue driving around the Gaspé coast, beginning with
a tour of Forillon National Park, a dramatic product of
erosion, and then heading along the south Gaspé coast.
Other highlights include the famous Percé Rock, one of
the most popular tourist draws in Quebec, and Île de
Bonaventure, a sanctuary a few kilometers off shore from
Percé that attracts dozens of species of birds in their thousands. After that come a series of scenic coastal towns,
some of which have Loyalist or Acadian roots.

Having completed the Gaspé circuit, the route
crosses into northern New Brunswick. Overnight in the
Campbellton area. Entering New Brunswick also involves
setting your watches ahead one hour. New Brunswick,
Nova Scotia and Prince Edward Island are in the Atlantic
Time Zone, which is one hour later than the Eastern Time
Zone. When it's 5:00 p.m. in Toronto or New York, for
instance, it's 6:00 p.m. in the Maritimes.

Suggested Schedule	
9:00 a.m.	Tour Forillon National Park.
11:00 a.m.	See Percé Rock and tour Île Bonaventure.
1:00 p.m.	Lunch.
2:00 p.m.	Continue the drive along the south Gaspé coast, stopping at points of interest.
5:00 p.m.	Cross into New Brunswick.

Driving Route
Forillon to Campbellton (340 km/200 miles)
Continue on Highway 132 to Restigouche and neigboring
Pointe-à-la-Croix, where there is a bridge to Campbellton,
N.B. It's about 340 kilometers (roughly 200 miles) from
Forillon to the bridge.

Sightseeing Highlights
▲▲▲**Forillon National Park**—Located on a small
peninsula at the easternmost tip of the Gaspé Peninsula,

Forillon park has rugged, hilly forests inland that are
framed on the coast by soaring limestone cliffs, pebble
beaches, small sandy coves and rocks sculpted by the
pounding sea. From offshore, the park has the strangest
appearance—like a huge, jagged-edged block emerging at
an angle from the sea, with one side sloping gently down
to the water and the cliff side dropping precipitously. In
summer, thousands of birds nest on the cliffs. Wildlife
includes deer, moose, lynx, black bear and red fox, and
you might see whales and seals from coastal cliffs. There
is also an unusually wide cross-section of plant life, given
the relatively small size of the park (245 square kilometers). The theme of the park is harmony among
humanity, earth and ocean. For more information, phone
368-5505 locally.

▲**Gaspé**—Gaspé, the administrative center for the area, is
one of the oldest settlements in North America. Jacques
Cartier took possession of Canada on behalf of the king of
France and placed a cross on this location in 1534. If
you're interested in the history of the peninsula, stop in at
Musée de la Gaspésie at 80 Gaspé Boulevard. The permanent exhibition is titled *Un peuple de la mer*, or people of
the sea. The museum also houses temporary exhibits of
artwork from the region. Open daily from 9:00 a.m. to
8:30 p.m. from June 24 to Labor Day; 9:00 a.m. to 12:00
noon and 1:00 to 5:00 p.m. Monday to Friday and 2:00 to
5:00 p.m. Saturday and Sunday during the rest of the year.
Admission is $3.50 for adults, $2.50 for students and
seniors, and $1.50 for children aged 6 to 11.

▲**St-Georges-de-Malbaie**—Just south of the village of
St-Georges-de-Malbaie, there is a superb vista of Forillon
on one side and Île Bonaventure and Percé Rock on
the other.

▲▲▲**Percé Rock**—An enigmatic, arresting presence, this
monolith sits just offshore, brooding over the town of
Percé. It was once attached to the shoreline, and at low
tide you can still reach it on foot. It is 510 meters long,
100 meters wide and 70 meters high (roughly 1,670 by
330 by 230 feet). It is named Percé because the sea has
"pierced" holes in it to form archways. Way back in the

mists of time, there were reputedly four such arches, but now there is just one large opening some 30 meters (98 feet) wide. Together, Percé Rock and Île Bonaventure make up the *Parc de l'Île-Bonaventure-et-du-Rocher-Percé*; call (418) 782-2721 for more information.

▲▲▲**Île Bonaventure**—An estimated 220,000 birds nest every year on windswept Bonaventure Island, a conservation park a few kilometers offshore from Percé. The colony of gannets alone is 50,000 strong. The island is also rife with wildflowers, mosses and mushrooms. You can take a boat excursion to Île Bonaventure from Percé. Check in at the interpretation center, the *Centre d'interprétation du Parc de l'Île-Bonaventure-et-du-Rocher-Percé*, for information. You need at least an hour to see Île Bonaventure.

▲**Chandler**—The wreck of the Peruvian freighter *Unisol* lies off Chandler and is visible from shore. The ship didn't sink when it hit some rocks there in 1983—it got wedged between the rocks and half of it sticks out of the water at an angle. It's a rather eerie sight—it looks like it's in the process of going down.

▲**New Carlisle**—This is a largely English-speaking village, populated mainly with the descendants of Loyalist families—American colonists of varying ethnic backgrounds who supported the British cause during the American Revolution and came to Canada in great waves in 1783 and 1784. It's also the birthplace of the late René Lévesque, founder and leader of the Parti Québecois, champion of the separatist movement and eventually premier of the province during the late 1970s and early 1980s.

▲**Bonaventure**—The Acadians, the predominantly French-speaking, Roman Catholic settlers of eastern Canada, were at one point deported from Nova Scotia by the British, who were struggling with the French for control of North America. Some went to Gaspé after avoiding the deportation campaign in the mid-1700s. As an Acadian stronghold, Bonaventure is home to the *Musée acadien du Québec*, featuring antiques and period photos plus a slide show on the history of Acadians in Quebec (some one million Quebecers are of Acadian descent). Bilingual guided tours are available. The museum is at 97 Port-Royal Avenue, open from 9:00 a.m. to 9:00 p.m. daily from late June until early September and shorter hours the rest of the year. Admission is $3.50 for adults, $2.50 for students and seniors and $7.50 for families.

▲**New Richmond**—Founded by the Loyalists, New Richmond has an interpretation center that recreates the Loyalist era, complete with houses, period furniture and bilingual guided tours. Recommended time to see it all is two-and-a-half hours. The *Centre de l'Heritage britannique de la Gaspésie* is at 351 Perron Blvd. W, open early June to Labor Day, 9:00 a.m. to 6:00 p.m. daily. Admission is $3.50 for adults, $2.50 for senior citizens, $1 for children under 12 and $6 for families.

▲**Carleton**—Another Acadian stronghold, Carleton boasts a magnificent setting between the sea and the mountains. From the top of Mont St-Joseph, just north of town and accessible by car, there is a panoramic view of the bay, the Gaspé coast and the coast of New Brunswick across the Baie-des-Chaleurs.

▲**Restigouche**—The largest Micmac reservation on the peninsula is in Restigouche. Stop in at the *Centre d'interprétation de la culture Micmac* to learn how the Micmacs have lived in Gaspé through the centuries. The Micmacs fished and hunted an area that spread from the coast of Nova Scotia across the Gaspé peninsula. The interpretation center is at 4 Riverside West, open from 9:00 a.m. to 7:00 p.m. daily from June to September, shorter hours the rest of the year. It takes about half-an-hour to see. Admission is $3 for adults, $2 for seniors and students, $1 for children and $5 for families.

Campbellton

Campbellton, near the mouth of the Restigouche River, is the site of a major annual salmon festival because the river is so well known for its Atlantic salmon sportsfishing. The festival normally runs from late June through the first week of July. Half the population is English-speaking and half French, so expect to hear both languages. The skyline is dominated by Sugarloaf Mountain, an attractive provincial park that doubles as a skihill in winter. If there's time, take a chairlift to the 300-meter summit for a view of the town and surroundings.

Lodging
The **Wandlyn Maratime Inn** at 26 Duke Street offers double rooms at about $67; call 753-7606 locally or 1-800-561-1881 toll-free from within New Brunswick. Double rooms at the **Comfort Inn** go for about $62; it's at 3 Sugarloaf Street West, phone (506) 753-4121 or 1-800-668-4200 toll-free. At the **Howard Johnson Hotel** at 157 Water Street, double rooms run at $76; phone (506) 753-4133 or 1-800-564-2000 toll-free. One local B&B is the **Aylesford Inn Bed & Breakfast**, open year-round and offering double rooms for $50 to $60. Write to the inn at 8 McMillan Avenue, Campbellton, N.B., Canada, E3N 1E9, or phone (506) 759-7672.

Camping
The only campground in Campbellton is in **Sugarloaf Provincial Park**. It has 65 sites with electricity, at $13.49 per site. Take exit 416 off Highway 11 onto the 270. Open May to September; write Sugarloaf Provincial Park, P.O. Box 639, Atholville, N.B. E0K 1A0, Canada, or phone (506) 789-2366.

Helpful Hints
There are seasonal tourist information offices in Gaspé, Percé, New Carlisle, Bonaventure, New Richmond and Campbellton.

FREDERICTON

My favorite thing about Fredericton, a small, attractive city of 45,000 in south central New Brunswick, is its beautiful old Victorian houses. There is street upon street of them, and on a summer day, strolling those streets is just the ticket. You may notice elm trees everywhere; Fredericton is known as "the city of stately elms." It may be the provincial capital, but Fredericton, by virtue of its size and perhaps the character of its residents, has a small-town, laid-back feel. Stop in at the Beaverbrook Art Gallery on Queen Street during your stroll; its collection includes works by such luminaries as Gainsborough, Hogarth and Reynolds. Take time to explore Kings Landing Historical Settlement, a re-created Loyalist village outside Fredericton.

Suggested Schedule

8:00 a.m.	Drive from Campbellton to Fredericton.
12:00 noon	After lunch in Fredericton, check into your accommodation and wander the downtown area.
3:00 p.m.	Head out to Kings Landing, a half-hour from the city.

Driving Route: Campbellton to Fredericton (362 km/225 miles)

From Campbellton, get onto Highway 11 and follow it to Bathurst. In Bathurst, get onto Highway 8 and follow it to Fredericton. This is the shortest route between Campbellton and Fredericton, covering 362 kilometers (225 miles). For a couple of alternative routes that are longer but more scenic, see end of the chapter.

New Brunswick

New Brunswick, which lies east of Maine and south of Quebec, covers some 73,000 square kilometers (28,000 square miles, or slightly smaller than Maine) and is bordered on the north by the Baie des Chaleurs, on the east

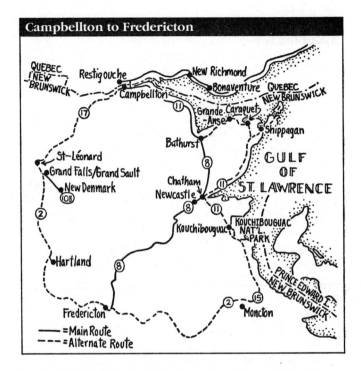

Campbellton to Fredericton

QUEBEC / NEW BRUNSWICK
Restigouche
New Richmond
Campbellton
Bonaventure
QUEBEC / NEW BRUNSWICK
⑰
⑪
Grande-Caraquet
-Anse
Shippagan
Bathurst
⑧
St-Léonard
Grand Falls/Grand Sault
New Denmark
⑩⑧
②
Chatham
Newcastle
GULF OF ST. LAWRENCE
⑪
KOUCHIBOUGUAC NAT'L PARK
Kouchibouguac
⑧
⑪
⑧
Hartland
⑧
PRINCE EDWARD I.
NEW BRUNSWICK
Fredericton
②
⑮
Moncton
—— =Main Route
---- =Alternate Route

by the Northumberland Strait, and on the south by the
Bay of Fundy. The entire province has a population of
724,000, a mix of French- and English-speaking people of
varying ethnic backgrounds. New Brunswick is the only
officially bilingual province in Canada (Quebec is officially
French, the other provinces English). For its size, the
province's geography is diverse, with cliffs and rocky
shores on some parts of the coast and sandy beaches and
salt dunes on other parts. Inland, there is a mix of river
valleys, farmland, forests, and wilderness.

Jacques Cartier and Samuel de Champlain were the
earliest European explorers of New Brunswick, then
populated by Micmac and Melcite Indians. When Cartier
sailed into New Brunswick in 1534, he was so impressed
by its beauty and the warmth of the waters that he named
the area *Baie des Chaleurs* (Bay of Warmth). The first
European settlers were French-speaking Acadians. Later,
Loyalists also settled in New Brunswick.

Sightseeing Highlights En Route

▲**Petit-Rocher**—If you take the coast road, Highway 134, instead of Highway 11 between Campbellton and Bathurst, you can stop off in Petit-Rocher for a visit to the New Brunswick Mining and Mineral Interpretation Center for a simulated ride down a mine shaft. You can also explore caverns and mine passageways drilled through mineral deposits. At Bathurst, get onto Highway 11.

▲**MacDonald Farm Historic Park**—Twenty kilometers (12 miles) northeast of Newcastle, this is a recreation of a 19th-century working farm, complete with a stone manor house, outbuildings, orchards and dock on the Miramichi River, which arches inland from Miramichi Bay on the Atlantic coast and is known for its salmon fishing. The farm, where costumed tour guides take visitors on inter- pretive tours, is at Bartibog Bridge on Route 11 off Highway 8. Call (506) 773-5761 for information.

▲**Newcastle**—Its major claim to fame is that Lord Beaverbrook was raised here. He was born William Maxwell Aitken, the son of a Presbyterian minister, in Maple, Ontario in 1879; in 1880 his family moved to Newcastle and "Max" later became a law clerk in Chatham, across the Miramichi River. It was the beginning of an astounding career that saw him move to Britain and become a financier, politician, author and newspaper publisher. In 1917, when he became a peer of the realm, he took the title Beaverbrook after a stream near his Canadian home. The town square in Newcastle features a monument to Lord Beaverbrook that contains his ashes plus various gifts from his lordship, and his boyhood home, the Old Manse Library, is open to the public.

Fredericton

Fredericton, which sits astride the Saint John River, was settled originally by the French, but eventually the British took control of what was then a tiny trading post and small numbers of British settlers came to the area. Some 2,000 Loyalists who arrived at the end of the American Revolution spent a very rough first winter huddled in tents. The survivors helped build what became Fredericton.

It was named the capital in 1785 chiefly because of its location on a river—accessible, yet distant enough from both the sea and the U.S. border that it was less prone to attack than Saint John, the largest city in the province.

Getting Around
Coming in to Fredericton from the north, Highway 8 becomes Gibson. Follow Gibson to Union, which runs along the north shore of the Saint John River, and turn left onto Union, which takes you to the Westmorland Street Bridge. Cross the bridge and you're right down-town. Coming in from the TransCanada, get off the TransCanada onto Highway 102, or Riverside, which becomes Woodstock Road and then King Street in the downtown core.

The city core is so compact that the only sensible way to see Fredericton is on foot; just about everything you want to see is in within a few square blocks downtown.

Fredericton has a program whereby visitors can park for free when they put a special ticket in their windshield. This comes in handy if you're staying outside the center of town. Check in at the Tourist Information Center at City Hall on the corner of Queen and York streets, or call them at 452-9500. It's open daily from 8:00 a.m. to 8:00 p.m. from May 15 to Labor Day and from 8:00 a.m. to 4:30 p.m. the rest of the year. The tourism people can also provide you with a Fredericton Visitor Guide that includes a helpful suggested five-block walking tour.

Fredericton Sightseeing Highlights
▲▲**Legislative Assembly Building**—This silver-domed Victorian building on Queen Street between St. John and Church streets has been the seat of government in New Brunswick since 1882, the previous legislative building having burned down a couple of years earlier. When the legislature is in session, visitors can sit in the public gallery (appropriate attire only, and no applauding under any circumstances). When it's not in session, you can actually go into the Assembly Chamber.

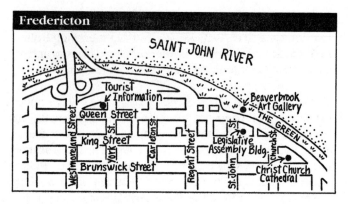

▲▲▲Beaverbrook Art Gallery—Across Queen Street from the Legislative Assembly Building, this art gallery, while small, houses a remarkable collection of British paintings spanning the 16th to 20th centuries. There are works here by Thomas Gainsborough, Sir Joshua Reynolds and John Constable, among others. The Canadian collection covers the years from the early 19th century to the present, including works by the Group of Seven. The first painting you see on entering the building is Salvador Dali's massive masterpiece, "Santiago el Grande." A bench faces the painting; sit and contemplate it for a while. The art gallery, one of several gifts to the city from the late Lord Beaverbrook, is open daily year-round, beginning at 10:00 a.m. Tuesday to Saturday and at 12:00 noon on Sunday and Monday. Admission is $3 for adults, $2 for seniors, and $1 for students.

▲▲The Green and Waterloo Row—Beginning behind the Beaverbrook Art Gallery, The Green is a tree-shaded area stretching east along the riverbank, parallel to Waterloo Row, where Fredericton's toniest houses sit. Make that mansions. Some of them are breathtaking. With the river on one side and the mansions on the other, The Green makes for an idyllic pathway to stroll.

▲Christ Church Cathedral—An imposing example of decorated Gothic architecture, Christ Church Cathedral was consecrated in 1853. Free guided tours are available from mid-June to Labor Day. The cathedral stands in the block between Queen, Brunswick and Church streets.

▲▲▲**Kings Landing**—To get to Kings Landing, head
west on the TransCanada (Highway 2) to exit 259; it's
clearly marked from the highway. Kings Landing, a re-
created Loyalist village in a lovely setting on the Saint
John River, is one of the province's major tourist draws
(rivaled perhaps by the Acadian Historical Village outside
Caraquet). There are some 70 buildings on the sprawling
site, ranging from a sawmill to a country inn to a one-
room schoolhouse to an assortment of furnished houses,
each reflecting the occupant's wealth and status in village
life in the 1800s. Costumed staff and volunteers work in
and around the buildings and can answer just about any
question you throw at them. On summer weekends, the
site is crowded despite its size, so try to go on a weekday.
Kings Landing is open daily from early June through to
Thanksgiving Monday in October (Columbus Day in the
U.S.), from 10:00 a.m. to 5:00 p.m. in June, September,
and October, and 10:00 a.m. to 6:00 p.m. in July and
August. Admission is $7.50 for adults, $6 for seniors, $4.50
for children aged six to 18, and $18 for families. For more
information, call the province's toll-free tourist line (see
the end of this chapter) or the Kings Landing administration office at (506) 363-5805.

Lodging
The **Lord Beaverbrook Hotel** at 659 Queen Street is
probably the most famous hotel in town, and among the
ritziest. Room rates, lower than in comparable hotels in
bigger cities, range from $89 to $119. Call 455-3371
locally or 1-800-561-7666 toll-free. The **Sheraton Inn
Fredericton**, at 225 Woodstock Road on the riverfront,
is another luxury establishment that opened in 1992. Its
room rates run from $65 to $112 depending on the
season; it also offers specials such as a family package
featuring two nights' accommodation and passes to Kings
Landing for a family of four for $229. Call (506) 457-7000
or 1-800-325-3535 toll-free. Also new is the **Kingsclear
Hotel and Resort**, which interestingly was developed by
the native community of the Kingsclear Reserve at
Mactaquac, 12 kilometers west of Fredericton off the

TransCanada at exit 274. The resort is just across from the 18-hole Mactaquac Golf Course. Rates range from $69 to $130, depending on the room and season. Call 363-5111 locally or 1-800-561-5111 toll-free.

For lower rates and a Victorian kind of atmosphere, try a B&B, of which there are several in and around Fredericton. The **Carriage House** is a lovely old Victorian mansion, more the size of an inn than a private home, with some exquisitely furnished rooms. It's also very centrally located and offers rooms for between $55 and $75. Write to Frank and Joan Gorham, 230 University Ave., Fredericton, N.B., Canada, E3B 4H7, or phone (506) 452-9924 locally or 1-800-267-6068 toll-free. There are complete B & B listings in the Fredericton Visitor Guide and in a brochure put out by the New Brunswick Bed & Breakfast Association Guide, both available from either the Fredericton or New Brunswick tourist information centers.

There is a motel strip along the TransCanada, which skirts the south end of the city.

Camping
The closest campgrounds to the city include those in **Mactaquac Provincial Park** at (506) 363-3011 and **Hartt Island Campground**, 10 kilometers west of the Princess Margaret Bridge, at (506) 450-6057.

Restaurants
The one restaurant everybody seems to recommend for either lunch or dinner is **La Vie en Rose** at 570 Queen Street, 455-1319. Its prices are moderate, it serves everything from chicken wings to steak, and it also offers fabulously rich desserts. Otherwise, there are assorted fast-food and family restaurants in the central district, or if you want upscale, try the **Maverick Room Steak House** in the Lord Beaverbrook Hotel at 455-3371.

Helpful Hints
For information on New Brunswick, write to Economic Development and Tourism, P.O. Box 12345, Fredericton, N.B., Canada E3B 5C3, or phone toll-free 1-800-561-0123.

They can supply the annually updated New Brunswick Travel Guide, a comprehensive 200-page publication with accommodation and campground listings, maps and travel information.

Note, however, that you can't make reservations for accommodations through New Brunswick's tourism information office.

For information on Fredericton, write to the Fredericton Tourism Department, City Hall, P.O. Box 130, Fredericton, N.B., Canada E3B 4Y7, or phone (506) 452-9500.

In person, you can drop in to tourist information centers in Campbellton, Bathurst, or Chatham, as well as in Fredericton.

For travelers going the B&B route, a handy book called *Bed & Breakfast—The Great Atlantic Adventure*, by Peter Gates and Elizabeth Stark, describes B&Bs in all four Atlantic provinces. It costs $9.50 plus $2 for postage and handling and can be ordered from Atlantic Adventure, 645 Manawagonish Road, Saint John, N.B., Canada E2M 3W4.

Finally, there are all manner of annual events and festivals throughout New Brunswick. Most take place in the peak summer months. Fredericton, for example, turns into a party town each year on Canada Day, July 1. It also hosts an annual jazz festival, the Harvest Jazz and Blues Festival, around mid-September. For detailed information and dates, consult the New Brunswick Travel Guide.

Alternate Routes
The Acadian Coast: The coastal route between Campbellton and Fredericton involves following New Brunswick's Acadian coast virtually all the way from Campbellton to Shediac and then turning inland. This scenic drive includes the so-called Acadian Peninsula. The distance is about 520 kilometers (310 miles).

The Acadian Historical Village, a recreated settlement just outside Caraquet on Highway 330, tells the story of the Acadians in this part of the world by depicting their lives from 1780 to the early 1900s. The Acadians who came to northern New Brunswick were the victims of the colonial struggle between Britain and France over

L'Acadie, made up of Nova Scotia and southern New Brunswick. When Britain deported some 75 percent of L'Acadie's French residents in 1755, many fled to northern New Brunswick. The Acadian Historical Village features costumed "residents" and special events and is one of the most popular tourist attractions in the province. Open June 1 to Sept. 27, 10:00 a.m. to 6:00 p.m. daily; admission is $7.50 for adults, $4.50 for kids up to 18, $5.50 for seniors and $18 for families. For information, call (506) 727-3467.

The Popes Museum and Art Gallery in Grande-Anse is, indeed, a museum that's unique in North America. It's devoted to portraits of all the Popes, plus a showcase dedicated to the current Pope and a model of St. Peter's Basilica in Rome. It's at 184 Acadie Street in Grande-Anse, near the Acadian Historical Village. Opening hours are 10:00 a.m. to 6:00 p.m. daily, June to early September; admission is $4.25 for adults, $2 for children up to 18 and $3 for seniors. Call (506) 732-3003 for information.

The Aquarium and Marine Center on 2nd Avenue in Shippagan houses a collection of 125 species of aquatic life, a marine museum plus a restaurant and outdoor patio. It's open daily May 23 to Sept. 12, 10:00 a.m. to 6:00 p.m.; admission is $5.35 for adults, $2.15 for children up to 18, $3.25 for seniors and $10.75 for families. Call (506) 336-3013 for more information.

Kouchibouguac National Park, the province's largest park, has coastal beaches, sand dunes, swimming, camping, hiking, canoeing and bicycling. From June 25 to September 6, the cost is $5 per day per vehicle, or $10 for four days. The park is open Monday to Thursday from 10:00 a.m. to 6:00 p.m. and from 8:00 a.m. to 8:00 p.m. on Friday, Saturday, and Sunday. Call (506) 876-2443 for information.

The TransCanada: The TransCanada route meanders through bucolic countryside and is about 400 kilometers (240 miles) long. Head southwest from Campbellton on Highway 17 to St-Leonard and turn south there onto the TransCanada (Highway 2), which winds along the

Quebec-New Brunswick border and then turns east, following the Saint John River, towards Fredericton.

The waterfalls at Falls and Gorge Park in Grand Falls/Grand-Sault, one of the largest cataracts east of Niagara Falls, drop 23 meters (75 feet) into a dramatic gorge. Call (506) 473-6013 for information. Check out the main street in Grand Falls/Grand-Sault, believed to be the widest main street in Canada. Would you believe, 38 meters (124 feet) wide? Once upon a time it was a military parade ground.

New Denmark, about 15 kilometers southeast of Grand Falls/Grand-Sault on Highway 108, is the largest Danish colony in North America. The time to be there is June 19, when the town celebrates Founders Day each year with song, dance, traditional costumes and food. A local museum portrays the history of the area.

Hartland is home to the longest covered bridge in the world, spanning 391 meters (1,279 feet) across the Saint John River.

THE FUNDY COAST

The Bay of Fundy coast along the southern New Brunswick shore is a panorama of serene inlets, rugged cliffs, picturesque villages and the fabled Fundy tides, the highest in the world. At the western end of the bay, the late president Franklin D. Roosevelt spent childhood summers on his beloved Campobello Island, one of the Fundy islands, in a humble "cottage" that has 34 rooms. Today's coastal drive also includes the venerable and picturesque summer resort of St. Andrews, with a short sidetrip to St. Stephen that's a must for chocoholics. Spend the night in Saint John, a historic port city whose picturesque waterfront area has been beautifully restored in recent years.

Suggested Schedule

9:00 a.m.	Depart Fredericton.
10:30 a.m.	Stop in St. Stephen.
11:30 a.m.	Wander around St. Andrews, have lunch.
1:00 p.m.	Stop in St. George to see the waterfalls.
1:30 p.m.	Catch the ferry for Deer Island and from there to Campobello.
6:00 p.m.	Arrive Saint John.

Driving Route: Fredericton to Saint John (270 km/162 miles)

Take the TransCanada west from Fredericton as far as Longs Creek, where you turn onto Highway 3 south. Follow Highway 3 to Lawrence Station, turn east on Highway 1 and follow it into St. Stephen. After visiting St. Stephen, drive back along Highway 1 to Highway 127 south and follow it down to St. Andrews. It's about 150 kilometers (90 miles) from Kings Landing to St. Andrews. The St. Stephen side-trip is about 20 kilometers (12 miles) roundtrip. From St. Andrews, take Highway 127 towards Chamcook and get onto Highway 1 east after Bocabec. St. George is just off Highway 1, about 30 kilometers (18 miles) from St. Andrews. From St. George, head south on

Highway 772 to Letete to catch the ferry for Deer Island. In summer, there is a ferry service between Deer Island and Campobello. Otherwise, the only way to get to Campobello is across the international bridge from Lubec, Maine. Then it's back to Highway 1 and on to Saint John.

Sightseeing Highlights

▲**St. Stephen**—St. Stephen is home to the Ganong chocolate factory, where Arthur Ganong invented the chocolate bar in 1906 when he wrapped blocks of chocolate in paper as snacks for fishing trips. The factory is on Chocolate Drive (what else) on the outskirts of town. Tours are available only during the annual Chocolate Fest, usually in early August. The Chocolatier shop on Milltown Boulevard has historic candy-making equipment, chocolate-dipping demonstrations and the world's tallest jelly bean display. St. Stephen is also a major entry point for visitors from the United States.

▲▲**St. Andrews**—One of the oldest towns in the province, St. Andrews-by-the-Sea (actually, it's by Passamaquoddy Bay, a small inlet near the mouth of the Bay of Fundy) was founded in 1783 by United Empire Loyalists. It's also where you'll find Canada's first pre-fab houses: Many of the Loyalists dismantled their homes in Castine, Maine, brought them over in barges and reassembled them in St. Andrews. Over half the town's buildings are more than 100 years old. Walking-tour brochures are available at the St. Andrews Tourist Bureau where Highway 1 crosses Highway 127. There is also a tourist information outlet on Harriet Street in town. The center of town, crowded with restaurants and shops, runs for four blocks along Water Street, anchored by the Market Wharf and the town square at the end of King Street. For decades the wealthy from New England flocked to St. Andrews in the summer, many of them to stay at the famous turret-topped Algonquin Hotel that broods over the town from a nearby hill.

▲**St. George**—This fishing village is tattooed with granite outcrops that make for some dramatic scenes. Magaguadavic Falls ranks among the most picturesque of them. In

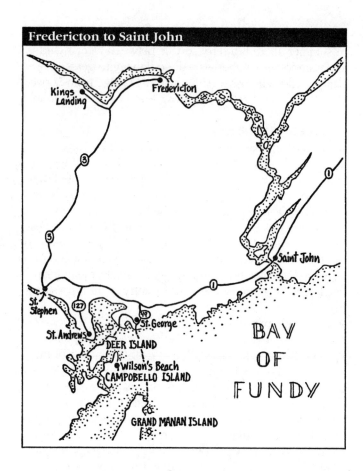

Fredericton to Saint John

summer, salmon on their way upriver to spawn struggle
up the man-made fish ladder next to the falls; it was built
so they could circumnavigate the falls. For some reason,
St. George is also reputed to have the best drinking water
in all of Canada.

▲**Deer Island**—Catch the free government-operated ferry
from Letete to Deer Island, home to what's billed as the
world's three largest lobster pounds, in Northern Harbour
on the island's west shore. Old Sow, one of the world's
largest whirlpools, can be seen off the Point Park on
Deer Island.

▲▲▲**Campobello Island**—From Deer Island, a small

private car ferry makes regular 45-minute crossings to Campobello. Confirm departure times at local information centers, since weather conditions can affect the ferry's operations. Note also that the ferry runs from late June until mid-September. Campobello contains a 2,800-acre international park, a joint Canada-U.S. venture that is supposed to symbolize the friendship between the two countries. The centerpiece of Roosevelt-Campobello International Park is U.S. President Franklin D. Roosevelt's summer "cottage," a red mansion with a green roof and 34 rooms where Roosevelt spent most of the summers of his youth. He also came to Campobello three times during his presidency (1933 to 1945). The house is surrounded by attractive gardens, and there are several walking trails on the island, plus lighthouses, a golf course and a stretch of pebbly beach. The park is open from 10:00 a.m. to 6:00 p.m. from late May until early October. For more information, phone (506) 752-2922.

Saint John

With a population of 125,000, Saint John is New Brunswick's largest city. It was the first city in Canada to be incorporated and is known as the Loyalist City because it was incorporated by Loyalists who arrived from the United States during the American Revolution. The city, particularly the downtown area with its lovely old buildings, is steeped in history. Saint John is also the New Brunswick terminal for the ferry to Digby, Nova Scotia, so there are plentiful facilities for visitors.

Getting Around

The famous Reversing Falls are off Highway 1 before you reach downtown, so you can stop there first to pick up tourist information and a schedule for the falls. The downtown core sits on a square peninsula of land at the mouth of the Saint John River; exit Highway 1 at Main Street and you're practically at Market Square, the harborside development that has rejuvenated the city in the last decade. Everything you want to see is within easy strolling distance of the centre of town, which can be placed at King

Square, a small park off King Street. The waterfront is two blocks down King Street from King Square.

Sightseeing Highlights
▲**Reversing Falls**—If you get the timing right, you can see the Reversing Falls in action. Twice daily, the tides of the Bay of Fundy reach such heights that they actually force the Saint John River to flow upriver in a raging torrent of foam and whirlpools, creating this unique phenomenon. Stop in at the Reversing Falls Information Center at the western end of Falls Bridge on Highway 100 in Saint John West, where there is also a lookout over the falls.

▲▲**The Old City Market**—Open every day except Sunday, this market is reputedly the oldest in Canada and offers a mind-boggling array of seafood, vegetables, antiques and myriad other goods. The block-long building, constructed in 1876, was one of the few public buildings to survive an 1877 fire that razed more than half the city. Its interior was modeled after the inverted hull of a ship. It's at 47 Charlotte Street, kitty-corner to King Square.

▲▲**Market Square**—Market Square, part of the extensive restoration of Saint John's riverfront, is lined with boutiques, restaurants and outdoor cafes. There's a harborfront boardwalk to stroll and plenty of atmosphere to absorb. Market Slip, where the Loyalists landed in 1783, adjoins Market Square. A tourist information center is in a 19th-century red schoolhouse next door to Market Slip. Pick up a pamphlet that describes the Loyalist Trail, a walking tour of central Saint John that includes the Loyalist Burial Ground, the 19th-century emporium known as Barbour's General Store (also on Market Square), the Old Loyalist House with its authentic period furniture and eight fireplaces, and other Loyalist-related sites in the downtown area.

Lodging
Saint John has a good selection of bed & breakfasts. **Country Wreath 'n' Potpourri**, a restored century-old home filled with the scent of home-made potpourri, has

doubles for $50 just five minutes from downtown at 125
Mount Pleasant Avenue North, Saint John, N.B. E2K 3T9,
Canada (506) 636-9919. **Five Chimneys Bed and
Breakfast** is midway between the Digby ferry slip and the
city centre and bills itself as a four-star property; rates for
a double run around $55. The address is 238 Charlotte
Street West, Saint John, N.B. E2M 1Y3 (506) 635-1888.
Cranberry's B&B is right downdown, in one of the city's
elegant old Victorian houses; rates begin at $55. The
address is 168 King Street East, Saint John, N.B. E2L 1H1,
Canada (506) 657-5173.

The luxurious **Saint John Hilton** at One Market
Square is right in the middle of things. Rates run $135 to
$160 a night. Call 693-8484 locally or 1-800-561-8282 toll-
free. A beautiful old Victorian house, the **Parkerhouse
Inn**, is on Sydney Street a block from King Square. Rates
begin at $65, including breakfast and parking. Call (506)
652-5054 or write to 71 Sydney Street, Saint John, N.B.
E2L 2L5, Canada.

There are motels along Manawagonish Road and another
strip of them along Rothesay Avenue, which crosses the
TransCanada, otherwise known as Highway 100.

Camping

A huge campground, **Rockwood Park**, lies just north of
the downtown area. It has small lakes, attractive sites and
a view of the city. It's also close to the centre of things,
just north of Rothesay Avenue, and is open from May
through October. The rate for tenters is $12, for fully ser-
viced sites $14. Write to Rockwood Park, Horticultural
Association, P.O. Box 535, Saint John, N.B. E2L 3Z8,
Canada, or phone (506) 652-4050.

Restaurants

The restaurants in the Market Square area range from fast-
food to elegant. **Grannan's Seafood Restaurant and
Oyster Bar** (634-1555) offers the catch of the day, oysters
or seafood platters at prices ranging from $11 to $25. The
Food Hall at Market Square offers an assortment of
fast-foods. **Mexicali Rosa's** at 88 Prince William Street

(652-5252) specializes in "Cali-Mex" food and is moderately priced. **Incredible Edibles** at 42 Princess Street
(633-7554) offers rich cheesecake and other desserts as
well as salads, pasta dishes and sandwiches. The cost is
moderate—usually less than $15 for a meal.

Festivals

Saint John hosts two fine festivals each summer, plus a
third smaller but particularly entertaining one. The Loyalist
Days Festival, usually the third week of July, features
re-enactments of the landing of the United Empire
Loyalists in 1783, complete with period costumes, plus
parades, street casinos, horse-racing and an antique fair.
Festival by the Sea, a cultural festival normally held the
second week of August, brings together up to 300
Canadian and international performers who provide some
125 performances in a 10-day period, with a special children's festival during the final two days. For sheer fun,
usually over the first weekend of August, the four-day
Buskers on the Boardwalk festival features magic, mime,
and music on the harborfront boardwalk at Market Square,
plus fireworks.

Itinerary Option: Grand Manan Island

Grand Manan Island, south of Campobello, is worth seeing but would require at least a full day to explore properly.
(Just to get there and back by ferry takes nearly four
hours.) With Deer Island and Campobello, Grand Manan
is the largest of the so-called West Isles Archipelago.

To visit Grand Manan, turn south off Highway 1 about
five kilometers (three miles) east of St. George, onto
Highway 785. It leads to Blacks Harbour, from whence
there are car ferries to Grand Manan. The ferries run year-
round, three times a day from Labor Day until late June
and six times a day from late June to Labor Day. Round-
trip rates are $8.20 for adults and $4.10 for children aged
5 to 13, plus $24.60 per vehicle. Call Coastal Transport in
Saint John at (506) 636-3922 for more information. The
crossing to North Head on Grand Manan takes between

90 minutes and two hours. The largest of the three Fundy Isles, Grand Manan is at once tranquil and exotically beautiful, with a mix of forests, towering cliffs and long beaches. You can whalewatch, birdwatch or just bake on the beach. In spring and summer, huge numbers of birds nest on the island's cliffs. Awed when he visited in the 1800, John James Audubon did many of his sketches there. Indeed, the island is a wonderful place to sketch, paint or take photos. The Hole-in-the-Wall, a massive shore-line rock formation that has a huge hole right through the middle of it, may be the most photographed scene on the island; it's in the North Head area, along a trail that begins near the Marathon Hotel. With scenic walking trails all over the island, a full day on Grand Manan would pass quickly.

There are several small communities on Grand Manan and it's possible to stay overnight—bearing in mind it's wise to book ahead, since there isn't that much accommodation. The town of North Head offers a couple of interesting places. The **Compass Rose**, a heritage inn, is actually two old houses with antique-furnished rooms looking out towards the sea. Breakfast, lunch, afternoon tea and dinner are all available in the dining room. The rooms are priced around $45 single and $55 double, including breakfast. Write to Compass Rose, North Head, Grand Manan, N.B. E0G 2M0, Canada, or phone (506) 662-8570 or (506) 446-5906 off-season. The century-old **Marathon Inn** in North Head is relatively luxurious, complete with a heated swimming pool. Rates run from $49 to $89. Write to Marathon Inn, North Head, Grand Manan, N.B. E0G 2M0, Canada, or phone (506) 662-8144. The **Fundy Folly Bed & Breakfast** offers rooms plus breakfast for $45 double; write to them at Box 197, North Head, Grand Manan, N.B. E0G 2M0, Canada, or phone (506) 662-3731. There are also inns or B&Bs in Seal Cove, including **Rosalie's Guest House** for $40 double (506-662-3344), and **McLaughlin's Wharf Inn** for $60 (506-662-8760).

The only campground on Grand Manan is in **Anchorage Provincial Park**. It has 50 sites, with a little over half having partial service and the rest for tenters. Write Anchorage Provincial Park, Grand Manan, N.B. E0G 3B0, Canada, or phone (506) 662-3215.

When it comes time to eat, go for seafood, since fishing is the major occupation on the island. Restaurants on Grand Manan tend to be casual, including the **Griff-Inn** in North Head and the **Water's Edge** in Seal Cove, which serves home-made Italian dishes plus seafood dinners.

For more information on Grand Manan, call the toll-free provincial tourist information line at 1-800-561-0123.

Helpful Hints

In Saint John, the grand old Imperial Theater re-opened in 1994 after extensive renovations. To find out what's on, ask at the Market Square tourist information center.

For more information on Saint John, contact the Saint John Visitor & Convention Bureau, Box 1971, Saint John, N.B., Canada E2L 4L1, or phone the bureau at (506) 658-2990. Ask for a brochure titled Reversing Falls Tide Tables, so that you can be sure to be there when it happens.

SOUTHEAST NEW BRUNSWICK

If you haven't explored downtown Saint John as much as you'd like, spend an hour or two doing that this morning. Then strike out for Sussex, which calls itself the Covered Bridge Capital of Atlantic Canada, and Fundy National Park, where steep sandstone cliffs tower over the craggy shoreline. The Rocks Provincial Park, with its striking rock formations that resemble massive flowerpots, is another must-see on this route; if the tide is out, you can walk right up to them. In Moncton, famous Magnetic Hill is a weirdly entertaining experience for some, a disappointment for others—but either way, you have to try it. From Moncton, it's only about an hour to Cape Tormentine and the ferry to Prince Edward Island, Canada's smallest province and home to Anne of Green Gables.

Suggested Schedule

9:00 a.m.	Explore downtown Saint John.
10:00 a.m.	Leave for Sussex, stopping at some of the covered bridges in the area.
11:30 p.m.	Fundy National Park, and perhaps a picnic lunch.
1:30 p.m.	The Rocks Provincial Park.
3:00 p.m.	Magnetic Hill.
4:30 p.m.	Shediac, the "Lobster Capital of the World."
5:30 p.m.	Catch the ferry to P.E.I. from Cape Tormentine.

Driving Route: Saint John to Cape Tormentine (370 km/222 miles)

Head east on Highway 1 from Saint John as far as Sussex, where you get onto the TransCanada (Highway 2) heading east. To get to Fundy National Park, take Highway 114 south, about 15 kilometers (9 miles) east of Sussex. Follow Highway 114 through the park and up the west shore of the Petitcodiac River, stopping en route at The Rocks Provincial Park, between Riverside-Albert and

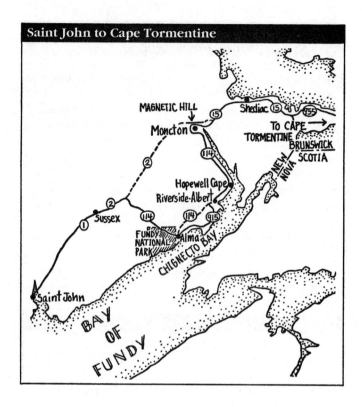

Saint John to Cape Tormentine

Hillsborough. The 114 leads to Moncton; to get to
Magnetic Hill, follow the 114 across the river, where it
becomes Highway 15. From Highway 15, get onto
Highway 126 north. The 126 meets the TransCanada just
east of Magnetic Hill. After visiting Magnetic Hill, take the
TransCanada east to Highway 15 east and stay on the
15 as far as Highway 955, which leads to Cape
Tormentine.

Car ferries run from Cape Tormentine to Borden,
Prince Edward Island; you don't pay to get on to the
island, you only pay when leaving it. Nor do you need
to reserve. In fact Marine Atlantic, which operates the
ferry, won't take reservations. In peak season ferries leave
every hour from 6:30 a.m. until 1:00 a.m. For a complete
schedule for Marine Atlantic's various ferry routes, drop
into a tourist information center or contact Marine Atlantic

at head office in North Sydney, N.S., at (902) 794-5700 from Canada or 1-800-341-7981 toll-free from the U.S. The crossing takes about 45 minutes.

▲**Sussex**—There are 17 covered bridges, many on bucolic country roads, in Sussex and the surrounding Kings County. Stop in at the Kings County Tourist Center in Sussex, or call (506) 433-3764, for a locator map for the bridges. If you happen to come through during the third week of August, that's when Sussex hosts Country Living Days, a week of family-oriented events like horse and livestock shows, auctions, woodsmen's competitions, a parade, and a farmer's market.

▲▲▲**Fundy National Park**—This 207-square-kilometer park on the shores of the Bay of Fundy is a sanctuary of sloping cliffs, tide-washed beaches, clear streams and hiking and nature trails. Driving through it takes from one to three hours, depending on how often you stop. During the summer, two information centers are open, and in the off-season information panels at Wolfe Lake and at the park administration building provide basic orientation. In summer there is also an interpretive program whereby bilingual guides can take you walking on the bottom of the sea at low tide or on nature walks. Entrance to the park is $5 per car. Phone (506) 887-2000 for more information.

▲▲▲**The Rocks Provincial Park**—Sculpted by the mighty Fundy tides, the curious rock formations called the Flower Pot Rocks are known as the world's largest flower pots because that's what they look like, sort of, when the tide is out. Some are 15 meters (50 feet) tall. You can see them at any time, but only at low tide can you go down and explore the rock columns and caves. When the tide is in, the Flower Pot Rocks become ordinary islands. Schedules for low tides are posted. The park is off Route 114 at Hopewell Cape. Phone (506) 734-3429 for more information.

▲▲▲**Magnetic Hill**—What happens at Magnetic Hill, the little dirt road outside Moncton that "defies gravity" by pulling your car backwards up what seems to be an uphill slope, is difficult to describe. You drive into Magnetic

Hill Park, a tourist trap if there ever was one, complete with a mini-train, a "wharf village" of restaurants and stores, a water slide park and so on. Ignore all that; for one thing, it costs $53.25 for a family pass to the water park, and all you want to do is Magnetic Hill itself. Staff members direct you to the top of a gentle slope, although if there's a lineup of cars—and this is a hugely popular attraction, make no mistake—it'll take a while to get there. When you get to the front of the line, you're instructed to drive slowly down the slope and swing over to the left side of the road when you get to the bottom, where there's a kind of dip in the road. Then you put the car in neutral and sure enough, the car starts coasting backwards *up* the slope. It's all an optical illusion, I reckon, but don't tell anyone. The actual experience lasts about 45 seconds. Magnetic Hill Park is just off the TransCanada northwest of Moncton and well marked on the highway. It's open from mid-May to mid-October, from 8:00 a.m. to 9:00 p.m. from late June to early September and slightly shorter hours in the other months. Admission is $2 per car if you're only trying out the hill. For information, phone (506) 384-0303 or 853-3516.

Moncton's other natural phenomenon is the tidal Bore of the Petitcodiac River. Like the Reversing Falls in Saint John, this happens twice daily because of the tides, when the rising waters in the Bay of Fundy cause the water in the river to roll back upstream in one wave. As the Bay of Fundy tides come in twice a day, one hundred billion tons of sea water rush up the shores of the bay. At the bay's eastern extremity, the tide has been measured at 14.8 meters, or 48.4 feet. That's the height of a four-story building, and the reason why the Bay of Fundy tides are said to be the highest in the world. Tidal bores take place in several rivers around the bay. In Moncton, the river-wide wave ranges in height from a few inches to two feet. If you're interested, the best vantage point is Bore Park on Main Street at the corner of King. For more information on Moncton, refer to the New Brunswick Travel Guide or contact Moncton Convention and Visitor

Services, City Hall, 774 Main Street, Moncton, N.B., Canada E1C 1E8, (506) 384-0303.

▲**Shediac**—The temperate waters of Shediac Bay are said to be the warmest salt waters north of the Carolinas; in summer, the water temperatures reach 24°-28°C (75°-85°F). Combined with the three-kilometer (two-mile) sandy beach in nearby Parlee Beach Provincial Park, this makes Shediac a favorite summer tourist resort. Shediac, which calls itself "The Lobster Capital of the World," also hosts a lobster festival, usually during the second week of July, that's worth stopping off for.

Arriving on Prince Edward Island

There is a tourist information center in Borden as soon as you get off the ferry, so if you don't already have the Visitors Guide, stop in and pick one up. Then head for Charlottetown, the provincial capital, which I recommend as a base for the two nights and one full day on the island. Charlottetown is 56 kilometers (33 miles) from Borden on the TransCanada (Highway 1). It also has direct access to two of the island's three scenic drives and is only 60 kilometers (36 miles) from Wood Islands, from whence ferries cross to Nova Scotia (see *Day 16*).

You can't go wrong as a visitor to P.E.I., which is geared towards looking after tourists. The Prince Edward Island Visitors Guide, a 200-page publication updated annually by the provincial tourist board, conveniently divides the island into three scenic drives: Lady Slipper Drive, around the western end of the island; Blue Heron Drive, around the central part; and Kings Byway Drive, around the eastern end. The routes are marked clearly both in the Visitors Guide and on the roads themselves. If you *do* go wrong, the worst thing that can happen is you go off down some side road and find red sandstone cliffs over a deserted beach or emerald hills rolling gently away towards the sea. P.E.I is so small that the sea is visible from most anywhere on the island, "if only in a tiny blue gap between distant hills," Lucy

Maud Montgomery wrote, "or a turquoise gleam through the dark boughs of spruce fringing an estuary. . . ."

Lodging

P.E.I. has numerous country inns, B&Bs, farm vacation homes and seaside cottages. Many are open only in season, meaning generally May to October.

Following are some suggestions in Charlottetown or within about 20 minutes of it, on or close to the Blue Heron route.

Dunrovin Lodge Cottages and Farms, with a large lawn, a barn kids can play in and a horse they can ride, is especially suitable for families. It overlooks the village of Victoria, about a third of the way to Charlottetown from Borden on the TransCanada. Room rates begin at $37; call Mrs. Kay (MacQuarrie) Wood at (902) 658-2375. In Bonshaw, about 10 kilometers further east on the TransCanada, the **Strathgartney Country Inn** is a 100-year-old homestead set amid 30 acres of countryside and gardens. Room rates at this smoke-free establishment range from $69 to $125; call (902) 675-4711. In Cornwall, 10 minutes east of Charlottetown, **Chez Nous Bed & Breakfast**, a rambling country house set among birch and maple trees, has four spacious guest rooms and a solarium where breakfast is served. Rates are $50 to $65; call Sandi and Paul Gallant at (902) 566-2779.

In Charlottetown, **The Duchess of Kent Inn** is an 1875 designated heritage home that's now a three-star bed & breakfast inn, with eight guest rooms and period furniture throughout. Rates are $48 to $60; no smoking. Call (902) 566-5826. **Heritage Harbour House**, another historic property built in the 1900s, is in a quiet area downtown. Rates start at $55; call (902) 892-6633. If you want real luxury in Charlottetown, and can afford it, stay at **The Charlottetown**, a grandly elegant hotel built by the Canadian National Railway in 1930-31. Rates range from $99 to $139; call 1-800-565-7633 toll-free.

In Brackley Beach on the north shore, 20 kilometers (12 miles) northwest of Charlottetown on Highway 15,

Windsong Farm is a pre-Victorian farmhouse nestled in the countryside with antique-furnished guest rooms. Rates are $55 to $65 and no smoking is allowed; call Jean and John Huck at (902) 672-2874. Or try **Shaw's Hotel**, a white-shingled, red-roofed 1860 building that claims to be Canada's oldest continuously family-operated inn. Rates for rooms run from $170 to $190, call (902) 672-2022.

Finally, **Dalvay-By-The-Sea Country Inn** is renowned for its dining room, but the rest of the inn is attractive too. None of the 26 guest rooms in the gingerbready Victorian mansion has a telephone, radio or TV, and the main activity is relaxing. The inn is near the eastern boundary of Prince Edward Island National Park, which runs along the central north shore. From Charlottetown, about 20 minutes away, take Highway 2 east for 10 kilometers (6 miles) and turn left on Highway 6. From Highway 6, turn off into the park. Rates range from $150 to $270; call (902) 672-2048.

You might also want to consider staying on a farm. Farm families on the island have opened their homes to guests for many years. They're all working farms of one sort or another and most have housekeeping units or cottages on their land. "Farm Vacations," a pamphlet put out by the Prince Edward Island Farm Vacation Association, lists more than two dozen such establishments around the island; call the provincial tourist information line for a copy. Individual farm homes are also listed in the province's visitors guide.

No matter what kind of accommodation you choose, reservations are advised, especially in July and August.

Camping

There are campgrounds and trailer parks throughout the province; 13 are in provincial parks and three in Prince Edward Island National Park, while some three dozen are privately run. One of the most convenient ones for this itinerary is in **Strathgartney Provincial Park**, 20 kilometers (12 miles) southwest of Charlottetown on the TransCanada, with rates of $12.50 and $15.75 and grounds that include a nature trail and playground.

Campgrounds in provincial parks accept reservations through any of the province's tourist information centers scattered around the island, or write to Provincial Parks, Box 2000, Charlottetown, P.E.I., Canada C1A 7N8. National park campgrounds do not accept reservations but visitor information centers can supply information about vacancies. In the case of privately operated campgrounds, call directly.

Restaurants

Surrounded by waters abundant with lobsters, mackerel, scallops, mussels, oysters and clams, the entire island is clearly a seafood lover's paradise. (This is not to say you can't eat other types of meals; even the seafood restaurants tend to offer steak as well). Partake of a lobster supper if you can. These all-you-can-eat feasts of lobster, fresh vegetables and home-made breads are offered by many local church and community groups. You'll see ads for them all over the place.

Shopping

In addition to the usual goods, more than 80 craft outlets throughout the island offer everything from pottery and woodworking to hand-painted silk. There are also antique shops aplenty.

There is a 10-per-cent provincial sales tax on most purchases, including accommodation (except campgrounds) and restaurant meals. Clothing and shoes are exempt to a limit of $100 apiece.

Theater

Many visitors consider the musical *Anne of Green Gables* a must. In summer it's performed nightly at the Confederation Centre of the Arts as part of the annual Charlottetown Festival. For information, call (902) 566-1267 or 1-800-565-0278 toll-free from New Brunswick, Nova Scotia, and P.E.I.

Helpful Hint

For information on Prince Edward Island, contact the Prince Edward Island Department of Tourism and Parks, Visitor Services, P.O. Box 940, Department 74, Charlottetown, P.E.I., Canada C1A 7M5, or phone 1-800-463-4PEI toll-free.

PRINCE EDWARD ISLAND

Prince Edward Island is a tranquil place, with gently rolling hills and soft pink beaches that are among the best in Canada. Granted, it gets crowded in summer, when visitors swell the population of 130,400 fivefold. Even so, long stretches of beach are deserted. Situated in the Gulf of St. Lawrence and separated from Nova Scotia and New Brunswick by the shallow Northumberland Strait, the crescent-shaped island is a mere 224 kilometers (135 miles) long and 60 kilometers (36 miles) wide at its widest point. Island life is based chiefly on the treasures of the sea and on farming the fertile red soil, notably potatoes, as well as on tourism. Canadians in other provinces generally refer to Prince Edward Island as "P.E.I.," while residents call it simply "the Island" and refer to non-residents as being "from away." The Island has other names that reflect its history and character: the "Garden of the Gulf," the "Million-acre Farm," the "Cradle of Confederation," or, less lyrically, "Spud Island."

Suggested Schedule

9:00 a.m.	Explore downtown Charlottetown.
10:00 a.m.	Prince Edward Island National Park and Green Gables House.
12:00 p.m.	Lunch.
1:00 p.m.	Lady Slipper Drive north, stopping at will.
2:30 p.m.	Lady Slipper Drive south, stopping at will.
4:00 p.m.	Blue Heron Drive south, stopping at will.
5:30 p.m.	Back to Charlottetown.

Prince Edward Island

French explorer Jacques Cartier described the Island in 1534 as "the fairest land that may possibly be seen," and indeed, its beauty helped provide Lucy Maud Montgomery with inspiration for her perennial bestseller, *Anne of Green Gables*. The coastline is indented with tidal inlets, steep sandstone bluffs and long sandy beaches. But the most startling aspect of the island's topography is its rust-red soil, caused by heavy concentrations of iron oxide.

Some 8,000 to 10,000 years ago, ancestors of the Micmac Indians were the first humans to live in P.E.I., spending summers along the shore and feasting on the abundant shellfish. Eventually they stayed year-round, naming the island Abegweit, or "cradle in the waves." The first Europeans to arrive were the French, who began to settle the island in the 1720s. But after 1758, when Louisbourg (the capital of the French colony of Île Royal, or what is now Cape Breton Island) fell to the British, the Island was settled mainly by English, Scottish and Irish immigrants. Today its population remains overwhelmingly British in origin; in fact it's arguably the most Celtic place in North America.

In 1864, representatives of Canada (Ontario and Quebec), Nova Scotia, New Brunswick and P.E.I. met in Charlottetown to discuss federal union of the British North American colonies. It was the first of a series of meetings which led eventually to the Confederation of Canada. Charlottetown still calls itself the Birthplace of Canada, even though when other colonies joined in the new federation in 1867, P.E.I. did not do so until 1873.

P.E.I.'s major claim to international fame, of course, is *Anne of Green Gables*, the novel by Lucy Maud Montgomery. Rescued from an orphanage, Anne wins the hearts of Matthew and Marilla Cuthbert and the community of Avonlea. But how could she not? She is articulate, plucky, sensitive, caring and fiery all at once. First published in 1908, the novel eventually won world-wide acclaim, and now some one million visitors descend each year on Green Gables House, the recreation of the Cuthbert home in Cavendish, P.E.I.

Catherine Callbeck, premier of Prince Edward Island since 1993, is Canada's only sitting woman premier.

Part of P.E.I.'s unique character probably stems from its physical separation from the rest of the country. But it appears this might change; the federal government is talking about building a 14-kilometer (8.5-mile) bridge to replace the federally subsidized Borden-Cape Tormentine

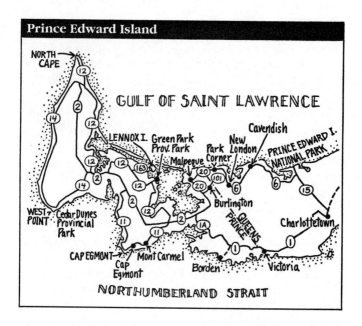

ferry service. A majority of Islanders voting in a 1988 plebiscite favored a fixed link, whether a tunnel, causeway or bridge. But critics say a fixed link could spoil the Island's intangible mystique. Whatever happens, the ferry linking the eastern end of P.E.I. with Nova Scotia will remain in service.

Driving Route

Because of the limited time on P.E.I., our focus is on the Blue Heron and Lady Slipper scenic routes, which cover the central and western part of the Island. They offer a wider range of interesting areas than Kings Byway Drive, the scenic route around the eastern end of the island. Furthermore, Kings Byway Drive is almost as long as the other two routes combined. For travelers who have more time, there is information on Kings Byway Drive at the end of the chapter. Ideally, three days is probably the optimal time to spend on P.E.I.—one day for a leisurely circuit of each of the scenic drives.

Blue Heron Drive is 190 kilometers (120 miles) long, Lady Slipper Drive 288 kilometers (180 miles) and Kings Byway 375 kilometers (234 miles).

From Charlottetown, follow the northern loop of Blue Heron Drive to Travellers Rest on Highway 2, where Lady Slipper Drive begins. Lady Slipper Drive travels in a rough circle around the western end of the island, ending back at Travellers Rest. From there, head south on the Blue Heron, which takes you back into Charlottetown.

Together, the Lady Slipper and Blue Heron routes comprise 478 kilometers (300 miles). However, you needn't stick to the routes exactly. There are all manner of shortcuts if you want to skip some of the sights. For example, instead of following Lady Slipper Drive all the way around the western end of the island, you could travel up Highway 2 and make occasional forays to the coast from it. Have on hand a copy of the map of the province that comes with the Visitors Guide, and you shouldn't go wrong.

The Blue Heron Drive route is clearly marked with blue road signs featuring the silhouette of a heron. It follows a circular route around the center of P.E.I. Lady Slipper Drive is marked with red roadsigns depicting the lady slipper, P.E.I.'s provincial flower. The route winds around the contorted coastline of the western end of the island, providing views of red sandstone cliffs, pearly white beaches on the north shore and red-sand beaches on the south shore. Part of Lady Slipper Drive also skirts Malpeque Bay, famous for its oyster beds.

There are numerous attractions along both routes—possibly too many to enjoy in one day, although driving distances between them tend to be short.

Sightseeing Highlights
▲▲**Province House (Charlottetown)**—This was the site in 1864 of the historic Charlottetown Conference. Today it is a national historic site; the Confederation Chamber where the meeting was held has been restored to appear as it did in the 1800s. The building also houses the

provincial legislature. It's at the corner of Great George and Richmond streets, right downtown. Open weekdays year-round and daily from June through August. Entrance is free and regular guided tours are available. Province House is at the top of Great George Street; call 566-7626 for more information.

▲▲**Confederation Centre Art Gallery and Museum (Charlottetown)**—Housed in the Confederation Centre of the Arts adjacent to Province House, the art gallery's extensive permanent collection of works by Canadian artists makes it one of Canada's major art galleries. Open daily from June to September, from 10:00 a.m. to 8:00 p.m.; $3 for adults, $5 for families. Call 628-6111 for information.

▲▲▲**Prince Edward Island National Park**—This park of lovely beaches, sand dunes and sandstone cliffs runs in a narrow strip along 40 kilometers (24 miles) of the Island's north shore, facing the Gulf of St. Lawrence. Unfortunately, the incursion of tourists has done its share of damage here, and parts of the beach are closed to the public in summer to protect the Piping Plover, a small shore bird that nests in certain areas of the park's beaches and has been declared an endangered species. Drive the Gulf Shore Parkway, which skirts the dunes, and stop to take one of the boardwalks and paths that lead to the water's edge (the boardwalks were built to protect the dunes from foot traffic). There is a park interpretive center at the Cavendish Visitor Centre at the western extremity of the park. For information, call 963-2391 or 672-6350 in winter.

▲▲**Green Gables House (Cavendish)**—If you loved *Anne of Green Gables*, you naturally must visit Green Gables House, the house where author Lucy Maud Montgomery's cousins lived and on which she based her heroine's house. It is now a museum that recreates the house as described in the novel. There is also an exhibit about the author and her works (there were, in all, eight books about Anne). On the grounds outside, visitors can explore the Haunted Wood, Lover's Lane and other famil-iar settings from the novel, not to mention the graves of

Montgomery and her husband. Expect to encounter hordes of visitors, including busloads of Japanese tourists; they adore the novel and visit P.E.I. in great numbers to see Green Gables. The house is at the western end of Prince Edward Island National Park. Open daily from mid-May to November 1; free entrance. Call 672-6350 for information.

▲**Lucy Maud Montgomery Birthplace (New London)**—The author was born in 1874 in this house, which now contains period furniture and Montgomery memorabilia. Intersection of routes 6 and 8. Open June 1 to early October; nominal entrance fee. Call 886-2099 for information.

▲**Anne of Green Gables Museum at Silver Bush (Park Corner)**—This was the home of Montgomery's uncle; she often visited it and her wedding was held in the drawing room. Now it contains an exhibit that includes the first editions of some of her books. Route 20. Open daily from June through October; $2.50 for adults, 75 cents for children under 16. Call 886-2884 or 436-7329.

▲**Woodleigh (Burlington)**—Woodleigh is a collection of large-scale models of historic British buildings and castles, constructed painstakingly by hand by the late, and presumably eccentric, Lt. Col. E.W. Johnston. You'll find the Tower of London, York Minster Cathedral and Dunvegan Castle, among other famous structures, plus a Shakespeare section with replicas of his mother's home and Anne Hathaway's cottage in Stratford-upon-Avon. Some of the replicas are large enough to walk into and are furnished with authentic items imported from Britain. On Route 101 north of Kensington. Open daily from late May to mid-October; $7.35 for adults, $6.75 for seniors, $4.10 for children from 6 to 12. Call 836-3401 for more information.

▲**Malpeque Gardens**—The gardens feature an array of annuals and perennials, as well as the Anne of Green Gables Gardens with a miniature model of Green Gables surrounded by flower beds shaped to look like Anne's flowered hat and other items from the novel. Route 20 north of Kensington. Open daily from mid-June to mid-October; $4 for adults, $2 for children under 14. Call 836-5418 for information.

▲**Green Park Provincial Park**—A shipbuilding museum in the park traces the history of shipbuilding, the major industry on the island in the last century. Also worth seeing is Yeo House, the gabled Victorian home of James Yeo, wealthy owner of the shipyard that once occupied Green Park. Route 12 on Lady Slipper Drive north. Open June 15 to Labor Day; $2.50 for adults, free for children under 12. The phone number is 831-2370 for the park and 831-2206 for the museum.

▲**Lennox Island Micmac Nation**—The Micmac families now living on the Lennox Island reserve are descendants of P.E.I.'s first human inhabitants. At the southern tip of the Island, there is a small museum with native artifacts and paintings, plus an arts and crafts shop nearby with a selection of silver, beaded jewelry, pottery and carvings. From Route 12, take Route 163 to the island. For information, phone 831-2653.

▲**Atlantic Wind Test Site (North Cape)**—At the tip of the western end of the island, there is a series of wind turbines operated by the national wind test lab, which evaluates wind generators. At the visitors' center you can view a video and there are guides to answer questions. At the north end of Route 12, open daily in July and August. Admission is $2 for adults and $1 for seniors and students; children under 10 get in for free. Call 882-2746 for information.

▲**West Point Lighthouse (Cedar Dunes Provincial Park)**—This black-and-white striped structure, now a museum, was built in 1875 and offers a fine lookout from its top across the park's red dunes to Northumberland Strait. Route 14 in the park. Open daily from mid-May to mid-October; $2 for adults, $1.25 for children, $1.65 for seniors, $6 for families. The phone number is 859-3605.

▲**The Bottle Houses (Cap-Egmont)**—These are so bizarre you must stop off and see them—a chapel, a house and a tavern all made entirely of bottles cemented together. It's the work of the late Edouard Arsenault, a retired fisherman who began the project in the mid-1970s and used more than 25,000 bottles by the time he was

through. You can go right inside each structure. Lady
Slipper Drive south, Route 11; open daily from mid-June
to late September, $3.25 for adults, $1 for children 6 to 16.
For more information, phone 854-2987.

▲▲**Acadian Pioneer Village (Mont-Carmel)**—This is
a re-creation of the 1820s Acadian settlement of Mont-
Carmel, complete with church, school, blacksmith shop,
store and houses. They're all log structures, and even the
church's altar is made from logs. Route 11 south of
Miscouche, on Lady Slipper Drive south. Open mid-June
to mid-September; $3 for adults and $1.50 for children.
Call 854-2227 for more information.

▲▲**Victoria**—As one of the few planned villages on the
island, Victoria has a neat, symmetrical layout. Nestled
between hills and overlooking a harbor, it's pleasantly
quaint. The operating lighthouse has a museum that
relates Victoria's history, but mostly Victoria is just a nice
place to stroll around. Stop in at Island Chocolates if
you're a chocoholic, and at The Studio Gallery for a sampling of photographs, batiks, etchings and watercolors by
local artists.

▲**Fort Amherst/Port-La-Joye**—Port-La-Joye (roughly,
Joyous Port), the first French settlement on the island, was
renamed Fort Amherst after it fell to the British in 1758.
The fort overlooked Charlottetown Harbour, but now only
the earthworks of the original fort remain. It's a National
Historic Site so there is an interpretive center that tells you
all about it.

Itinerary Option
If you have extra time on the Island, the third scenic
drive, Kings Byway Drive, winds around the particularly
placid eastern end of Prince Edward Island, dotted with
quiet fishing villages and tidy farming communities. Some
highlights:

▲**Orwell Corner Historic Village**—A restored 1800s
crossroads farming village, Orwell Corner is now a historic
site featuring farms, a school, a church and various other
buildings. One of the most interesting structures is a farm-

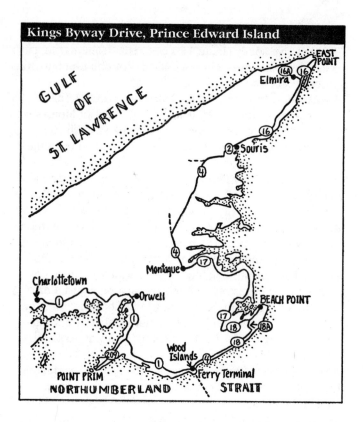

Kings Byway Drive, Prince Edward Island

house that also serves as a store and post office, and it has a dressmaker's shop upstairs. All the buildings have been restored and all are on their original sites. Open mid-May to mid-October; $3 for adults, free for children under 12. The village is off the TransCanada 30 kilometers east of Charlottetown; just follow the signs. For more information, call 651-2013.

▲**Point Prim Lighthouse**—Built in 1845, the oldest lighthouse on the island is still in use. It's also billed as the only round brick structure in Canada. The lantern house at its peak provides a view over Northumberland Strait. Open mid-June to Labor Day; free admission. Point Prim is at the end of Route 209, 10 kilometers (6 miles) south of the TransCanada between Orwell and Wood Islands. The phone number is 659-2572.

▲**Garden of the Gulf Museum (Montague)**—Some of the relics in this museum date back several centuries, such as a 1698 Bible. More recent artifacts include letters written by Lucy Maud Montgomery. Open mid-June to mid-September daily except Sunday; $2 for adults, free for children under 15. Montague is on Route 4 on the eastern coast of the island. For information, call 838-2460.

▲**Souris**—Souris, oddly enough, means "mice" in English. The thinking is this fishing port and ferry terminal may have been so-named after it was overrun with plagues of field mice in the 1800s. Souris is the terminal for ferries to and from Quebec's Magdalen Islands (more correctly, *Îles-de-la-Madeleine*), an archipelago of windswept but charming islands in the middle of the Gulf of St. Lawrence that are closer to P.E.I. and Nova Scotia than to Quebec. In fact other than the ferry service to and from Souris, the Magdalens are accessible only by plane from Montreal, Halifax, Gaspé or Quebec City. If you have the time, the islands are well worth roaming around, with their long sand dunes, cliffs, lagoons, bright wooden houses and hospitable inhabitants. (For more information on the Magdalens, contact Quebec's toll-free tourist information line at 1-800-363-7777).

▲**East Point**—At the easternmost tip of the island, the East Point lighthouse is one of only three manned lighthouses out of the island's 60-plus lighthouses. The others are Souris and Wood Islands. Climb to the top and you'll have a view of the "meeting of the tides," where the waters of the Gulf of St. Lawrence and the Northumberland Strait meet and swirl together. Open June through early October; $2.50 for adults, $2 for seniors, $1 for children, and $4 for families. The phone number is 687-2295.

▲**Elmira Railway Museum**—This used to be a real railway station but is now a railway museum housing a display of photographs and information about the railway system of the 19th and early 20th century. A must for railway buffs. Open mid-June to Labor Day; $2 for adults, $1 for kids. Elmira is on Route 16A between North Lake and South Lake near the eastern extremity of the island. For more information, call 357-2481.

Helpful Hints

With a few exceptions, I've concentrated on sites that reflect the island's relatively unspoiled aspects. But you'll find as you drive around quite a range of baldly commercial attractions, the sort of places where access is through the gift shop. Some are rather appealing because they're a little weird, like the House of International Dolls with its 1,800 dolls from around the world or the British Royalty Collection, a private collection of royal family memorabilia.

P.E.I.'s tourism industry, it must be said, is geared in many ways towards families with young kids, and you'll find all manner of theme and amusement parks. Just for starters, there is Santa's Woods, billed as a Christmas Theme Park; Fantasyland Provincial Park, featuring statues of favorite storybook characters and a playhouse in the shape of a fort; and P.E.I. Fairyland, where visitors can take a mile-long ride on a miniature train.

Prince Edward Island is also dotted with golf courses; if you're interested, call Golf Prince Edward Island at (902) 368-4130 or the tourist information line for details.

For a copy of the Visitors Guide and other information, contact Prince Edward Island Tourism, Visitor Services, P.O. Box 940, Charlottetown, P.E.I., Canada C1A 7M5, or phone 1-800-463-4PEI toll-free. The Tour the Island Visitor Information Center in Oak Tree Place on University Avenue in Charlottetown is open year-round. Seven other provincial tourist information centers operate seasonally, in Borden, Portage, Summerside, Cavendish, Wood Islands, Montague and Souris.

There are also about a dozen privately operated tourist information centers scattered around the island.

Finally, the City of Charlottetown Visitor Information Center is at Queen and Kent streets downtown; the phone number is (902) 566-5548.

HALIFAX

Nova Scotia is a peninsula that hangs beneath New Brunswick, and on a map has a vague lobster shape. Inland, there are fertile river valleys, glaciated rock formations, and, on Cape Breton Island at the northeastern end of the province, highlands that are eerily reminiscent of Scotland. Nova Scotia is only 560 kilometers (340 miles) long and never more than 130 kilometers (78 miles) wide, but its serrated coastline runs for 7,400 kilometers (4,600 miles) past harbors, inlets, bays, long beaches, and rugged cliffs. Its physical beauty has made tourism into a major industry; in fact after a few days in Nova Scotia, a travelling companion remarked that the province is really one big tourist trap. But he didn't particularly mean it in a negative way; it had taken him a while to even realize it. While the province is markedly geared towards tourism, it manages for the most part to be tasteful about it.

Suggested Schedule

9:00 a.m.	Depart Charlottetown.
12:00 noon	Arrive Halifax, check into lodging, lunch.
1:30 p.m.	Tour the Citadel, which also provides a panoramic view of the city and harbor.
3:00 p.m.	Wander the waterfront for the rest of the afternoon, particularly Historic Properties, a renovated harborside area. Take a harbor cruise if you like, and stop in at the Maritime Museum of the Atlantic.

Driving Route

From Charlottetown, head east on the TransCanada (Highway 1) to Wood Islands, where ferries depart for Caribou, Nova Scotia, starting at 6:00 a.m. daily. There is a Nova Scotia tourism information center to the left of the ferry terminal. The 22-kilometer (14-mile) crossing takes an hour and 15 minutes. The rates are $8.50 for adults, $6.25 for

Charlottetown to Halifax

senior citizens, and $4.10 for children aged 5 to 12, plus
$27.25 per automobile. This particular ferry service is run
by NFL Ferries, which stands for Northumberland Ferries
Limited. NFL doesn't accept reservations; in the peak summer season, plan to board before 10:00 a.m. or after 6:00
p.m. to avoid the rush-hour sailings the rest of the day. For
information, call (902) 566-3838 in Charlottetown or, from
Nova Scotia and P.E.I., 1-800-565-0201 toll-free.

From Caribou, follow the TransCanada (Highway 104)
south and west to exit 15 near Truro. Take exit 15 onto
Highway 102 and follow it right into Halifax. This is about
170 kilometers (105 miles) on good roads; it should take
less than two hours.

In Halifax, Highway 102 merges with Bayers Road.
Follow Bayers Road to Windsor Street and turn right.

When you pass the North Common, a big green space, on your left, turn left at the next street and follow Cogswell Street to Barrington. Turn right on Barrington, which runs through the downtown core.

Nova Scotia

Colonial Nova Scotia changed hands several times as the British and French fought over it. At one point in the mid-1700s, the British expelled 6,000 French-speaking Acadians from Nova Scotia; the "Cajuns" in modern-day Louisiana are descended from some of those deportees. Some Acadians eventually returned to Nova Scotia, and French is still spoken in parts of the province, notably on the northwest coast.

The French were finally defeated after building the magnificent Fortress of Louisbourg on Cape Breton Island. The British later ordered the fortress destroyed, but it is now slowly being reconstructed and is open to visitors.

Nova Scotia drew settlers mainly from Britain, although an influx of German Protestants led to the founding of German-flavored Lunenberg, famous for both its ship-building and its annual Octoberfest. Thousands of New Englanders and, later, Loyalists, also came to Nova Scotia from south of the border. The indigenous people, the Micmacs, were decimated by European diseases and territorial clashes and now number about 10,000.

The major industries are fishing, agriculture, mining, mainly of coal, and forestry. And, of course, tourism.

Halifax

The event that most people connect with Halifax, a sea-faring city of 115,000 on the south-central coast, is the famous Halifax Explosion of Dec. 6, 1917. On that wartime morning, the French munitions ship *Mont Blanc* barely bumped the Belgian relief ship *Imo* in the Halifax harbor and exploded with such force it was the most powerful manmade blast before the atom bomb. The ship's anchor flew almost 3 kilometers (2 miles), landing in a field off the Northwest Arm. The blast shattered windows as far away as Truro, some 100 kilometers (60 miles) to the northeast, and was heard on Prince Edward Island. It also emptied the harbor beneath the *Mont Blanc*'s keel, creating a tidal wave that roared up streets, sweeping away people and vehicles in its path. When the horror was over, more than 1,600 people were dead and 9,000 injured. A fifth of the seaport, which had a population of 50,000 at the time, was devastated, with some 1,600 buildings leveled and another 12,000 damaged.

Today, Halifax is the largest city in Atlantic Canada and sits on one of the largest harbors in the world. The central part of the city occupies a fat peninsula of land girded by Bedford Basin to the north, a long, slender inlet called the Northwest Arm to the southwest, and Halifax Harbor and the Atlantic to the south. Across the Narrows, which link Bedford Basin and Halifax Harbor, lies the city of Dartmouth. Commuter ferries cross regularly between the two cities.

Halifax is also the cultural centre of Nova Scotia, offering all manner of music, art, and theater. It further boasts that it has the highest ratio of educational facilities per capita of any city in North America, and because it's a university town, there are numerous second-hand bookstores and a lively nightlife.

Getting Around

On foot is the way to go. The major sights are all in a fairly compact area in central Halifax. Begin at the Citadel and work your way down toward the waterfront. If you get lost in central Halifax and can't see a street name, walk to the nearest corner and look down. For some reason, the names of streets are carved into the sidewalk at each corner.

Parking isn't the problem in Halifax that it is in some other Canadian cities. If you want to drive, there is parking both at the Citadel and at Historic Properties.

There is a provincial tourist information center in the Red Store Building in Historic Properties, while Tourism Halifax runs a year-round information center in City Hall at the corner of Barrington and Duke Streets and a sea-

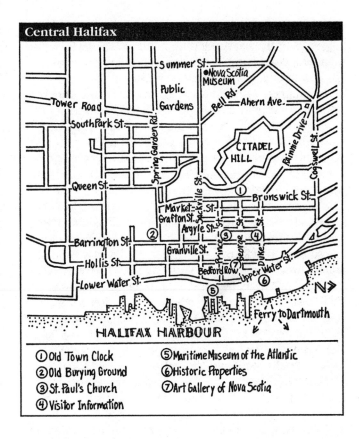

Central Halifax

Summer St.
●Nova Scotia Museum
Public Gardens
Tower Road
Bell Rd.
Ahern Ave.
SouthPark St.
Spring Garden Rd.
CITADEL HILL
Rainnie Drive
Cogswell St.
Queen St.
① Brunswick St.
Market St.
Grafton St.
Sackville St.
② Argyle St.
③
④
Barrington St.
Granville St.
Prince St.
George St.
Duke St.
Hollis St.
⑦ Bedford Row
Upper Water St.
Lower Water St.
⑥
⑤
Ferry to Dartmouth
N➤
HALIFAX HARBOUR

① Old Town Clock
② Old Burying Ground
③ St. Paul's Church
④ Visitor Information
⑤ Maritime Museum of the Atlantic
⑥ Historic Properties
⑦ Art Gallery of Nova Scotia

sonal information center in the Public Gardens at the top of Sackville Street.

Sightseeing Highlights

▲▲▲**The Halifax Citadel**—This star-shaped fortress provides not just a history lesson but a dramatic view of the city and harbor below. Halifax was for years the bastion of British imperial control in North America. The present fortress, constructed between 1828 and 1856, is actually the fourth citadel on this site. The previous fortifications date back to 1749, the year Halifax was founded. The citadel was never attacked. When the British garrison finally departed in 1906, the site was handed over to the

Canadian militia. It was manned by Canadian forces during both world wars and, during World War Two, served as a temporary barracks for troops heading overseas. It was declared a national historic park in 1956.

In summer, 19th-century soldiers drill on the parades, and there's usually a bagpiper on hand. The firing of the noon gun is worth seeing. (The last time I visited, the gun misfired, much to the crowd's amusement. Disconcerted soldiers assured spectators that it almost never happens.) There are sentries, vaulted barracks and other rooms and a musketry gallery. For the best view of the city and the Old Town Clock, go up on the ramparts. The Old Town Clock, almost as much a Halifax landmark as the Citadel, was completed in 1803 and served as the garrison clock. It's so big it blocks part of the view of the city. Guided tours of the Citadel leave every half-hour between 9:30 a.m. and 5:00 p.m. from near the entrance. Admission is $2 for adults, $1 for children aged 5 to 15, free for seniors and children under 5 and $5 for families. Open 9:00 a.m. to 6:00 p.m. from June 15 to Labor Day, 9:00 a.m. to 5:00 p.m. the rest of the year. For information, call (902) 426-5080.

▲▲**St. Paul's Anglican Church**—To get to St. Paul's, walk down Prince or George Street to Argyle Street. Constructed in 1750, St. Paul's is the oldest standing building in Halifax as well as the oldest Protestant church in Canada. Its greatest claim to fame is the third window on the right on the upper level after you enter the church. You'll notice immediately there seems to be a silhouette of a man's profile etched on the pane. Local lore has it that a piece of flying debris crashed through this window during the Halifax Explosion and left a hole whose outline duplicates the profile of the parson of the day. The parson was killed in the explosion. The church is at the Grand Parade between Barrington and Argyle streets. The Grand Parade, a one-time parade ground in the middle of the city, has ample green space and often hosts live entertainment in summer.

▲▲**Art Gallery of Nova Scotia**—The permanent collection includes mainly Nova Scotian artists but gives some space to Canadian, British and European works as well.

There is also an extensive folk art section on the mezzanine level. Temporary exhibits change every 6 to 12 weeks. The gallery is at 1741 Hollis Street, between George and Prince streets, not far from Historic Properties. Open year-round, 10:00 a.m. to 5:30 p.m. Tuesday to Saturday, 10:00 a.m. to 9:00 p.m. Thursday, 12:00 noon to 5:30 p.m. Sunday, closed Monday. Admission is free on Tuesday, otherwise $2 per person. For information, call (902) 424-7542.

▲▲▲**The Maritime Museum of the Atlantic**—If for nothing else, stop in here to see an exhibit about the Halifax Explosion called *A Moment in Time*. It takes up only one small corner of the museum and it's fascinating, maybe simply because the story of the explosion is so compelling. The display includes photographs, artifacts such as a comb and pencil belonging to school kids and a 17-minute video about the disastrous event. Elsewhere in the museum is a collection of quite extraordinary ship models plus some real life-size boats, ranging from Queen Victoria's Royal Barge and a beautiful *Bluenose*-class sloop to a couple of dories (small boats used for almost a century aboard fishing schooners because they were easily hoisted and lowered and could carry two men, their gear, and the catch). Upstairs, a display called *The Age of Steam* has models of everything from Arctic patrol vessels and Great Lakes freighters to magnificent Cunard liners. (Company founder Samuel Cunard was born in Halifax.) Berthed at the dock outside the museum is the C.S.S. *Acadia*, a onetime hydrographic survey vessel that is now a museum ship. The Maritime Museum of the Atlantic is at 1675 Lower Water Street between Prince and Sackville streets; nominal admission. Open May 15 to October 15 from 9:30 a.m. to 5:30 p.m. Monday to Saturday (to 8:00 p.m. on Tuesday) and 1:00 to 5:30 p.m. Sunday; slightly different hours the rest of the year. Phone (902) 424-7490 for more information.

▲▲▲**Historic Properties**—This is a picturesque waterfront complex of boutiques, restaurants, and pubs in 10 restored wood and stone buildings that date back to the early 1800s and are said to be Canada's oldest waterfront buildings. With a waterside boardwalk and outdoor cafés,

it's a nice area just to stroll, even if you're not in a shopping mood. It's also where harbor cruises depart. Take
one; you get to see much more of the cityscape, including
Point Pleasant Park at the southern end of the city and
McNabs Island in the harbor. Evening cruises are available
as well. If you haven't time for a two-hour cruise Prices for
a two-hour cruise on the *Harbor Queen*, for example, are
$15 for adults, $14 for seniors, $12 for youths ages 13 to
18, and $9.50 for kids from 5 to 12 years old. The family
rate is $29.50, while a dinner cruise costs $29.50 per person. If you haven't time for a two-hour cruise, take the
ferry across to Dartmouth and back; the ferry terminal is
just south of Historic Properties, and the seven-minute
roundtrip provides a good view of the skyline and some of
the harbor for $2. The complex is off Upper Water Street at
the base of Duke Street. A replica of the original *Bluenose*,
the schooner depicted on the Canadian dime, used to dock
at Historic Properties each summer. She is currently out of
commission due to needed repairs and her owner (the
Nova Scotia government) can't find the money for them.

▲**The Old Burying Ground**—The oldest burial ground
in Halifax has gravestones dating as far back as 1754. It
was declared a national historic site in 1991 and is being
gradually restored as an outdoor museum and park. It's
on Barrington Street at the corner of Spring Garden Road.

▲▲**Public Gardens**—The peaceful and picturesque
Public Gardens lie just to the southwest of Citadel Hill at
the corner of Spring Garden Road and South Park Street.
Formal Victorian gardens, lush with roses, hibiscus, dra-
caenas and other varieties, are laid out around a lovely
Victorian bandstand where there are musical performances
on Sunday afternoons. The gardens are open from spring
to late fall, and admission is free.

▲**Point Pleasant Park**—The other major green oasis in
Halifax is Point Pleasant Park at the southern tip of the
city. With an unimpeded view of the Atlantic ocean and
miles of paths, it's a perfect place for a picnic, a walk, or a
swim off Black Rock beach. No cars are permitted inside
the park, but there is ample parking at both eastern and
western entrances.

Lodging

Staying in one of Halifax's attractive old inns is a good bet for their prices, their atmosphere, and their central locations. The **Waverley Inn** is a charming antique-furnished Victorian establishment at 1266 Barrington Street, with double rooms running from $55 to $90, including breakfast; call (902) 423-9346. The **King Edward Inn** at 2400 Agricola Street is another Victorian-style inn with room rates ranging from $65 to $89; call (902) 422-3266. The **Queen Street Inn** at 1266 Queen Street is in an old stone house near downtown, with rates running around $50 for a double; call (902) 422-9828.

At the upscale end of things, the **Halifax Sheraton** is right in the heart of the action on Upper Water Street next to the Historic Properties area. Double rooms begin around $165; phone 421-1700 locally or 1-800-325-3535 toll-free. The **Delta Barrington** is less pricey but also right next to Historic Properties. Room rates begin around $90; call 429-7410 locally or 1-800-268-1133 from Canada, 1-800-877-1133 from the U.S. The **Chateau Halifax** at 1990 Barrington Street offers doubles for $125 to $160; call 425-6700 locally or 1-800-441-1414 toll-free. Room rates at the **Halifax Hilton** at 1181 Hollis Street begin around $100; call 423-7231 locally or 1-800-HILTONS toll-free. At the **Prince George Hotel** at 1725 Market Street, double rooms begin around $160; call 425-1986 locally or 1-800-565-1567 toll-free.

The 300-page visitors guide put out the Nova Scotia Department of Tourism and Culture contains pages and pages of accommodation listings, conveniently broken down by location. There is also a handy brochure put out by the Metropolitan Area Tourism Association called "Guide to Bed and Breakfast and Country Inns of Metropolitan Halifax-Dartmouth," listing more than 30 B&Bs and inns.

The province's toll-free tourist information line doubles as a booking service called Check In. You can reserve hotels, motels, inns, bed & breakfasts, resorts, campgrounds and car rentals simply by calling the number, but have a particular place or two in mind before phoning to make a reservation. From Canada, the phone number

is 1-800-565-0000; from the U.S., 1-800-341-6096; and
in Halifax, 425-5781.

Camping

Nova Scotia has an abundance of campgrounds in its two
national parks (Kejimkujik in the centre of southwestern
Nova Scotia and Cape Breton Highlands National Park),
in some provincial parks, and in more than 100 privately
run operations.

There are four campgrounds within easy driving distance of Halifax-Dartmouth. **Laurie Provincial Park** is a
wooded campground on Route 2 at Grand Lake. Rates
begin at $7.50; call (902) 861-1623. **Shubie Park** is on
Route 318 in Dartmouth and offers swimming, fishing,
nature trails, a play area and a tennis court. Rates begin at
$12; call (902) 464-2334. **Woodhaven Park** is a wooded
campground on Hammonds Plains Road. Rates are $12
and up; call (902) 835-2271. **Colonial Camping** in Upper
Sackville is on a river and offers swimming, boating, play
ground, boat rental, and mini-golf. Rates begin at $11.50;
call (902) 865-4342.

Restaurants

The **Privateer's Warehouse** is a three-restaurant complex in Historic Properties; the higher you go, the higher
the prices. The **Lower Deck** is a pub on the ground floor,
with long communal tables and inexpensive, fresh
seafood; call 425-1501. The **Middle Deck** offers ocean
views and local food; call 425-1500. **Bradley's** on the
upper deck serves up dishes like smoked salmon tartare
appetizer and other culinary delights, all at upscale prices;
call 422-1289.

Other noteworthy seafood places (and seafood is
naturally the way to go in Halifax) include **The Five
Fishermen**, an informal establishment in a 175-year-old
building at 1740 Argyle Street at the corner of George
Street (422-4421); and **Clipper Cay**, a two-level place at
the end of the Historic Properties Pier with pub-style dining downstairs and seafood aplenty upstairs (423-6818).

But Halifax has other types of restaurants too. The

Granite Brewery serves up bitters, stout, and other beers along with pub-style food in a warm atmosphere at 1222 Barrington Street. There's a vegetarian restaurant, **Satisfaction Feast**, at 1581 Grafton Street (422-3540). For a fine lunch, dinner or just dessert (like Chocolate Decadence Cake), try the **Silver Spoon** at 1813 Granville (429-6617). The **Green Bean Coffeehouse** serves up excellent coffee and food at 5220 Blowers Street. A large complex of interconnected restaurant-bars at 1740 Argyle Street at the corner of George Street includes **The Atrium**, **My Apartment**, and **Cheers**. If you can't immediately decide what kind of food or decor you want, wander through the place until something strikes your fancy.

Nightlife
This is a port city, so consider a pub crawl. Pick up a copy of a *Halifax Pub Guide* from the tourist office in the Old Red Store and start crawling. The aforementioned **Privateer's Warehouse** in Historic Properties is popular for drinking as well as eating, since two of its three levels offer live music in the evenings. A guitarist or jazz group plays from 10:00 p.m. to 12:00 midnight, Monday through Saturday, at the **Middle Deck** (425-1500). Things are more boisterous one floor below at the **Lower Deck** (425-1501), where a singer leads the crowd in maritime folk songs from 9:00 p.m. on.

Culture vultures also have ample choice, with pro-fessional concerts and drama offered by the Neptune Theater, the Dalhousie University Arts Centre, and Symphony Nova Scotia. Check the *Chronicle-Herald* or the *Mail Star* for up-to-date listings.

Shopping
Halifax's smartest shops are on the Granville Promenade, on Granville Street north of Duke Street. The promenade has been restored and is part of Historic Properties.

Helpful Hints
Nova Scotia likes to call itself the Festival Province because it offers something like 350 festivals a year,

would you believe. Needless to say, many of them are
pretty small local affairs, and you may well come across
one or two as you're travelling around. In Halifax-
Dartmouth, the most interesting summertime fests include
the **Summer Entertainment Series** of outdoor concerts,
running in Dartmouth throughout July; the **Festival of
Light** fireworks extravaganza jointly hosted by both cities
around mid-July; Yarmouth's **Seafest**, a seaside festival
the third week of July; the annual **Atlantic Jazz Festival**
in Halifax around the same time; and Halifax's
International Buskerfest the second week of August.
The Nova Scotia visitors guide contains long listings of
what's afoot throughout the province.

The provincial tourist information line, Check In, can
supply all manner of information, chiefly in the bulky
annual visitors guide to the province, titled *Nova Scotia—
The Doers and Dreamers Complete Guide*. Another handy
publication, at least for travelers who enjoy fine dining, is
a booklet titled *Taste of Nova Scotia*; it lists restaurants
throughout the province that meet high standards set by
the Taste of Nova Scotia program. The toll-free numbers
for Check-In are 1-800-565-0000 from Canada and 1-800-
341-6096 from the United States. In Halifax, the local
phone number is 425-5781. Tourism Halifax's phone
number is (902) 421-8736.

THE WESTERN COAST: THE LIGHTHOUSE ROUTE AND THE EVANGELINE TRAIL

The Lighthouse Route runs along the south coast from Halifax to Yarmouth, at the western tip of the province, through such picturesque towns as Peggy's Cove, Mahone Bay, and Lunenburg. The Evangeline Trail leads from Yarmouth along the part of the Bay of Fundy coast known as the Acadian shore. Evangeline was a young Acadian woman who was separated from her betrothed, Gabriel, by the deportation of the Acadians from Nova Scotia. The lovers were reunited only at the end of their lives, as Gabriel lay dying. American poet Henry Wadsworth Longfellow heard the story and immortalized it in his poem *Evangeline: A Tale of Acadie*. The Evangeline Trail continues on through the lush Annapolis Valley, but it's too much to do the whole circuit in one day. Stop in Annapolis Royal for the night, leaving the Annapolis Valley for tomorrow.

Suggested Schedule

8:00 a.m.	Depart Halifax so that you get to Peggy's Cove before everyone else does.
9:15 a.m.	Depart Peggy's Cove and proceed at your own pace through Chester, Mahone Bay, and Lunenburg, among the most scenic spots on today's itinerary.
12:00 noon	Lunch, maybe in Lunenburg, maybe in Liverpool.
1:30 p.m.	Continue the circuit at your own pace.
5:00 p.m.	Arrive in Annapolis Royal.

Driving Route: Halifax to Annapolis Royal (400 km/ 245 miles)

From Halifax, follow Highway 333 to Peggy's Cove. After that, just follow the road signs for the Lighthouse Route (silhouette of a lighthouse) to Yarmouth. After Yarmouth, follow the signs for the Evangeline Trail (silhouette of a

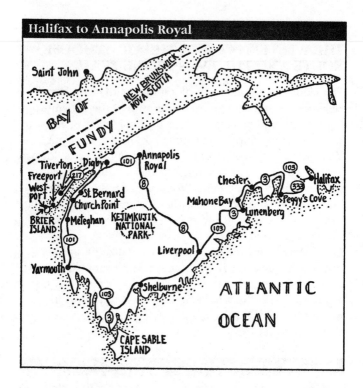

Halifax to Annapolis Royal

church) as far as Annapolis Royal. Both routes hug the coast. Allowing for stops plus the fact that the average driving speed on this route is about 70 kilometers an hour (42 MPH), it will take a good part of the day to drive.

Sightseeing Highlights

▲▲▲**Peggy's Cove**—Peggy's Cove is a tiny fishing village, renowned for its picturesque setting and rustic buildings, about a half-hour's drive southwest of Halifax. It's such a well-known attraction that it's always crowded. The only way to see it properly without elbow-to-elbow crowds is to get there first thing in the morning. And I mean early—get in and out before 9:00 a.m., when the tour buses start arriving. It's a beautiful spot and well worth a visit if you can do it that way. Park in the parking lot at the edge of the village and walk down the slope. Peggy's Cove sits in a calm little inlet, and when you get into the center of the village you'll understand why it's one of the most photographed parts of Nova Scotia. Take a few shots; they'll come out looking like picture-perfect postcards, because that's exactly how Peggy's Cove looks. Then continue along the road towards the lighthouse, which sits on a point and doubles as a post office during tourist season. The coastline here is made up of huge, gently rounded granite boulders with surf splashing against them. It's a powerfully stark scene; take some time to walk over the rocks (wear sneakers and be careful!) and sit a while contemplating the sea. Steer clear of the restaurant-souvenir shop near the rocks. Of all the souvenir shops in Peggy's Cove, the one worth searching out is Beales Bailiwick, which offers wares from pewter and oilcloth coats to pretty pottery, mohair sweaters, and high-quality sweatshirts and t-shirts.

▲▲**Chester**—Chester is an old resort town where lots of wealthy Americans used to spend their summers. It has some lovely old mansions, including the Sword and Anchor Inn, built in the early 1800s. If you're getting hungry, the recommended restaurant is the Captain's House. The town has long drawn sailors and yachters, and the busiest week of the year is Chester Race Week, held the second week of August. It's Atlantic Canada's largest sailing regatta, and everybody goes to it.

▲**Oak Island**—Oak Island, five minutes outside Mahone Bay, has a fascinating history. Legend has it that Captain Kidd's treasure is buried in a pit on Oak Island, and for decades serious treasure hunters have been trying to figure out how to solve the mystery of the so-called Money Pit. It contains an elaborate system of shafts and tunnels that were apparently designed to cave in or flood with sea water when disturbed. So far, nobody has succeeded in this great treasure hunt, though searchers have spent literally millions trying to get to the bottom of it all. In summer, you can tour the island by bus and view a video about the continuing exploration. The cost is $3.50 for adults and $2 for children.

▲▲▲**Mahone Bay**—Mahone Bay is famous for its three churches, which stand in a row (Anglican, Lutheran, and

United) at the head of the town's harbor. Perhaps less well-known but equally interesting is the nearby heritage cemetery; take the time to stroll through it. Mahone Bay, which likes to call itself "one of the prettiest towns in Canada," is a fine place in which to stroll, shop, and eat. For eating, try the Innlet Cafe, which has fresh seafood, salads and sandwiches plus a view of the three churches from its location in the Kedy's Landing complex at the head of the bay. The Teazer, named after a ghost ship, is popular for souvenir shopping. And stop in at Suttles & Seawinds, located in a giant pink house on Main Street. It sells clothes and quilts, and is worth a visit just to see the inside of the house. For pewter goods, try Amos Pewterers, also on Main Street.

▲▲▲**Lunenburg**—This is the famous ship-building center where both the original *Bluenose* and the replica *Bluenose II* were built. It was long one of Canada's great fishing ports. Stop in at the Fisheries Museum of the Atlantic, consisting of two floating vessels moored at the quay as well as museum buildings. The most interesting ship is the restored *Theresa E. Connor*, the last Canadian schooner to fish Newfoundland's Grand Banks. The other ship is the *Cape Sable*, a steel-hulled trawler. The adjacent museum buildings house an aquarium, a display of *Bluenose* mementos, a theater, and a gift shop. Entrance is $2.25 for adults, 50 cents for children, and $5.50 for families. Lunenburg, an exceedingly picturesque place, boasts some beautiful old restored buildings. Pick up a walking-tour pamphlet from the local tourist information center, which is housed in a lighthouse replica in Blockhouse Hill, a public park that provides a panoramic view of the town and harbor. For a meal, consider the Compass Rose Inn, a small heritage inn in Old Lunenburg whose restaurant is open to the public. Should you fall in love with the place and decide to stay longer, see if there's room at the exquisite old Lunenburg Inn at 26 Dufferin Street, (902) 634-3963. One of the annual festivals in Lunenburg arises out of the town's German heritage: Octoberfest, with activities for all ages, takes place in early October.

▲**Liverpool**—Fine old houses dating from the Loyalist

influx still stand on Liverpool's tree-lined streets. Stop in at the Simon Perkins House, built in 1766 by a prosperous local merchant and now a provincial museum, at 105 Main Street. In addition to 18th-century furniture, the house contains a copy of Perkins' diaries, which he kept painstakingly for 40 years, providing succeeding generations with a vivid record of daily life in a colonial town. For some reason, he was particularly detailed about any illness in the family. Admission to the house is free. Liverpool also has a tourist information center, located in Centennial Park.

▲**Shelburne**—For a time after it was first settled by Loyalists in 1783, Shelburne was the third-largest town in North America. Eventually many Loyalists moved on, but the town's tourist literature encourages visitors to come trace their roots because so many colonists funnelled through Shelburne. You never know. Many of the town's houses date from Loyalist times, including the Ross-Thompson House, built in 1784 and now a provincial museum. Part of the museum is a restored Loyalist store displaying period merchandise. Settlers George and Robert Ross originally opened the store in the 1780s and sold salt, tobacco, molasses, and dry goods to the other settlers. Admission is free. There is a tourist information center on Dock Street in Shelburne, and the Shelburne County Genealogical Society is also on Dock Street. Near Shelburne, The Islands Provincial Park, connected to the mainland by a causeway, offers picnic tables and a campground.

▲▲**Cape Sable Island**—Cape Sable Island, Nova Scotia's most southerly point, is linked by a 1,200-meter causeway (3,925 feet) to Barrington Passage, a tiny village on the mainland south of Clark's Harbour. But Cape Sable Island's other claim to fame is that over the years, hundreds of ships have run afoul of the submerged shoals that stretch out around the island. The cape has long been known to sailors as one of the graveyards of the Atlantic. In the tiny community of Centreville on Cape Sable Island, the Archelaus Smith Museum exhibits items salvaged from vessels shipwrecked in the area. Admission is free.

▲**Yarmouth**—Yarmouth is the province's largest seaport east of Halifax, and also the terminal for the ferry service from Bar Harbour and Portland, Maine. Downtown, many 19th-century buildings have been preserved. The Yarmouth County Museum at 22 Collins Street displays model ships and paintings and is one of the largest collections of this kind in Canada. Several major Acadian festivals take place in Yarmouth, notably the Seafest, a week of activities in July. Yarmouth marks the beginning of the Evangeline Trail.

▲**Meteghan**—Just before the village of Meteghan, stop in at Smugglers Cove Provincial Park, which offers a vista of St. Mary's Bay. Meteghan, a small but busy port, is where a mystery man known only as Jerome is buried. He apparently materialized on the beach at Sandy Cove, across the bay from Meteghan, in 1854. He was dressed in clean clothes and had a supply of water and biscuits, but his legs had been amputated above the knees. He was unable to speak and never revealed his origins. He was named Jerome by local residents, who cared for him until his death 58 years later.

▲**Church Point (*Pointe de l'Église*)**—Church Point boasts St. Mary's Church, one of the largest wooden churches in North America. It was built between 1903 and 1905. The spire reaches 56 meters (183 feet) into the air and is weighted down inside with tons of rock to act as ballast in the strong winds that come in off St. Mary's Bay. Guided tours are available in summer.

▲**Belliveau Cove**—Stop here to see what the tide is doing. Belliveau Cove has a well-protected harbor, and the tides of St. Mary's Bay, a Bay of Fundy inlet, are extremely high.

▲**St-Bernard**—There is another big church here, an enormous gothic granite building that dominates the village and seats 1,000 people. Guided tours are available.

▲**Kejimkujik National Park**—One of Nova Scotia's two national parks lies inland, about 55 kilometers (33 miles) north of Liverpool on Route 8. Kejimkujik is a wooded, gently rolling wilderness area dotted with lakes, rivers, and hiking trails. There is also a campground.

Canoeing is a particularly popular activity; rentals are available. In summer, park naturalists give lectures and lead guided walks and canoe trips. For information, call (902) 682-2772.

▲**Brier Island**—This side trip shows you tall, strange rock pillars that extend from the shore hundreds of meters into the sea like ragged rows of marching columns. The site is called the Giant's Causeway. Ask for directions in Westport, the only community on the island. Brier Island is at the tip of a thin peninsula called Digby Neck and the Islands that stretches west from Digby. To get to it, take Route 217 from Digby, catch a ferry from East Ferry to Tiverton on Long Island and, at the far end of Long Island, catch another ferry from Freeport across to Westport. Ferries run regularly. Brier Island, about 65 kilometers (40 miles) from Digby, is also known for whale-watching and bird-watching. Tours are available out of Westport. Whale-watching cruises are also available from Tiverton. Ask at the Tiverton Tourist Bureau for directions to Balancing Rock, a strange coastal rock formation that looks like it's about to keel over into the water.

Annapolis Royal

When French explorers Samuel de Champlain and Sieur de Monts first came across the Annapolis River basin in 1604, they named the area Port-Royal. Within a couple of years, a small band of French farmers had settled in Port-Royal, making it the oldest European settlement in Canada. Port-Royal changed hands several times as the French and British battled over Nova Scotia. At one point, when the British were in control, it was renamed Annapolis in honor of Queen Anne, and it served as the capital of Nova Scotia for a time before Halifax was founded.

Eventually, after the Acadians were expelled, the area was resettled by New Englanders and Loyalists, and the two names merged to become Annapolis Royal. Today, it's a lovely little place, retaining its unspoiled small-town atmosphere and beauty despite its popularity as a tourist destination. The part of St. George Street that runs parallel to the waterfront downtown claims to be the oldest town

street in Canada, lined with restored buildings housing
small historical museums, shops, and restaurants. Pick up
a walking tour pamphlet from the local tourist information
bureau in the railway station at the base of Victoria Street.

Running parallel to St. George Street behind King's
Theater, a waterfront promenade overlooks the Annapolis
River and the village of Granville Ferry, where the falling
Fundy tides leave vessels berthed at the wharf—high and
dry. And drop in at the Annapolis Royal Historic Gardens,
located at the traffic lights on Route 8 (St. George Street).
The grounds boast pretty theme gardens and winding
pathways in a setting that slopes gently down to the
Allains River. The gardens are open daily from May to
October. Admission is $3.50 for adults, $3 for seniors and
children and $9.75 for families. History buffs should also
visit Fort Anne National Historic Park, which has earthwork
fortifcations dating from the 1600s and a reconstructed
British Field Officers' Quarters dating from 1797.

Just outside town is the Annapolis Royal Tidal Power
Generating Station, the continent's only tidal power plant.
An interpretation center on the site demonstrates how the
plant generates hydroelectric power from some of the
world's highest tides. Also on the site is a provincial
tourist information center.

Lodging

Several exquisite old Victorian inns in town offer rooms in
the $50 to $85 range. The **Queen Anne Inn** is just up the
road from the Annapolis Royal Historic Gardens at 494
Upper St. George Street; phone (902) 532-7850 (no smoking). **The Garrison House Inn** at 350 St. George Street
also boasts a wonderful restaurant; call (902) 532-5750.
The **Bread & Roses** at 82 Victoria Street is a restored
Victorian brick mansion; call (902) 532-5727 (no smoking).
Located on a large estate with a duck sanctuary, **The
Hillsdale House** at 519 St. George Street is a registered
heritage property furnished with antiques. Children are
welcome. Call (902) 532-2345.

A number of B&Bs in the area have rates beginning

around $40 for a double room. Try **English Oaks B&B**,
a modern house on lovely riverside property just outside
town; call (902) 532-2066. The **St. George House Bed &
Breakfast** at 548 Upper St. George Street is a registered
heritage property with antique furnishings; call (902) 532-
5286 (no smoking). **The Turret Bed & Breakfast**, yet
another registered historic property, is at 372 St. George
Street; call (902) 532-5770 (no smoking). Or try **Amulree**,
a comfortable old home at 703 St. George Street; (902)
532-7206. In Granville Ferry a few minutes from Annapolis
Royal, **Bayberry House Bed and Breakfast** is an early
Victorian home overlooking the river basin and Annapolis
Royal; call (902) 532-2272.

Digby, 38 kilometers (23 miles) west of Annapolis
Royal, has plentiful hotels, motels, and B&Bs because it's
the terminal for the ferry to Saint John, N.B. Digby's most
famous hotel is **The Pines**, a grand resort with prices to
match ($127 to $250, depending on the season); the
phone number is (902) 245-2511. You'll find a wide range
of much lower-priced accommodations in and around
Digby as well. In Digby, the area to stroll is Water Street,
a waterfront section of shops and restaurants with a view
over the Annapolis Basin and Diby's scallop fleet.

Camping

There are several campgrounds in the area around
Annapolis Royal. **Dunromin Campsite and Trailer
Court**, a wooded and open campground with a grocery
store, laundromat, swimming area and play area, is minutes west of town on Route 1. Rates begin at $12. Call
(902) 532-2808. **House of Roth** in Clementsport, another
campground offering both wooded and open sites plus
a pool, hiking trails and play areas, is 13 kilometers (8
miles) west of Annapolis Royal; call (902) 638-8053.
Fundy Trail Campground is on the Bay of Fundy, 19
kilometers (12 miles) north of Route 1, and has a recreation hall, lanudromat, canteen, pool, and walking trails as
well as wilderness sites on a freshwater brook. Rates
begin at $10. Call (902) 532-7711.

Restaurants

The Old Post Office serves three-course country suppers every night from 5:00 to 9:00 p.m.; call 532-POST. For more upscale dining, try the aforementioned **Garrison House Inn** at 350 St. George Street (532-5750) or **Newman's Restaurant** at 218 St. George Street (532-5502).

Helpful Hints

If you're short of time or beginning to overdose on scenic fishing villages and ocean vistas, you can cut across from Liverpool straight to Annapolis Royal on Route 8, a 117-kilometer (70-mile) drive that passes the edge of Kejimkujik National Park.

Families might want to stop in at the Upper Clements Family Vacation Park, five minutes west of Annapolis Royal on Route 1. The theme park combines re-creations of Nova Scotia's heritage and history with latter-day amusement-park rides. It's open from mid-May to mid-October. Entrance to the theme park is free, but you pay for each ride and attraction once inside. It's open daily in July and August; on weekends only in June and September. From Atlantic Canada, call toll-free 1-800-565-PARK.

THE ANNAPOLIS VALLEY TO CAPE BRETON ISLAND

Blessed with more sunny days and milder weather tnan most other parts of the Maritimes, the fertile Annapolis Valley is dotted with small, peaceful villages and apple orchards. This is apple-growing country in a big way. In May and June, the apple trees turn a marvelous pink with blossoms and an annual five-day Apple Blossom Festival is held throughout the valley at the height of the blossoms in late May. The Annapolis Valley is flanked by ridges known locally as the North and South Mountains, with the North Mountain running along the Bay of Fundy shore. The Evangeline Trail runs through the center of the bucolic valley, passing through tranquil villages that boast some glorious old Victorian houses. On a sunny day, it's like drifting through a little piece of heaven on earth.

Suggested Schedule

9:00 a.m.	Spend the morning driving through the valley at your own pace, exploring as you go. A sidetrip to Halls Harbour and The Lookoff will take about 90 minutes.
1:00 p.m.	Lunch, probably in Windsor.
2:00 p.m.	There's a lot of driving to do after Windsor. With brief stops in Truro and Antigonish, you should arrive in Baddeck by about 5:00 p.m.

Driving Route: Annapolis Royal to Baddeck (530 km/320 miles)

The Evangeline Trail follows Route 1, which snakes through the heart of the Annapolis Valley. If you want a change of scenery, there are numerous side roads leading to fishing villages along the Minas Channel shoreline. In fact the shoreline is never more than 15 kilometers (9 miles) due north. The channel empties into the Bay of Fundy, which means the tides are high. Because of the bay's shape, the great volume of the incoming tide is squeezed into a narrowing space as it pours up the channel and into Minas Basin. This forces the water to rise very high along the shoreline as the tide comes in, and to recede a long way as it goes out. The most dramatic effect occurs in the Minas Basin, but the rise and fall is significant along the entire Bay of Fundy and its inlets and you can see its effects at any of the fishing villages along the Minas Channel.

I recommend a sidetrip to picturesque Halls Harbour; to get there, take Route 359 north from Kentville. To see what's known as The Lookoff, which provides a remarkable vista of the Annapolis Valley, backtrack from Halls Harbour along the 359 for a few kilometres and turn left when you see a sign for Glenmount. Stay on the same road through and past Glenmount until it becomes Route 358. The Lookoff is a couple of kilometers further along Route 358. Then backtrack along Route 358 and stay on it until you're back at Route 1.

At Windsor, get onto the Glooscap Trail, another of the province's scenic routes, and follow it as far as Truro. From there, the TransCanada leads straight to Cape Breton Island. Aim to spend the night somewhere around Baddeck (for lodging suggestions and other information on Baddeck, see the end of this chapter). Cape Breton Island is connected with the mainland by the 1,370-meter (4,480-foot) Canso Causeway. On the mainland, the Trans-Canada is Highway 104; on Cape Breton Island, it becomes Highway 105.

Sightseeing Highlights

▲**Lawrencetown**—The annual Annapolis Valley Exhibition is held in Lawrencetown the third week of August. It's a big country fair, with animals, flowers, fruits, vegetables, livestock, art and entertainment, even photography and art exhibits.

▲**Middleton**—Middleton bills itself as the "Heart of the Valley" and hosts a Heart of the Valley Festival in mid-July, complete with parades, contests and fireworks.

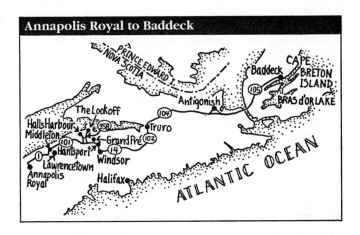

Annapolis Royal to Baddeck

▲▲▲Halls Harbour—Halls Harbour is a lovely little fishing village that slopes steeply down to the shore, where the tides rise and fall to an astounding extent. When we were there, the tide was out, and fishing boats were grounded way down below wharf level. Stranded fish flopped about in small pools of water left behind.

▲▲▲The Lookoff—The Lookoff, about 20 minutes from the Evangeline Trail, is well worth the sidetrip for its panoramic view over the Minas Basin and the patchwork fields of the Annapolis Valley.

▲Grand Pré—Grand Pré National Historic Park marks the site of the explusion of the Acadians. The park contains formal gardens, a commemorative church, and a statue of Evangeline. A growing number of artisans are settling in Grand Pré, so it's a good place to browse for arts and crafts. Grand Pré is also the centre of Nova Scotia's wine industry; locally, the Grand Pré Winery offers tours, tastings, and a wine and gift boutique.

▲Hantsport—If you want to see more ship models, stop here at the community centre, which houses models and other maritime mementos.

▲▲Windsor—This is a good place to view the tidal bore, the tumbling wave that moves upriver with the advancing tide from the Bay of Fundy. It can vary from a few inches to a several feet in height and is most dramatic as it enters certain rivers that empty into the bay. Along this shore, the bore is most pronounced in the Meander River near Windsor. Ask at the Windsor Tourist Bureau for tidal times and directions. Stop in at Shand House, a magnificently gingerbready late-Victorian home that is now a provincial museum furnished with just about everything ever acquired by the Shand family, down to trophies won by Clifford Shand in high-wheeled bicycle races. Windsor calls itself the Giant Pumpkin Capital of the World. How big are these gargantuans? The annual pumpkin festival at Thanksgiving has produced pumpkins and squash in excess of 275 kilos (600 pounds). Windsor is the eastern gateway to the Annapolis Valley.

▲**Truro**—Truro, a manufacturing, railway, and shipping centre known as "the hub of Nova Scotia," is another place to view the tidal bore as it comes up the Salmon River on the northern edge of the city.

▲**Antigonish**—Worth a stop if the Highland Games are happening. The Antigonish games have been held every year since 1861, making them the oldest Highland Games in Canada. They're held in July, and they're a major blow-out. Main Street in the heart of town is worth a browse.

▲▲**Bras d'Or Lake**—Between Whycocomagh Bay and Baddeck on Cape Breton Island, the TransCanada follows the shoreline of Bras d'Or Lake, an inland sea which despite its name is actually an arm of the Atlantic Ocean. Bras d'Or (Gold Arm) divides much of Cape Breton Island into two large peninsulas; the Cabot Trail runs in a circuit around the highlands to the north, while the flank of land to the south and southeast is more densely populated and industrial.

▲▲**Alexander Graham Bell National Historic Park**— Besides inventing the telephone, the Scottish-born genius conducted aviation research leading to the first-ever flight in the British Empire when, in 1909, his *Silver Dart* flew over Baddeck Bay. The park houses a museum displaying the *Silver Dart* and such other Bell inventions as a huge HD-4 hydrodrome (a forerunner of hydrofoil boats), a vacuum jacket (an early version of the iron lung), and, of course, early telephone equipment. Located in the summer resort area of Baddeck, the gateway to the Cabot

Trail, the site is open year-round, from 9:00 a.m. to 9:00 p.m. from July 1 to Sept. 30 and 9:00 a.m. to 5:00 p.m. the rest of the year. Admission is free. For more information, call (902) 295-2069. $2 for adults, $1 for children and $5 for families.

The museum is near Bell's family home, Beinn Breagh, where Bell lived for many years. Bell first visited Baddeck in 1885 and built Beinn Breagh seven years later on a headland overlooking Baddeck Bay amid scenery that he said reminded him of his native Scotland. He died there in 1922 and was buried on the summit of his "beautiful mountain" (In Gaelic, Beinn Breagh). The home is not open to the public; the inventor's descendants still live there.

Lodging

As the official start and end of Cabot Trail circuit, Baddeck has plentiful tourist facilities. Accommodations run the gamut from motels to stately resorts. Rates tend to be rather high except at the B&Bs because this area draws so many visitors.

Duffus House Inn is a country inn overlooking Bras d'Or Lake with room rates running from $60-$85; phone (902) 295-2172. Another country inn, **MacNeil House**, is particularly upscale, offering one- or two-bedroom suites, each with a Jacuzzi, fireplace, and kitchen, beginning at $125 a night; call (902) 295-2340. The **Inverary Inn Resort** at Exit 8 on Route 205 is a large resort offering rooms from about $70 to $160; call 1-800-565-5660 toll-free.

At the budget end of things, local B&Bs offer rooms for around $40. **Try The Bay Tourist Home Bed & Breakfast** at Exit 10 off the TransCanada (902-295-2046); **Au Seanne Mhanse**, in the same area (902-295-2538); or The **Restawyle Tourist Home** on Shore Road (902-295-3428).

Cape Breton also runs a bed & breakfast program whose members offer common rates ($40 for a double at last notice). All members are listed in a brochure titled *Cape Breton Bed & Breakfast Program*; you can get it from the provincial tourist information people or by contacting the Cape Breton Tourism Distribution Centre, 20 Keltic Drive. P.O. Box 1448, Sydney, N.S., Canada B1P 6R7, or phoning 1-800-565-9464 toll-free.

Book ahead for accommodations in Baddeck. Contact the establishment directly or call the provincial Check In line (1-800-565-0000 from Canada or 1-800-341-6096 from the United States).

Camping

There are three campgrounds in the immediate Baddeck area, all offering plentiful facilities. **Baddeck Cabot Trail KOA Campground**, on a river 8 kilometers (5 miles) west of town off the TransCanada, offers rates of $14 and up; call (902) 295-2288. **Bras d'Or Lakes Campground** is on the lake, 5 kilometers (3 miles) west of Baddeck off the TransCanada, with rates starting at $11; call (902) 295-2329 or 295-3467. And **Silver Spruce Resort** is 8 kilometers (5 miles) west of town off the TransCanada, with a minimum rate of $11; call (902) 295-2417.

Restaurants

Baddeck has a full range of eateries to choose from. One of the best restaurants in the area is the **Bell Buoy**, on the lower end of Chebucto Street; call 295-2581 for reservations.

Itinerary Options

Sunrise Trail: The Sunrise Trail, another of the province's scenic routes, follows the Northumberland Strait coast from Pictou to the New Brunswick border. There are something like 25 beaches along the 130-kilometer (80-mile) route—ideal if you just want to lay back and relax awhile. This shoreline boasts the warmest salt water north of the Carolinas. To get to Pictou, take exit 22 off the TransCanada. Aside from beaches, sights along the Sunrise Trail include the Balmoral Grist Mill, a restored water-powered grist mill in a lovely setting on a deep gorge, and the nearby Drysdale Falls.

Marine Drive: The Marine Drive scenic route runs from Halifax along the length of the southeastern coast

(the so-called eastern shore) and around the shore of
Chedabucto Bay to Antigonish. This is a coastal drive
all the way, zigzagging along bays, inlets, headlands,
beaches, and coves. The route is about 340 kilometers
(200 miles) long. It is a particularly unspoiled part of the
province, with no big tourist resorts or amusement parks
to mar the landscape. It has beaches, museums, and cultural attractions, including the Black Cultural Centre in
Westphal and the Railway Museum in Musquodoboit
Harbour, and offbeat attractions like a smokehouse at
Tangier that produces smoked salmon, mackerel, and eels.
Sherbrooke Village, a restored riverside pioneer village
that's part of the provincial museums system, is a short
sidetrip from the Marine Drive. The village includes a
printshop, sawmill, blacksmith, tailor's shop, boat builder,
weaver, jail, post office, and general store. Woolens,
quilts, and other products are for sale. Sherbrooke Village
is open from 9:30 a.m. to 5:30 p.m. daily from mid-May to
mid-October; phone (902) 522-2400 for information.

Glooscap Trail: If you want to continue on the
Glooscap Trail scenic route instead of breaking away from
it at Truro, it follows the northern shore of Minas Basin
and then the rim of Chignecto Bay to the New Brunswick
border. According to Micmac legend, Glooscap was the
Indian god who created the land and the tides hereabouts.
The Five Islands in Minas Basin were created when an
enraged Glooscap threw some huge clumps of earth out
into the basin. The islands are strewn in a rocky line
across the bay. If you go this route, you should also stop
in at the Springhill Miners Museum, where you can tour a
coal mine. Hours are 9:00 a.m. to 8:00 p.m. in July and
August, 10:00 a.m. to 5:00 p.m. in June, September, and
early October, closed the rest of the year. Admission is $3
for adults and $2 for seniors and children ages 5 to 12.
The Springhill Mine is notorious because of several explo-
sions and other disasters over the years in which scores of
miners have died. The museum, with its diaries and letters
of trapped men and other relics of the worst accidents,
reflects the town's stoicism in the face of such tragedies.
The Glooscap Trail is also known for the semi-precious

stones, including agate and amethyst, found in the beaches and cliffs near Parrsboro. The Geological Mineral and Gem Museum is in Parrsboro.

Ceilidh Trail: Another of the province's scenic routes, the 107-kilometer (65-mile) Ceilidh Trail leads north along Route 19 from the Canso Causeway to Margaree Harbour on the Cabot Trail, running along the coast most of the way. All over Cape Breton Island and the rest of Nova Scotia, but particularly along this route, you'll see the phrase "Ciad Mile Failte." It's Gaelic for "A Hundred Thousand Welcomes" to this region originally settled by Scottish highlanders. There are beaches, clifftop views, sheep on the hillsides, and landscapes eerily reminiscent of Scotland. Stop in at Mabou Provincial Park, which offers a panoramic view of the Mabou Valley.

Fleur-de-lis Trail: This scenic trail leads south from the Canso Causeway along the southern rim of Bras d'Or Lake all the way to Louisbourg. It's Acadian country mainly. Pondville Beach Provincial Park boasts a sandy beach that's a kilometer long (more than half a mile), plus picnic tables and a lagoon. At Marble Mountain, a museum tells the story of the marble quarrying industry in the late 1800s and early 1900s. The village also has a marble-chip beach. Île Madame, an island to the south accessible by causeway, has a strong Acadian heritage and several shoreline picnic areas. In July, Big Pond, a tiny village on Bras d'Or Lake, is the site of a major Cape Breton folk concert. Pig Pond is also the home town of famous Cape Breton singer Rita MacNeil; Rita's Tea House in town displays her awards and records.

THE CABOT TRAIL

The Cabot Trail on Nova Scotia's Cape Breton Island, one of Canada's most famous scenic routes, offers up astounding natural beauty that can take your breath away. It follows the Gulf of St. Lawrence shoreline around the magnificent Cape Breton Highlands National Park and along the Atlantic coast. The scenery is rapturously beautiful, all cliffs and crashing waves and remarkable vistas. Fortunately, the route is dotted with lookouts where you can pull off the road to absorb the panorama without causing an accident.

Suggested Schedule

9:00 a.m.	Set out from Baddeck toward Margaree and travel the entire circuit at your own pace. If the weather's fine (and let's hope it is), pack a picnic lunch.
1:00 p.m.	Arrive in Cape North or South Harbour, more than half-way around the route. Picnic at Cabot's Landing Provincial Picnic Park.
5:00 p.m.	Complete the Cabot Trail drive and head for North Sydney.

Driving Route

The route, which runs in a loop, is about 300 kilometers (180 miles) long and can be done in a day or a week, depending on how much you dawdle. It doesn't particularly matter which direction you travel in. The bigger of two park information centers is at the western entrance outside Cheticamp, inviting clockwise travel. At South Gut St. Ann's, when you've nearly completed the circuit, turn left onto the TransCanada toward North Sydney. Ferries depart from there for Newfoundland. North Sydney is about 50 kilometers (30 miles) away. Depending on when ferries for Argentia depart, you can catch the overnight ferry or spend the night in North Sydney before catching

The Cabot Trail

the daytime ferry. If you opt to go to Newfoundland's west coast, ferries run regularly between North Sydney and Port aux Basques.

Sightseeing Highlights
▲**Margaree Valley**—Formed by the Margaree River and its many branches, this pastoral valley is renowned for salmon fishing. Northeast Margaree, one of several villages in the valley (the others are Margaree Centre, Margaree Forks, Margaree Valley, East Margaree, and Margaree Harbour) has a salmon museum describing the river's features and displaying fishing gear. In Margaree Harbour, a restored schooner, the *Marion Elizabeth*, built by the same Lunenburg company that built the *Bluenose*, is now a floating museum and restaurant. Margaree Harbour also offers several souvenir shops. If you're lacking tourist information, there is a tourist bureau in Margaree Forks.

▲**Cheticamp**—This Acadian fishing village at the western entrance to Cape Breton Highlands National Park was originally settled by Acadians who were expelled from the mainland in 1755. Its streets are lined with shops and restaurants with French signs. Stop in at *Les Trois Pignons* (The Three Gables), a museum and cultural centre where one of the galleries houses hooked rugs, something Acadian artisans have elevated to an art form. The Cape Breton Highlands National Park information center is just north of Cheticamp.

▲▲▲**Cape Breton Highlands National Park**—Here's where you'll get the most scenic vistas—sandy beaches and plunging cliffs along the coast and dizzying canyons when the road swings eastwards across the top of the peninsula. There are 28 hiking trails in the park, ranging from 20-minute strolls to challenging treks. At French Lake, for instance, you can take a walk along the Bog Trail, a short, wheelchair-accessible path into the heart of bog life. Elsewhere, you can visit Mary Ann Falls, one of the prettiest and most accessible waterfalls in the park. Signs along the route indicate lookoffs and nature trails. In summer, the Cabot Trail is like a hilly ocean of green dropping steeply to the water below; in autumn, when the leaves change, it's truly incredible, and some people swear it's the best time of all to visit. You never know what you'll find around the next corner; at one lookoff not far north of Cheticamp, for example, there is a moving inscription dedicated to all the Canadians who have died overseas in the service of their country "who will never know the beauty of this place or the changing of the seasons." If you want to stay in the area longer, there are eight campgrounds in the park. Wildlife is abundant, including deer, bobcat, mink, moose, eagles, and dozens of bird species. Admission to the park is $5 per vehicle. The information center at Cheticamp (or the one at Ingonish at the park's eastern entrance if that's the way you're traveling) has everything you need to know about the park. Both information centers are open from 8:00 a.m. to 9:00 p.m. from late June to Labor Day and from

9:00 a.m. to 5:00 p.m. from mid-May to late June and from Labor Day to late October. In winter, information is available only by phone. Call (902) 285-2691 or (902) 285-2270.

▲**Cabot Landing**—The Cabot's Landing Provincial Picnic Park near Cape North features a monument to explorer John Cabot, who is presumed to have made landfall here in 1497. The Cabot Trail is named after him. The park is near Cape North.

▲**Ingonish Beach**—This is the eastern entrance to Cape Breton Highlands National Park. It is also the site of Keltic Lodge, a lovely old resort set atop cliffs overlooking the ocean. Call (902) 285-2880 or 1-800-565-0444 toll-free, if you're interested in staying there.

▲**Cape Smokey**—At 366 meters (1,200 feet) high, you can't miss this massive headland just south of Ingonish. Cape Smokey Provincial Park provides a magnificent look-out over the ocean and coastline. Drive carefully and slowly; there are a lot of hairpin turns coming down off Cape Smokey.

▲**South Gut St. Ann's**—This is the site of the Gaelic College of Celtic Arts and Crafts, the only Gaelic educational institution in North America. In summer it offers courses ranging from bagpipe playing to tartan weaving to Gaelic language courses. The college's Great Hall of the Clans depicts Scottish history and culture. The town was originally settled by a group of Highland Scots whose ship had blown off course. The town is the site of an annual week-long festival of Celtic culture, the Gaelic Mod, usually held during the first week of August.

Lodging

Depending on when the ferries are running, you may need to spend a night in North Sydney. (For detailed information on the Newfoundland ferries, see end of chapter.) The North Sydney-Sydney area is referred to by the provincial tourism people as "industrial Cape Breton" and there isn't much to see. But North Sydney, the terminal for ferries to and from Newfoundland, has ample roadside accommodations and eateries to cater to all the tourists passing through. **MacNeil's Motel** on the TransCanada, about 5 kilometers (3 miles) before you get to the ferry terminal has room rates beginning around $45; call (902) 736-9106 or 736-2692. The **Clansman Motel** on Peppitt Street has rates from $58 to $75 for a double; call (902) 794-7226. The **Heritage Home B & B** at 110 Queen St. offers doubles for $45 to $55; call (902) 794-4815. The pricier **North Star Inn** at 39 Forrest Street has rates beginning at $80; call (902) 794-8581.

Optional Sightseeing Highlights: Industrial Cape Breton

▲▲**Miners' Museum**—You can tour a real coal mine at this museum in Glace Bay, with a retired miner as your guide. The site tells the story of coal mining in this area and contains typical miners' houses, a company store, and a restaurant. For information, call (902) 849-4522. Glace Bay, 45 kilometers (27 miles) southwest of North Sydney, is the start of another of the province's scenic drives, the Marconi Trail (so named because Glace Bay had the first trans-Atlantic wireless station in North America). Admission is $2.75 for adults and $1.75 for children.

▲▲▲**Fortress of Louisbourg**—Louisbourg, the best re-created historic village in Canada, lies 55 kilometers (35 miles) south of North Sydney on Route 22. The Louisbourg fortress was the centre of French power in the region and covered 20 hectares (50 acres), surrounded by a wall almost 3 kilometers (2 miles) long. The French took more than 20 years to build Louisbourg, but when an army of New Englanders backed by the British Royal Navy attacked the following year, the Louisbourg garrison was unprepared and its defences weak, and it fell after a 49-day seige. Three years later, in 1748, Louisbourg was handed back to France only to be recaptured by the British in 1758. The fall of Louisbourg, along with the fall of Quebec City, marked the end of French colonial power in North America. A few years later the British prime minister ordered the demolition of all fortifications at Louisbourg.

Nowadays, the Fortress of Louisbourg National Historic Site is the largest historical reconstruction project in

Canada. One-quarter of the town has been reconstructed, including many buildings and some of the fortifications. You can visit all manner of period buildings, from homes to soldiers' barracks to a noisy waterfront tavern. From June to early September, it's all brought to life by costumed guides, soldiers, merchants, sea captains, and other "residents" who re-create the community of the summer of 1744 and regale visitors with stories, dances, music, and the "latest" local gossip. The weather tends to be cool and damp even in summer, so bring a sweater and raincoat and wear comfortable walking shoes. Admission is $6 for adults, $3 for children, and $15 for families. For taped information, phone (902) 733-3100; for specific information, call (902) 733-2280. Louisbourg is at the south end of the Marconi Trail.

Helpful Hints

There are a variety of whale- and bird-watching cruises available from different places along the Cabot Trail. For instance, whale-watching cruises are offered from Cheticamp, Pleasant Bay (at the northern end of the west-coast section of the route), Bay St. Lawrence (north of Cape North) and Dingwall (between Cape North and Ingonish on the eastern coast). Tours to Bird Islands are available from South Gut St. Ann's. Bird Islands, two small islands off St. Ann's Bay, are the nesting site of thousands of seabirds, including Atlantic puffins, cormorants, gulls, and razor bills.

As noted, there are eight campgrounds in Cape Breton Highlands National Park. Should you wish to linger, there are motels, hotels, cottages, inns and B&Bs in various towns along the Cabot Trail outside the park, including Cheticamp, Pleasant Bay, Ingonish, Ingonish Beach, and Ingonish Centre as well as Baddeck. Check the provincial visitors guide for complete listings, and if you'll be there in summer, book well ahead.

The Newfoundland Ferry

From North Sydney, separate ferries go to Argentia (pronounced Ar-JEN-cha, more or less) on Newfoundland's

Avalon Peninsula on the east coast, and to Port aux Basques (pronounced Port-o-BASK) on the west coast. This itinerary explores the Avalon Peninsula, which incorporates the provincial capital, St. John's, and the peninsula's varied landscape.

It's a tough call. The other route, along Newfoundland's west coast, contains Gros Morne National Park, one of Atlantic Canada's most scenic areas. Exploring both coasts would be the ideal solution, and travelers with plenty of time should by all means do so. You could take the ferry to Port aux Basques, travel through Gros Morne and beyond, then drive across to the east coast, explore St. John's and the Avalon Peninsula and return to North Sydney via the ferry from Argentia. It would probably take a minimum of a week; it's a 900-kilometer (540-mile) drive across the province from Port aux Basques to St. John's. (For more on Newfoundland's west coast, see the Posttour Options at the end of this book.)

The ferry schedule can vary slightly from summer to summer. In 1994, the ferry to Argentia ran twice a week between mid-June and the end of September, departing at 7:00 a.m. on Tuesday and Friday from mid-June to September 10, and at 4:00 p.m. on Tuesday and Friday from September 11 to September 30. The crossing takes 14 hours. One-way rates in 1994 were $103 per car plus $47 per adult passenger, $23.50 for children aged five to 12 and $35.25 for seniors. Rates for cabins ranged from $95 to $125 extra.

The afternoon departure means you spend the night on the ferry and have to sit up if the cabins are all booked. It's a huge, modern, cruise-ship-like ferry, with large lounges, a casino with slot machines, a cafeteria, a dining room, a playroom for kids, and lots of quite comfortable chairs scattered throughout the vessel.

The morning departure means you're on the ferry for an entire day and arrive in Newfoundland after dark. Be sure to reserve ahead for accommodation in the Argentia area (see end of chapter).

In the opposite direction, in 1994 the ferry ran twice a week from Argentia to North Sydney between June and late September, departing at 9:00 a.m. on Wednesdays and Saturdays. It meant passengers arrived in North Sydney around 11:00 p.m. Again, remember to reserve accommodation in North Sydney.

The ferry from North Sydney to Port aux Basques runs between one to four times daily in peak season. In 1994, one-way rates were $53 per vehicle, plus $17 per adult, $8.50 for children aged 5-12 and $12.75 for seniors. The crossing takes about five hours.

It's important to call well ahead of time to find out the schedule, nail down your itinerary, reserve passage on the ferry and, depending on the time of sailings, book accommodation at both ends of the ferry crossing. The ferries are operated by Marine Atlantic; call (902) 794-5700 from Canada (except Newfoundland and Labrador) or 1-800-341-7981 toll-free from the United States. From Newfoundland and Labrador, call (709) 772-7701 in St. John's or (709) 695-7081 in Port aux Basques. Or write to Marine Atlantic Reservations Bureau, P.O. Box 250, North Sydney, N.S., Canada B2A 3M3.

Lodging in Newfoundland

As noted, you should reserve ahead for accommodation in Newfoundland if you're travelling on the day ferry to Argentia. Placentia (pronounced Pla-SEN-cha), the town nearest the Argentia ferry slip, has several hotels and motels. Those cited here all offer room rates around $50 for a double. **Ocean View Apartments** has rooms with cooking facilities and the rates include Continental breakfast; call (709) 227-5151. Similarly, the **Harold Hotel** on Main Street has 23 rooms with cooking facilities in each, continental breakfast included; call (709) 227-2107. **Rosedale Manor** has five rooms; call (709) 227-3613. The **Unicorn Guest Home** has three rooms; call (709) 227-5424. The **Coffey House** has two double and three single rooms, and its rates include a full home-cooked breakfast; call (709) 227-2262 or 227-7303.

ARGENTIA TO ST. JOHN'S

Newfoundland sits at the easternmost edge of Canada and is known as The Rock; you'll understand why once you see it. It doesn't attract the huge numbers of tourists the other three Atlantic provinces do, which is both fortunate and unfortunate: fortunate because it remains largely unspoiled; unfortunate because Newfoundland is the poorest province in Canada and could use the revenues. Travelers who are interested in things other than amusement parks and beaches should make a real effort to visit this province. It is different from the rest of Canada— different from anywhere else in North America, in fact. The landscape ranges from forests to barrens, the rugged coast is steep and rocky and wild, and the people are warm and wry. "When you live in this province," one St. John's native said to me, "all you've got going for you is your sense of humor."

This itinerary concentrates on the Avalon Peninsula, an H-shaped land mass that juts from the southeast corner of Newfoundland and presents a richly diverse landscape in a relatively small area.

Suggested Schedule

9:00 a.m.	Wander around Placentia and visit Castle Hill.
9:45 a.m.	Drive down the coast, stopping at will to take pictures.
11:00 a.m.	Stop in at the Cape St. Mary's Bird Sanctuary. Driving into it takes about 20 minutes and walking along the cliff and back takes at least an hour.
12:30 p.m.	Picnic lunch.
2:30 p.m.	Salmonier Nature Park.
4:30 p.m.	Arrive in St. John's.

Driving Route: Argentia to St. John's
(200 km/120 miles)

Take the first day in Newfoundland to drive leisurely to
St. John's from the Argentia-Placentia area by way of the
Cape Shore, which skirts around the southwest arm of the
H-shaped Avalon Peninsula. Argentia was an important
American naval base during and after World War II; the
base is still there. Nearby Placentia, the closest town to the
ferry terminal, was once a French fortification and is now
a fishing community and service centre for Placentia Bay.
After Placentia, the route leads past tiny villages nestled in
"dokes"—long, wooded river valleys that all seem to end
in calm blue lagoons separated from the sea by stretches
of sandy beach. The hilltops offer great opportunities for
photography. Cape St. Mary's wondrous Bird Rock, where
more than 20,000 birds nest, is a must-see, as is Salmonier
Nature Park.

From Argentia, head south on Route 100, which follows
the coastline to St. Bride's. Watch for sheep wandering on
the road. After St. Bride's, the road turns inland across
windswept moors. The turnoff for Cape St. Mary's is 5
kilometers (3 miles) past St. Bride's. Back on Route 100,
keep going in the same direction. Shortly after it turns
north just beyond a tiny place called Branch, it becomes a
dirt road. After North Harbour you're back on asphalt and
the road is now Route 92. Follow to Route 91 and turn
right; at St. Catherines, head north on Route 90, stopping
in at Salmonier Nature Park. When Route 90 crosses the
TransCanada (Highway 1), head east into St. John's. The
entire route is roughly 200 kilometers (120 miles).

If the desolate dirt-road drive through scrubby forests
puts you off, backtrack from St. Mary's Bay to Argentia and
stay on Route 100 until it crosses the TransCanada. Head
east toward St. John's and turn south onto Route 90 to get
to Salmonier Nature Park. There are tourist information
centres in Dunville on Route 100 and on the TransCanada
just east of the junction with Route 100. Doing it this way
makes it a drive of about 240 kilometers (145 miles).

If you're coming off the ferry in the evening, spend the
night in Placentia (for accommodation suggestions, see

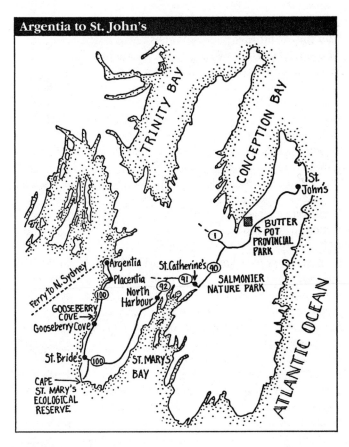

Argentia to St. John's

Lodging in Newfoundland in Day 19) and set out on the drive for St. John's in the morning. I advise strongly against driving at night in the Newfoundland countryside. The roads are winding and badly marked, often with no outside lines and only faint center lines. Furthermore, sheep and moose may wander across the road and you won't see them in the dark until you're practically on top of them.

Newfoundland
There are actually two parts to the province—Newfoundland, a vast island, and Labrador, on the mainland to the northwest, separated from the island of Newfoundland by

the Strait of Belle Isle. Labrador, the much larger of the two but by far less populated, lies north of the province of Quebec. It is remote and undeveloped except for small ports along the coast and a few towns inland. It's home to the largest caribou herd in the world. Officially, the province is called Newfoundland and Labrador, but everyone refers to it as Newfoundland unless referring specifically to Labrador.

The indigenous people, the Beothuks, are extinct and almost nothing is known about their society or history. In the 10th century, the Norse established a temporary settlement at L'Anse aux Meadows on the Great Northern Peninsula on Newfoundland's west coast. Explorer John Cabot, sailing for England, is believed to have made landfall somewhere on Newfoundland's coast in 1497. By the 16th century, fishermen from a variety of European countries were fishing the prolific waters around Newfoundland and Labrador. To this day the vast majority of Newfoundlanders are descended from English and Irish fishermen who settled Newfoundland's shores. A government with full colonial status was established in 1855, and Newfoundland remained a British colony until 1949, when it finally joined Canada more than 80 years after Confederation. Newfoundlanders lived a hardscrabble existence in a remote area, and perhaps nothing better illustrates their psychological and physical apartness than the long years of resisting confederation. Even when Newfoundland finally became Canada's youngest province, it was only after a hard-fought referendum won by a narrow margin.

Major industries include forestry, oil (an offshore megaproject called Hibernia is scheduled to begin producing oil in 1997), and the fisheries. The richest fishing grounds in the world lie off the coast of Newfoundland and Labrador—except that lately the supply has dwindled sharply. In 1992, the federal goverment imposed a two-year moratorium on Newfoundland's northern cod fishing because supplies were so drastically depleted. Cod is an important part of the Newfoundland fishery, accounting for 40 percent of all fish landed in 1991.

Fortunately for visitors, the whales remain. Seventeen species of whales frequent the waters of Newfoundland and Labrador, and the best time to see them is in summer, when they're migrating northward. The most common species are the humpback, minke, and fin whales, with less frequent sightings of white-sided dolphins, harbor porpoises, belugas, sperm whales, and common dolphins. You can often spot whales from shore, but the best hope of seeing them is out on the ocean.

If you're there in late spring or early summer, the other large bodies you may see floating in the waters off Newfoundland are icebergs. Some years they're still drifting southward as late as August, other years there are no more after early June. Some years there are hardly any, other years there are thousands.

The names of some communities and geographical features attest to Newfoundlanders' sense of humor—Backside Pond, Blow Me Down, Chase Me Further Pond. Newfoundland's natural beauty notwithstanding, the best thing about the province is its people. Spend as much time as possible getting to know them. You probably won't have to go out of your way to make friends; in Newfoundland, everybody says "hello" and usually much more.

A word about the Newfie accent. It takes some getting used to. It's a mixture of English and Irish dialects that have mingled into a quite distinct language. But don't worry. You'll be able to understand most of it right away and virtually all of it after a couple of days, when you get accustomed to some of the expressions. *"B'y,"* for instance, means "boy," while "away" means the mainland, as in "When I lived away I noticed the beer labels were different."

Sightseeing Highlights
▲**Placentia**—Visit the site of long-ago French fortifications at Castle Hill National Historic Park above town. The visitors center houses an exhibit about what life was like in Plaisance, as Placentia was called by the French. The

park provides a sweeping view over Placentia Bay. Admission is free.

▲Gooseberry Cove—About halfway between Placentia and Cape St. Mary's, Gooseberry Cove is a small provincial park with a long sandy beach and a lagoon surrounded by grassy banks.

▲▲▲Cape St. Mary's Seabird Ecological Reserve—The 12-kilometer (7-mile) dirt road that leads from Route 100 south to Cape St. Mary's is a bumpy drive pocked with mega-potholes; take it slowly. Park at the lighthouse and go into the sanctuary headquarters for information on the bird colony. Then follow the trail along the clifftops. It's an awesome sight when you get there—thousands upon thousands of huge, golden-headed gannets and other birds crowded onto near-vertical 150-meter (490-foot) cliffs, with waves crashing below. It's estimated that 53,000 birds blanket the cliffs at Cape St. Mary's in summertime, and it's one of the best spots in the province for seeing a seabird colony up close. If you go all the way, it's a 30-minute walk to Bird Rock, but you can get a good view after about 10 minutes of walking. Dress warmly; the weather can be cold and foggy, and it's always very windy. There will probably be sheep wandering around the clifftops, so if you're travelling with a dog leave it in the car. Take binoculars, and keep an eye out for whales in the water below. There's a picnic table near the lighthouse.

▲Cataracts Provincial Park—Just beyond North Harbour is Cataracts Provincial Park, where a huge rock gorge creates spectacular waterfalls. Steps, bridges, and a trail make it easy to move around and get the best views of the falls.

▲▲▲Salmonier Nature Park—Salmonier Nature Park is really a zoo, but a zoo with a big difference. It's beautiful and peaceful, with a 2.5-kilometer (1.5-mile) boardwalk and woodchip trail winding through woodlands and past ponds and streams. The animals in Salmonier are there because they cannot be released back to nature for one reason or another. Each species resides in a large area that resembles its natural habitat as closely as possible. The beavers, for example, live in a vast pond. There are a snowy owl, a peregrine falcon, and a bald eagle, as well as lynx, moose, mink, arctic fox, caribou, and other species. Stop in at the visitors center to see the displays there and then begin walking. More than two-thirds of the trail is on the boardwalk, which makes life easy for people in wheelchairs or with young kids in strollers. The rest of the trail is still woodchip, but eventually it will all be boardwalk. There are several shortcuts if you don't want to do the whole circuit. Wear comfortable shoes and remember to take binoculars and camera. Insect repellant will also probably come in handy if it's a warm day. Salmonier Nature Park is 12 kilometers south of the TransCanada on Route 90. It's open from 12:00 noon to 7:00 p.m. daily from early June until Labor Day but closed on Tuesdays and Wednesdays. Admission is free. Phone (709) 729-6974 for more information.

▲**Butter Pot Provincial Park**—This forested provincial park, 36 kilometers west of St. John's on the TransCanada, has a beach, a campground, and a mini-golf course set amid the woodlands (remember insect repellant!) and has a Newfoundland theme, complete with little replicas of Signal Hill, a ferry, Confederation Building and so on. "Butter pot," by the way, is the term for a prominent rounded hill; this park is named after Butter Pot Hill, found within its boundaries.

Helpful Hints

When you set foot on Newfoundland soil, set your watch ahead 30 minutes. Newfoundland's time zone is half an hour ahead of the Atlantic Time Zone and 90 minutes ahead of the Eastern Time Zone. When it's 5:00 p.m. in Montreal and 6:00 p.m. in Halifax, it's 6:30 p.m. in Newfoundland.

The retail sales tax in Newfoundland is a whopping 12 percent; with the cascading GST, you're paying a total tax of somewhere around 20 percent. The good news is that visitors who purchase goods and take them out of the province within 30 days are entitled to a refund of the sales tax paid. To apply for the visitors tax refund, you need to buy at least $100 worth of taxable goods with a total of $12 in provincial retail sales tax. You can pick up a refund application from provincial tourist information centres and mail it, along with original receipts, to the address on the form. Remember to apply first for the GST refund (see How to Use this Book), since the federal government will return your original receipts to you but Newfoundland won't.

In summer, a variety of festivals are held throughout the province, with everything from dory races to folk music festivals.

Speaking of summer, don't expect hot weather in Newfoundland even in July and August. It happens occasionally, but so do rain and fog and cool temperatures, so travel with appropriate clothing.

Newfoundland's Department of Development publishes a thick annual guide titled *Newfoundland and Labrador Travel Guide*. For a free copy of it plus any other information you might need, call 1-800-563-6353 toll-free or (709) 729-2830 in St. John's, or write: Department of Tourism and Culture, Box 8730, St. John's, Nfld., Canada A1B 4K2.

ST. JOHN'S

I've never really seen St. John's. I've been there, I've spent time there, but I haven't viewed the city from afar as I approached it, because it was always blanketed in fog. It became a running joke: here comes the fog, we must be getting near St. John's. Wandering around St. John's in such weather can be an agreeable if faintly eerie experience. This doesn't happen all the time, but when it does, it can last for days. Part of what makes Newfoundlanders so hardy is the weather in their part of the world. They talk a lot about it.

Suggested Schedule

9:00 a.m.	Explore Signal Hill and nearby Quidi Vidi Battery.
10:30 a.m.	Back in town, stop in at the Commissariat House Museum.
11:00 a.m.	Head for the downtown core on the waterfront, have lunch, and spend the afternoon exploring and window-shopping.
3:30 p.m.	Drive down to Cape Spear, the easternmost part of Canada.
5:00 p.m.	Return to St. John's.

St. John's

St. John's, one of the oldest settlements in North America, is built on high hills surrounding the harbor. The downtown core is more or less on level land but as soon as you venture further afield you're climbing steep hills lined with colorful wooden row houses. The hills, the harbor and the houses are what make this historic port city so picturesque. As the capital of Newfoundland and Labrador, St. John's, which has a population of 172,000, is home to most of the province's social, educational and religious institutions. It's eminently possible to explore the entire Avalon Peninsula in day trips from St. John's.

Getting Around

Coming in to St. John's from the TransCanada, enter the
northwest section of the city via Route 2, which leads to
the downtown area on the waterfront. St. John's was
destroyed by fire several times in the 19th century. The
worst, which raged for 24 hours in 1892 and razed more
than half the town, has come to be known as The Great
Fire. The town was rebuilt each time in a rather haphaz-
ard manner, so this city is anything but planned. Except
for the heart of downtown, finding your way around can
be confusing. Arm yourself with a good map and don't
hesitate to ask for directions. Except for the downtown
core, the best way to get around is by car. Harbour Drive
runs along the harborfront, with Water Street (reputedly
one of the oldest streets on the continent) and Duckworth
Street parallel to Harbour Drive. Signal Hill Road is off the
eastern end of Duckworth Street. At its western end,
Duckworth runs into New Gower Street.

The St. John's tourist information centre is in an old
restored railway car on the waterfront; you can't miss it.
You can pick up all manner of information there, including pamphlets described walking tours of four different
areas of the city, and join the free "Nice to Meet You" program, whereby you're issued a credit-card-style card that
provides for various discounts at shops, hotels, restaurants, and attractions around town.

Sightseeing Highlights

▲▲▲**Signal Hill**—Signal Hill, now a national historic
park, is the best place to start a tour of St. John's because
it affords a magnificent view over the city, the harbor, and
the Atlantic (when not fogged in). Signal Hill, a majestic
rock guarding the narrow harbor entrance, lies around a
curve of the shoreline east of the harborfront area. The
access road, Signal Hill Road, runs off the end of Duckworth Street. The English and French fought several times
for control of Signal Hill, and it was here that the last battle of the Seven Year's War was fought in North America,
in 1762. In 1901, Guglielmo Marconi received the world's
first transatlantic radio transmission on Signal Hill. It was

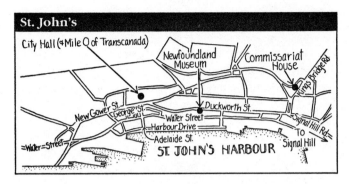

St. John's

City Hall (¾ Mile Q of Transcanada)
Newfoundland Museum
Commissariat House
Kings Bridge Rd
New Gower St.
George St.
Duckworth St.
Water Street
Harbour Drive
Adelaide St.
=Water=Street=
ST. JOHN'S HARBOUR
Signal Hill Rd.
To Signal Hill

the letter "S"; Marconi said it stood for Success. The Queen's Battery, fortifications dating from the Napoleonic Wars, and the imposing Cabot Tower, a monument built in 1897 to commemorate the 400th anniversary of the European arrival in Newfoundland, are also on Signal Hill. In July and August, the Signal Hill Tattoo performs twice a day from Wednesday through Saturday, at 3:00 p.m. and 7:00 p.m., weather permitting. The interpretation center, about halfway up Signal Hill Road, has exhibits on the history of New-foundland spanning 1,000 years from the Viking era to the province's entrance into Confederation in 1949. Gibbet Hill, to the right of the interpretation center, has a rather ghoulish history. In the 1700s, anyone who broke the law was hanged there and left there for a week as a deterrent to would-be criminals. From all over town, people could see the bodies swinging up on Gibbet Hill. After a week of dangling in chains, the bodies were stuffed into barrels, weighted and dumped into Dead Man's Pond. Signal Hill National Historic Park is open year-round, from 8:30 a.m. to 8:00 p.m. from mid-June to Labor Day and 8:30 a.m. to 4:30 p.m. the rest of the year. Admission is free. For more information, call (709) 772-5367.

▲▲**Quidi Vidi Battery**—Another dizzying view, this time of Quidi Vidi Village and Cuckold Cove. (Quidi Vidi is pronounced kitty vitty.) The battery was built by French troops during their brief occupation of St. John's in 1762. It was later manned by British troups and has now been restored to its 1812 condition. Guides dressed in period uniforms are on hand to answer questions. The battery, a provincial historic site, is open daily in summer. For information, call (709) 729-0862 or 729-2977.

▲**Commissariat House**—This gracious restored Georgian house was constructed in 1818-1821 and served as the home of the Assistant Commissary General. It's now a provincial historic site, furnished to the 1830 period, with costumed guides on hand. The house, on Kings Bridge Road, is open daily in summer from 10:00 a.m. to 6:00 p.m. Admission is free. For information, call (709) 729-0862 or 729-6730.

▲▲▲**St. John's Waterfront**—To get a real sense of this historic port city, stroll along the waterfront. The harbor will doubtless be crowded with vessels from all over the world, and with small fishing boats. The St. John's tourist information centre is in an old railway car on the waterfront. Pick up some walking tour pamphlets and wander Water Street and Duckworth Road, lined with restaurants, cafés, and stores. Stop in at the James J. O'Mara Pharmacy Museum, a heritage drug store depicting a working pharmacy circa 1895, at 488 Water Street. George Street, the hub of the city's nightlife, between Water Street and New Gower Street, is lined with restaurants and bars; walk up Adelaide Street to see it. Then continue another block along Adelaide to New Gower. City Hall is across the road; Mile "0," the point where the TransCanada Highway begins, is located at City Hall.

▲**Newfoundland Museum**—This museum depicts 1,000 years of Newfoundland and Labrador history, from the Vikings on. Exhibits describe the lifestyles of native people, settlers, fishermen, and townspeople. Located on Duckworth Street at Cathedral Street, the museum is open year-round from 9:00 a.m. to 4:45 p.m. weekdays and 10:00 a.m. to 5:45 p.m. weekends. Admission is free. The museum has a branch at Murray Premises, a restored 19th-century building on Water Street, that features maritime, military and natural-history displays. For information on either branch, call (709) 729-0916.

▲**Cape Spear National Historic Park**—This is the most easterly point of North America and lies roughly 10 kilometers (6 miles) from downtown St. John's. The oldest lighthouse in Newfoundland stands on a rocky cliff at Cape Spear. It was built in 1835, remained in use until 1955 and is now a museum. The scenery hereabouts is rugged and beautiful. Call (709) 772-5367 for information. To get to Cape Spear, head west on New Gower Street and take the first exist after crossing the Waterford River.

▲**Bowring Park**—If you're with children, make time for this large park. It boasts a replica of the famous Peter Pan statue in London's Kensington Gardens. The park was given to the city by the Bowrings, a wealthy business family. Legend has it that Sir Edward Bowring persuaded the sculptor of the original Peter Pan statue to make the replica in memory of his godchild, Betty Munn, who died in a disaster at sea in 1918. The park, which has picnic sites, a swimming pool, and a playground, is on Waterford Bridge Road in the west end of the city. Call (709) 576-8452 for information.

▲**Memorial University Botanical Gardens**—These gardens cover 45 hectares of land at Oxen Pond in C.A. Pippy Park, the vast park north of downtown. Flower gardens include a rock garden, peat and woodland beds, a cottage garden, a perennial garden and a heather bed. There is also a nature reserve with trials leading through a variety of habitats like boreal forests and bog. The gardens are open daily except Monday and Tuesday from 10:00 a.m. to 5:30 p.m. between May and November. There are guided tours every Sunday at 3:00 p.m. Admission is free, but donations are welcome. Call (709) 737-8590 for more information.

▲**Logy Bay**—The Ocean Research Laboratory, operated by Memorial University at Logy Bay (5 kilometers—3 miles—east of the city), specializes in cold-ocean biology and oceanography. Guided tours are available in summer, from 10:00 a.m. to 5:00 p.m. daily. Admission is $2.50 for adults and $1.50 for students and seniors. The facility is on Marine Lab Road at Logy Bay off Route 30; phone (709) 737-3706 for more information.

Lodging
One of the ritziest hotels in town is the landmark **Hotel Newfoundland** on Cavendish Square, with room rates starting at $150 for a double in high season; call 726-4980

locally or 1-800-268-9420 from Ontario and Quebec, 1-800-268-9411 from elsewhere in Canada and 1-800-828-7447 from the U.S. The other establishment for big spenders is the **Radisson Plaza Hotel**, which has a convention center connected to it and room rates ranging from $130 to $155. The Radisson is at 120 New Gower Street; call 739-6404 locally or 1-800-333-3333 toll-free.

Historic city that it is, St. John's also has a good number of heritage-style inns and B&Bs. The **Prescott Inn Bed and Breakfast** at 17-19 Military Road and **The Roses Bed and Breakfast** at 9 Military Road are two of the nicest such establishments and happen to be owned by the same people. Room rates are around $65 at both places, which are just down the road from the Hotel Newfoundland. Call (709) 753-6063 for reservations at either. **Victoria Station Inn** at 290 Duckworth is also centrally located, with room rates ranging from $65 to $85; call (709) 722-1290. **Fort William Bed & Breakfast,** at 5 Gower Street across from the Hotel Newfoundland, offers double rooms for around $65; call (709) 726-3161. **Compton House** is a Victorian mansion on a landscaped estate at 26 Waterford Bridge Road, with room rates of between $70 and $100; call (709) 739-5789. Another Victorian-era home, the **Kincora Hospitality Home**, at 36 King's Bridge Road, offers rooms beginning around $60; call (709) 576-7415. Other centrally located places offering double rooms for between $55 and $70 include **Gower House** at 180 Gower Street, (709) 754-0047 or 1-800-563-3959 toll-free, and **Bonne Esperance Bed & Breakfast** at 20 Gower Street, (709) 726-3835. **The Old Inn** at 157 Lemarchant Road is a rather eccentric old place that does not boast period furnishings, is not right in the downtown core and so is cheaper. Its rates run around $40 for a double; call (709) 722-1171.

Camping

The best bet for camping is the fully serviced 156-site trailer park-campground in C.A. Pippy Park, an enormous green space fully within city limits. Contact the **Pippy Park Trailer Park** at (709) 737-3669 or (709) 737-3655. The 1,343-hectare park also has a golf course, hiking trails, a fitness trail, playground, snack bar, convenience store, and other recreation facilities. Rates range from $5.50 to $15 a night.

Restaurants

For a small city, St. John's has quite a wide range of decent restaurants. Following are some suggestions in no particular order.

For lunch, try the **Cavendish Cafe** at 73 Duckworth Street, the **Classic Cafe** at 364 Duckworth or, for more elegant surroundings, the **Cabot Room** in the Hotel Newfoundland. For delicious fish and chips, try either **Ches's Fish and Chips** on Freshwater Road or **Leo's Fish and Chips**, also on Freshwater Road. The two have had a bit of a running feud for years and St. John's residents are divided on the merits of each place, but in fact both are excellent and both serve up huge orders of fish and chips for about $5. For evening dining, **The Blue Door**, a delightful little place at 252 Duckworth, specializes in seafood; call 726-7822. **Biarritz on the Square** at 188 Duckworth, another establishment that seats barely 30, specializes in both Cajun food and seafood; call 726-3885. **Stone House**, located in one of St. John's oldest houses at 8 Kenna's Hill, specializes in seafood, game, and traditional Newfoundland dishes; call 753-2380. For pub fare, try **The Rose & Thistle** at 208 Water Street. The **Casa Grande** is a good Mexican restaurant at 108 Duckworth; call 753-6108.

Nightlife

Newfoundlanders are great partyers, and St. John's is renowned for its lively nightlife and thriving live music scene, which encompasses everything from jazz and rock to toe-tapping jigs and reels. The center of it all is George Street, lined with pubs, dance bars, and restaurants; just wander until something strikes your fancy. In summer, outdoor concerts and other organized events take place on George Street.

Shopping

Both Water and Duckworth streets are lined with shops and boutiques selling wool sweaters and scarves, woven

goods, quilts, stonewear pottery, and handcrafted silver
jewelry. Nature lovers, stop in at Wild Things, 124 Water
Street, offering nature art and photography plus wildlife
T-shirts, locally handmade jewelry, and souvenirs, all featuring whales, puffins, eagles, and other Newfoundland
wildlife.

Festivals
A variety of festivals are held in St. John's each summer.
On the weekend closest to June 24, the city hosts **St.
John's Days Celebrations**, a four-day festival commem-
orating its birthday. (John Cabot arrived here on June 24,
1497.) Events include a parade, a street dance and indoor
and outdoor concerts.

Another major annual event is the **Newfoundland and
Labrador Craft Development Association's Summer
Craft Fair**, a three-day event in early July. The **St. John's
Regatta**, held the first Wednesday in August, dates from
the 1820s and is the oldest continuous sporting even in
North America. The regatta itself is actually a rowing race.
The attendant carnival is more fun.

Helpful Hints
One thing you should do today is make a reservation for
tomorrow's whale- and bird-watching cruise out of Bay
Bulls south of St. John's. Call **Bird Island Charters** or its
partner company, **Humpback Whale Tours**, at (709) 753-
4850 or 334-2355; **Bird Island Boat Tours** at (709) 334-
2002; or **Gatherall's Boat Tours** at (709) 334-2887 (for
details, see Witless Bay Ecological Reserve in Day 21.)

Speaking of cruises, there is a variety of other boat trips
you can take from St. John's and elsewhere on the Avalon
peninsula. Ask the staff about it at the St. John's tourist
information center.

THE SOUTHERN SHORE

Along the southeast arm of the Avalon Peninsula, you'll
come across windswept coastal villages, barren heathlands
where caribou wander, and a noisy seabird sanctuary on
three rocky islands offshore. The highlight is a cruise out
to the sanctuary. The rest of the circuit is remarkable for
its varied landscape and dramatic ocean vistas.

Suggested Schedule

8:45 a.m.	Depart St. John's before 9:00 a.m.
9:30 a.m.	Cruise to the Witless Bay bird sanctuary.
12:00 noon	Lunch in Bay Bulls or Witless Bay, or if picnicking, you can stop in La Manche Provincial Park.
1:00 p.m.	Continue the circuit at your own pace. Return eventually to St. John's.

Driving Route: South Shore Circuit (310 km/155 miles)

It's difficult to go wrong on this route, which runs in a
long loop from St. John's. It starts off as Route 10 and
turns into Route 90 at the bottom of what Newfoundlanders call the Southern Shore. When the 90 crosses the
TransCanada, head east back to St. John's. If for some reason you didn't stop in at Salmonier Nature Park on Day
19, you'll be passing it again on Route 90, about 12 kilometers (7 miles) south of the TransCanada. Bay Bulls is 30
kilometers (18 miles) south of St. John's; the rest of the
circuit totals about 280 kilometers (168 miles).

Sightseeing Highlights

▲**Bay Bulls**—Bay Bulls? The name comes from *Baie
Boules*, a French reference to the bull bird, or Dovekie,
which winters in Newfoundland. One of Newfoundland's
oldest settlements, Bay Bulls was repeatedly attacked
by the French and the Dutch, and several times was
destroyed by fire. You'll notice four massive old cannons

The Southern Shore

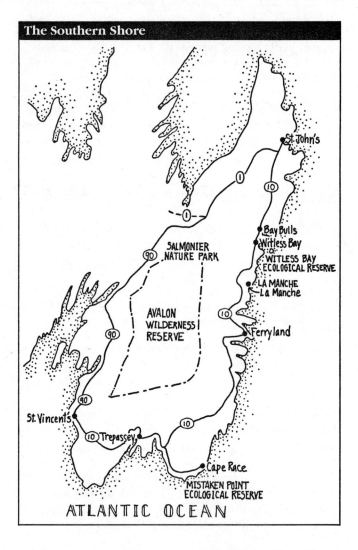

used as gateposts at the Roman Catholic church on the
waterfront. This is Irish, and Roman Catholic, territory).
The cannons, which stand on end, are topped with big
bronze statues of four saints, known locally as the "canon-
ized saints." Bay Bulls is the starting point for a cruise out
to the "bird islands" seabird sanctuary in Witless Bay.

▲▲▲**Witless Bay Ecological Reserve**—Even if you're not particularly a bird-, whale-, or nature lover, I strongly recommend a cruise out to Gull Island, Green Island, and Great Island. Together they comprise the Witless Bay Ecological Reserve. Whether you book aboard Bird Island Charters, Humpback Whale Tours, Bird Island Boat Tours, or Gatherall's Boat Tours (for phone numbers, see Day 20 Helpful Hints), you should have a great time. Not only do you get to see unbelievably dense colonies of Atlantic puffins, razorbills, murres, kittiwakes, and other species (the nesting season runs from mid-June to late July), you'll probably spot some whales, and you may even get to see some towering icebergs. Moreover, you'll be treated to some down-home Newfoundland-style hospitality on board, complete with music, songs, stories dancing, and nature lore. ("And do you know why there are no divorces among penguins? Because they're all Catholic.") By happenstance, we booked with Bird Island Charters, operated by Loyola O'Brien, a gregarious charmer who could talk the birds down off the cliffs. His brother Joe operates Humpback Whale Tours and cruises the identical route.

The seabird colonies provide a powerful sense of what the province means when it says it has one of the greatest concentrations of seabirds in the world. The cost for the two-and-a-half-hour cruise with either of the O'Briens (Bird Island Charters or Humpback Whale Tours) is $25 per adult, $15 for kids aged 6 to 15, and $10 for children aged 2 to 5. Gatherall's Boat Tours, operated by the Gatherall family, offers similar cruises at similar rates, while Bird Island Boat Tours' two-hour cruises, billed as the most economical way to see the birds and whales in Witless Bay, cost $20 for adults and $10 for kids. Remember to dress warmly and bring your camera and binoculars.

▲**La Manche Provincial Park**—La Manche, French for "sleeve," is named for the shape of the harbor at the abandoned fishing village of La Manche on the coast. The village was destroyed one January day in 1966 when a severe winter storm hit, bringing an enormous tide that washed away boats, anchors, many buildings, and the suspension bridge that connected the two sides of the harbor. Miraculously, no lives were lost, but with the entire village economy wiped out, residents agreed to be resettled by the government. You can visit what remains of the village—not much beyond house foundations—by hiking a trail in the park. Route 10 skirts the edge of the park, which encompasses the scenic La Manche River Valley. There are picnic facilities there if you brought lunch along.

▲▲**Ferryland**—No, this is not an amusement park. It's a village on a picturesque harbor rimmed with steep cliffs and it has a rather interesting history. In 1621, Sir George Calvert, who later became Lord Baltimore, established a colony at this location, but after a few harsh winters and some battles with the French, he up and transferred his colony to Virginia. Later, another settlement also failed, whereupon some of the cod fishermen who had been ousted by the colonists returned. In the 18th century, during periods of Anglo-French and Anglo-American conflict, the fishing settlement was fortified. The 1700s also saw a large influx of Irish to what had been a predominately English settlement. The main attractions in modern-day Ferryland are the lighthouse that dominates the harbor and the Ferryland Museum, which affords a particularly good view of the harbor. It's near the church, off Route 10, and is open daily in summer. After Ferryland, the coastline gets wilder and the landscape inland increasingly tundra-like. When the road veers away from the sea, it's a bit like driving across the moors, especially if it's misty, as it often is in these parts.

▲**Mistaken Point Ecological Reserve**—The world's richest find of Precambrian fossils—records of marine creatures that flourished some 500 million years ago—was made at Mistaken Point in 1968. The area was declared an ecological reserve to preserve the find. In fact Mistaken Point is one of the most important fossil sites in Canada. It's off Route 10, 16 kilometers (10 miles) southeast of Portugal Cove.

▲**Cape Race**—A little further along the same side-road past Mistaken Point, the Cape Race lighthouse, first operated in 1856, was proclaimed a federal heritage structure in 1990.

▲**Trepassey**—This town at the bottom of the southern shore drive has a history linked to aviation. The first plane to cross the Atlantic Ocean from west to east departed from here in 1919. Three U.S. Navy seaplanes attempted the trip; two were forced down at sea, but the third touched down in the Azores and then flew on to Portugal. In 1928 Amelia Earhart left from Trepassey on her first transatlantic flight—as a passenger. Reportedly, the thrill of that crossing convinced her to make aviation her career. The local museum has pictures of both the first transatlantic flight and Earhart. After Trepassey, you'll probably start seeing caribou scattered across the landscape, some quite close to the highway.

▲**St. Vincent's**—There's a long sandy beach running along the side of the highway as it passes through this town at the junction of Holyrood Bay and Holyrood Pond. It's not for swimming (Newfoundlanders can spend their entire lives never learning to swim because the water's so cold) but is a good place to stop, stretch your legs, and breathe in the sea air. You might also see whales, who can come in very close to shore to feed at that particular part of the coast because the ocean bottom drops sharply just off shore.

Itinerary Option: Avalon Wilderness Reserve

If you're a real outdoors type, this one's for you. But first you have to get a permit from the provincial Department of Environment and Lands. This vast protected region lies in the middle of the peninsula; the single road into it is just before Shore's Cove when you're traveling south on Route 10. The reserve has rolling barrens, panoramic viewpoints and thousands of roaming caribou; nowhere else in North America does such a large population of caribou dwell so close to a city. The area attracts mainly hikers, canoeists, wilderness campers, photographers, ar anglers. To reserve entry permits and find out more ab the reserve, contact the Department of Environment and Lands, Parks Division, P.O. Box 8700, St. John's, Nfld., Canada A1B 4J6, phone (709) 729-2431. From May to September, you can also get permits for Avalon at several other provincial parks, including Butter Pot (Day 20) and La Manche.

Helpful Hint

Have with you clothes for all climates. This is a relatively short drive, but it can aptly illustrate the vagaries of Newfoundland weather, ranging from cold rain and fog to medium-warm sunshine in a single day.

CONCEPTION AND TRINITY BAYS

Spend a day exploring the shorelines of Conception Bay and Trinity Bay, accented with brooding cliffs and dotted with dozens of small outports where wooden houses cling to the hillsides. Some of Newfoundland's most striking coastal scenery is along this route. The sightseeing highlights below outline the most noteworthy stopoffs, and you'll find as you go along there are many other places to pause. This is a day to wander at will, absorbing the atmosphere of life along the rugged Newfoundland shore. It's best done when the sun is shining, of course, though fog and misty rain are common.

Driving Route: From St. John's, follow Route 60 to Topsail and stay on it until it intersects Route 70 between Brigus and South River. Route 70 heads north along the western shore of Conception Bay. At Carbonear, turn onto Route 74, which crosses the peninsula to Heart's Content. From there, travel south on Route 80, which follows the eastern shore of Trinity Bay, until you reach the TransCanada. Take the TransCanada east back into St. John's. This route is roughly 280 kilometers (170 miles) long. Note that crossing from Carbonear to Heart's Content cuts out the entire north end of the peninsula that splits the two bays; going all the way to Bay de Verde near the tip of that peninsula adds about 120 kilometers (72 miles) to the driving distance.

Sightseeing Highlights

▲**Topsail**—Topsail provides a good view of Conception Bay and three islands in the bay, Bell, Little Bell, and Kellys Island. Until 1966, huge iron-ore deposits were mined at Bell Island, which was first settled 240 years ago as a fishing and farming community and has had its ups and downs since. The town's history is displayed in a series of huge murals on local buildings; if you're inter-

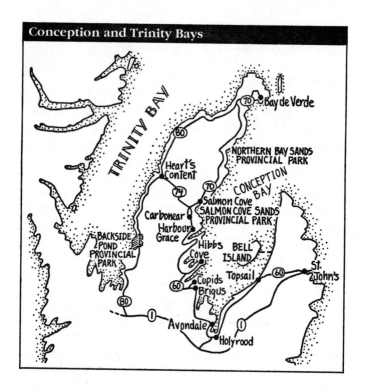

Conception and Trinity Bays

ested, there's a ferry to Bell Island from Portugal Cove, located about 25 kilometers (15 miles) north of Topsail. Kellys Island is named after a pirate who is said to have made his headquarters there some three centuries ago.

▲**Holyrood**—This summer resort area is known for both its scenery and excellent sailing. It's at the southernmost end of Conception Bay.

▲**Avondale**—Railway buffs should stop here to visit the Avondale Railway Station Museum housed in a restored 1864 railway station. Call 229-6579 for information.

▲▲**Brigus**—The view is lovely as you drive down into Brigus, a charming village on a long, thin inlet. Arctic explorer Robert Abram "Bob" Bartlett was born here in 1875. Bartlett commanded ships in the polar expedition of Commodore Perry. His former home, Hawthorne Cottage, stills stands in Brigus and has been designated an historic site. The local museum, Ye Olde Stone Barn Museum, is housed in an 1820s dwelling that's a rare example of stone-house construction in a province where the vast majority of houses are made of wood. The address is 4 Magistrate's Hill.

▲**Cupids**—Newfoundland's first official settlement was established here in 1610 by John Guy of Bristol, England, and 39 colonists. They settled in and built a fort, but the colony was disbanded after 18 years of pirate raids and the opposition of fishermen.

▲▲**Hibbs Cove**—Hibbs Cove, where the small, rock-ringed harbor is rimmed with square wooden houses, is so picturesque and yet so typical of Newfoundland outports that artists and photgraphers are much attracted to it. The Port de Grave Fishermen's Museum in Hibbs Cove displays furniture and artifacts used by early settlers and fishermen. Admission is $1 for adults and 50 cents for children; for more information, call (514) 786-3912.

▲▲**Harbour Grace**—This historic town was settled in the early 1500s, and one of its earliest claims to fame is that it was headquarters to a pirate by the name of Peter Easton, who was quite famous in that era. In this century, beginning in 1919, it was the departure point for several early attempts to fly across the Atlantic. In 1931, Wiley Post began a round-the-world flight from Harbour Grace. And in 1932, famed aviatrix Amelia Earhart left Harbour Grace to fly to Northern Ireland, becoming the first woman to fly solo across the Atlantic. The community museum in Harbour Grace, housed in a century-old former customhouse on the site of old fortifactions, has an exhibit chronicling the town's role in the history of transatlantic flight. An extensive collection of fishing boat models, period furniture, old photographs, and other articles round out the museum's depiction of the history of the area. Open daily in summer; admission is free.

▲**Carbonear**—This is a town, not just a village. There is a picnic area off the highway on a rise overlooking Carbonear. A 17th-century Irish princess, whose story is the stuff of pure romance, is buried in a private garden in Carbonear. Her gravestone reads: "Sheila Na Geira, wife of Gilbert Pike and daughter of John Na Geira, King of

County Down." During the reign of Elizabeth I, English pirate Gilbert Pike fell in love with Sheila Na Geira after he rescued her from a Dutch warship where she was being held prisoner after being kidnapped from a ship in the English Channel. The princess wed (and reformed) Pike and the couple decided to make a new life for themselves in the New World. They ended up in nearby Bristol's Hope. Shades of the Past Museum on High Road North in Carbonear tells the history of Conception Bay; admission is $2 for adults. One of the best times to visit Carbonear is when it's hosting the Conception Bay Folk Festival in late July or early August.

▲**Heart's Content**—One of Newfoundland's oldest fishing towns, Heart's Content also has a place in the history of international communications as the site of North America's first cable relay station. The cable ship *Great Eastern* landed the first successful transatlantic telegraph cable—and the longest, 4,447 kilometers (2,668 miles) of it—here in July 1866. She spent two weeks steaming across the ocean from Ireland, lowering cable more than three kilometers (two miles) to the ocean floor. Four earlier attempts to lay a telegraph cable from Ireland to Newfoundland had failed. After the ship arrived at Heart's Content, the first message sent to Ireland via the cable read simply, "All right." A series of stations across Nova Scotia relayed messages throughout North America from the cable station in Heart's Content. The old cable station, which saw nearly a century of service, is now a provincial historical site containing early telegraph equipment. Open daily in summer; admission is free. For more information, call (514) 729-0862.

▲**Backside Pond Provincial Park**—With a name like this, who can resist? The park includes a saltwater pond and beach, plus a hiking trail.

▲**Bay de Verde**—Possible stop-off points along the road between Carbonear and Bay de Verde include two provincial parks with sandy beaches (Salmon Cove Sands Provincial Park and Northern Bay Sands Provincial Park) and the scenic Lower Island Cove area. The isolated fishing community of Bay de Verde at the top of the western coast of Conception Bay was originally settled by "planters," colonists who were trying to avoid French raiders in the 1600s. In the early 1900s, two kegs of Spanish gold—believed to be pirate booty—were dredged up from a small cove here by local fishermen. Offshore is Baccalieu Island, a nesting site for puffins, gannets, gulls, and other birds. A short trail leads f om Bears Cove above town to a scenic lookout. From Bay·de Verde to Heart's Content, Route 80 travels the Trinity Bay shoreline through pretty villages such as New Melbourne, New Chelsea, and Winterton.

Saint-Pierre and Miquelon: Officially, the French islands of St-Pierre and Miquelon have nothing to do with Newfoundland, or for that matter Canada. I'm mentioning them here because they're only 15 kilometers (nine miles) off the south coast of Newfoundland in the Gulf of St. Lawrence, and there is ferry service to them from a town called Fortune. There are several crossings a day in summer; the trip lasts just under an hour. Fortune is about 350 kilometers (210 miles) from St. John's along the TransCanada and Route 210.

The tiny islands of St-Pierre, Miquelon, and Langlade, left over from the days of New France, form a little French outpost where you pay in French francs and chat with gendarmes. It's like visiting France without having to cross the Atlantic. The major industry has always been fishing. The only other economic activity is tourism, which has been growing in recent years. The climate is windy, damp and generally harsh. Aside from the ferry service, you can fly to St-Pierre and Miquelon from Sydney or Halifax in Nova Scotia, or from Montreal. For more information, write to the St-Pierre & Miquelon Tourist Office, B.P. 4274, 97500—St-Pierre & Miquelon, phone (508) 41-22-22; or contact the French Government Tourist Office, 1981 McGill College Ave., Suite 490, Montreal, Que., Canada H3A 2W9, phone (514) 288-4264 or (514) 987-9761. There is also a French Government Tourist Office in Toronto at (416) 593-6427, and in New York City at (212) 757-1125.

THE WEST COAST: GROS MORNE TO L'ANSE AUX MEADOWS

Newfoundland's west coast is a natural wonder, a panoply of cavernous fjords, dense forests, tufted heathlands, and ancient mountains that run from Port aux Basques in the south to L'Anse aux Meadows at the northern tip of the Great Northern Peninsula. The Viking Tail, a scenic route along the coast, links two UNESCO World Heritage sites—the magnificent Gros Morne National Park at its base and L'Anse aux Meadows at its tip, where Vikings settled some 1,000 years ago. Many of the place names along this route are corruptions of those used by the original French settlers of the area.

If you opt to see this part of the province rather than the Avalon Peninsula, take the ferry from North Sydney to Port aux Basques instead of to Argentia. If you're exploring both coasts, take the ferry to one port and return from the other (for more information on ferry schedules and prices, see Day 19).

The only other way to get to the west coast is to fly; there are small airports in Stephenville, Deer Lake and St. Anthony.

Driving Route: From Port aux Basques, follow the TransCanada north to Deer Lake. From there, the Viking Trail scenic route (Route 430) snakes all the way up the west coast to L'Anse aux Meadows. This is a long trip: 270 kilometers (162 miles) from Port aux Basques to Deer Lake and about 440 kilometers (265 miles) from there to L'Anse aux Meadows. Round trip, that's 1,420 kilometers (854 miles).

If you're driving across the province, return to Deer Lake and go east on the TransCanada. It's a little over 600 kilometers (360 miles) from Deer Lake to St. John's.

If you're going to Labrador, there is a ferry service from St. Barbe, about 100 kilometers (60 miles) south of L'Anse aux Meadows.

Lodging and Restaurants: For such a wild landscape, plenty of tourist facilities are available along this route. There are hotels and B&Bs in small communities as well

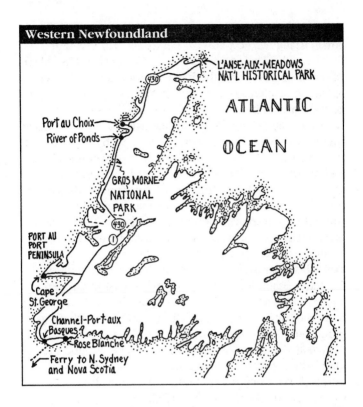

Western Newfoundland

L'ANSE-AUX-MEADOWS NAT'L HISTORICAL PARK

430

ATLANTIC

Port au Choix
River of Ponds

OCEAN

GROS MORNE NATIONAL PARK

430

PORT AU PORT PENINSULA

Cape St. George

Channel-Port-aux-Basques
Rose Blanche

Ferry to N. Sydney and Nova Scotia

as in larger centres like Corner Brook and Deer Lake. Most of the numerous provincial parks along the coast offer camping facilities.

Book ahead, especially if you're travelling in summer. Check the *Newfoundland and Labrador Travel Guide* for complete listings and locations (call 1-800-563-6353 for a free copy of the guide).

Sightseeing Highlights
▲**Rose Blanche**—The scenery along the 40-kilometer (24-mile) drive between Port aux Basques and Rose Blanche is what makes this short sidetrip worthwhile. Rose Blanche, a small fishing village, lies to the east of Port aux Basques.

▲▲**Port aux Port Peninsula**—A sidetrip from the TransCanada along Route 460 leads to the westernmost point of Newfoundland, Cape St. George at the tip of the small, triangular Port au Port peninsula. Turn west at Stephenville. The peninsula has 130 kilometers (78 miles) of rocky coastline and the highest proportion of French-speaking residents of any part of Newfoundland (15 percent). Battered by wind and water, the limestone and dolomite cliffs along the peninsula make for some dramatic scenes. Picadilly Head Provincial Park, with camping, hiking trails, picnic tables, lookouts and a playground, is located on the northeast shore. One of the best times to visit this area is during the annual *Une Longue Veillee* folk festival each August. Held to celebrate French heritage, the festival attracts performers from all over Newfoundland, Atlantic Canada, Quebec, and the French islands of St. Pierre and Miquelon.

▲**Marble Mountain**—This is for skiiers only. Marble Mountain, eight kilometers (five miles) east of Corner Brook, has been upgraded and expanded and is attracting increasing numbers of skiiers. It has 26 runs, with a top elevation of 472 meters (1,580 feet). The season usually begins at Christmas and peaks in February, around the time Corner Brook stages its annual 10-day Winter Carnival. For more information, call Corner Brook Ski Club at (709) 634-2160 or 634-4563.

▲**Wiltondale Pioneer Village**—Just outside the southern entrance to Gros Morne National Park, this recreated 19th-century logging village includes a house, a barn, a small school, a general store and church. Admission is $3 for adults, $1 for children and $6 for families. Call (709) 453-2464 for more information.

▲▲▲**Gros Morne National Park**—Gros Morne, which was declared a UNESCO World Heritage Site in 1988, may be the single most compelling reason to see the west coast of Newfoundland. Located northwest of Deer Lake, Gros Morne has an outstanding and remarkably varied landscape. Barren rock ridges, tundralike plateaus, densely forested foothills, glacier-carved fjords, boggy coastal plains, grasslands, lakes, huge sand dunes, and picturesque villages are all found within the 2,000-square-kilometer park. You may spot caribou, arctic hares, black bears, lynx, or moose. You could easily spend a week exploring the park. For example, some of the oldest and oddest rocks on the planet are part of The Tablelands. Or you could take a boat tour of a fjord named Western Brook Pond which runs for 16 kilometers (10 miles) through 600-meter (2,000-foot) cliffs that have some of North America's highest waterfalls cascading over them. Or, if you're feeling hale and hearty, you could hike the 16-kilometer (10-mile) James Callaghan Trial to the peak of Gros Morne Mountain, a challenging outing that would take a day. The park has five campgrounds, as well as hiking trails, fishing ponds, saltwater swims, and so on. Admission is $5 per vehicle. For detailed information, call the province's toll-free tourist information line at 1-800-563-6353.

▲**River of Ponds Provincial Park**—A display at this park includes whale bones that are an estimated 7,000 years old; the bones, found at nearby sites, offer proof that this part of Newfoundland's west coast was once under the ocean. The park, about 60 kilometers (36 miles) north of the edge of Gros Morne, includes a freshwater lake ringed by sand beaches and a forest. Visitors can camp, swim, hike, canoe, or fish.

▲**Port au Choix**—An interpretive centre at Port au Choix National Historic Park displays skeletons, tools, ornaments and other artifacts unearthed from a 4,000-year-old burial site here. The site was discovered by accident in 1967 by some construction workers as they dug foundations for a building. The next year, archaeologists found three ancient cemeteries and more than 100 skeletons of the Maritime Archaic People, hunters and gatherers who plied the coastal resources between Maine and Labrador more than 4,000 years ago. Also on display are relics from another major archeological site in this area discovered in the 1950s. It turned up the remains of a Dorset Inuit community that lived on nearby Pointe Riche around A.D. 100. There are picnic grounds at Pointe Riche lighthouse if you're toting food.

▲▲▲**L'Anse aux Meadows**—This is where the first authentic Viking site found in North America was discov-

ered. As far back as 1914, Newfoundlander William A.
Munn was suggesting that Norse landings had occured on
this spot, but the remains were not discovered until 1960,
when the Norwegian explorer and writer Helge Ingstad
and his wife, archaeologist Anne Stine, searched the area.
Stine excavated the site through much of the 1960s, after
which Parks Canada took over. Three building complexes,
each consisting of a large communal dwelling and work-
shops, were turned up. The site also contained evidence
of ironworking and carpentry, which means the Norse
here were doing the first known iron-smelting in the New
World. Archaeologists believe the Norse were here during
a relatively short time between A.D. 990 and 1050; it's further believed that Leif Eriksson established a colony here,
which he called Vinland. The site, which was declared a
UNESCO World Heritage Site in 1978, also contained evidence that Groswater, Maritime Archaic, and Dorset people were in the area before the Norse. Visitors can wander
through a recreation of the sod houses unearthed at the
site, while displays in the park's interpretive center
include the floorboard of a Norse boat and iron rivets
excavated at the site. The park grounds are open year-
round, the visitor center from 9:00 a.m. to 8:00 p.m. daily
from mid-June to Labor Day. Admission is free. For more
information, call 1-800-563-6353 toll-free.

Labrador—The most isolated part of Newfoundland,
Labrador is for those who want something other than a
run-of-the-mill vacation. Labrador lies north of Quebec,
and most of it is a wilderness of towering mountains,
wide rivers and broad lakes. Traditionally, Labrador has
attracted hunters and fishermen more than tourists, and if
you love the wild, unspoiled outdoors, it's worth a visit.

The native Innu (Indian) and Inuit (Eskimo) have sur-
vived in Labrador for thousands of years. The first
Europeans to settle the coast were Basque mariners who
set up a huge whale oil processing center at Red Bay in
the 16th century. The Labrador Heritage Museum in
Goose Bay depicts the history of the land and the people.

Getting there and getting around takes some planning.
There are sizeable airports at Goose Bay, Wabush, and

Churchill Falls, while coastal communities are served by smaller airfields. From Baie Comeau, Quebec, you can drive to Labrador City and Wabush in western Labrador. In summer, there's a ferry from St. Barbe to Mont Sablon, Quebec, right next to the Labrador border; from there, the road takes you to Red Bay. There are also ferries to Labrador from Lewisporte on the north-central part of the island of Newfoundland. Seasonal coastal boats operate along the north Labrador coast as far as Nain.

The provincial tourism people say you should plan your visit well in advance, and once there, visitors should never venture into unknown territory without an experienced guide. For more information, contact the province's toll-free tourist information line at 1-800-563-6353.

The shortest route back to Niagara Falls involves cutting across the northern part of Maine, New Hampshire, Vermont and New York.

After taking the ferry back to North Sydney, N.S., follow the TransCanada (Highway 105 in Cape Breton Island and Highway 104 on the Nova Scotia mainland) as far as Truro. From Truro, turn south on Highway 102 for 43 kilometers, then west on Highway 14 to Highway 101. Follow the 101 to Digby. Catch the ferry from Digby to Saint John, N.S. Take Highway 1 west from Saint John to the border crossing at Calais, where it becomes Highway 9. Follow Highway 9 until you get to Highway 2, just past Bangor, Me. Take Highway 2 to St. Johnsbury, Vermont, and turn south on Interstate 91. Follow the 91 to Brattleboro and turn west onto Highway 9, which becomes Highway 7. At the outskirts of Albany, take Interstate 87 south for seven kilometers to Interstate 90 and head west on the 90. When the 90 ends, take the 290 north as far as the 190, which goes into Niagara Falls, New York.

Altogether, the driving distance is about 1,800 kilometers (1,080 miles). Driving on average six hours a day, it would take three days. Overnighting in Saint John and Albany would tidily break up the driving into about 600 kilometers a day.

INDEX

Other Books from John Muir Publications

Travel Books by Rick Steves
Asia Through the Back Door, 4th ed., 400 pp. $16.95
Europe 101: History, Art, and Culture for the Traveler, 4th ed., 372 pp. $15.95
Mona Winks: Self-Guided Tours of Europe's Top Museums, 2nd ed., 456 pp. $16.95
Rick Steves' Best of the Baltics and Russia, 1995 ed. 144 pp. $9.95
Rick Steves' Best of Europe, 1995 ed., 544 pp. $16.95
Rick Steves' Best of France, Belgium, and the Netherlands, 1995 ed., 240 pp. $12.95
Rick Steves' Best of Germany, Austria, and Switzerland, 1995 ed., 240 pp. $12.95
Rick Steves' Best of Great Britain, 1995 ed., 192 pp. $11.95
Rick Steves' Best of Italy, 1995 ed., 208 pp. $11.95
Rick Steves' Best of Scandinavia, 1995 ed., 192 pp. $11.95
Rick Steves' Best of Spain and Portugal, 1995 ed., 192 pp. $11.95
Rick Steves' Europe Through the Back Door, 13th ed., 480 pp. $17.95
Rick Steves' French Phrase Book, 2nd ed., 112 pp. $4.95
Rick Steves' German Phrase Book, 2nd ed., 112 pp. $4.95
Rick Steves' Italian Phrase Book, 2nd ed., 112 pp. $4.95
Rick Steves' Spanish and Portuguese Phrase Book, 2nd ed., 288 pp. $5.95
Rick Steves' French/German/Italian Phrase Book, 288 pp. $6.95

A Natural Destination Series
Belize: A Natural Destination, 2nd ed., 304 pp. $16.95
Costa Rica: A Natural Destination, 3rd ed., 400 pp. $17.95
Guatemala: A Natural Destination, 336 pp. $16.95

Undiscovered Islands Series
Undiscovered Islands of the Caribbean, 3rd ed., 264 pp. $14.95
Undiscovered Islands of the Mediterranean, 2nd ed., 256 pp. $13.95
Undiscovered Islands of the U.S. and Canadian West Coast, 288 pp. $12.95

For Birding Enthusiasts
The Birder's Guide to Bed and Breakfasts: U.S. and Canada, 288 pp. $15.95
The Visitor's Guide to the Birds of the Central National Parks: U.S. and Canada, 400 pp. $15.95
The Visitor's Guide to the Birds of the Eastern National Parks: U.S. and Canada, 400 pp. $15.95
The Visitor's Guide to the Birds of the Rocky Mountain National Parks: U.S. and Canada, 432 pp. $15.95

Unique Travel Series
Each is 112 pages and $10.95 paperback.
Unique Arizona
Unique California
Unique Colorado
Unique Florida
Unique New England
Unique New Mexico
Unique Texas
Unique Washington

2 to 22 Days Itinerary Planners
2 to 22 Days in the American Southwest, 1995 ed., 192 pp. $11.95

2 to 22 Days in Asia, 192 pp. $10.95

2 to 22 Days in Australia, 192 pp. $10.95

2 to 22 Days in California, 1995 ed., 192 pp. $11.95

2 to 22 Days in Eastern Canada, 1995 ed., 240 pp. $12.95

2 to 22 Days in Florida, 1995 ed., 192 pp. $11.95

2 to 22 Days Around the Great Lakes, 1995 ed., 192 pp. $11.95

2 to 22 Days in Hawaii, 1995 ed., 192 pp. $11.95

2 to 22 Days in New England, 1995 ed., 192 pp. $11.95

2 to 22 Days in New Zealand, 192 pp. $10.95

2 to 22 Days in the Pacific Northwest, 1995 ed., 192 pp. $11.95

2 to 22 Days in the Rockies, 1995 ed., 192 pp. $11.95

2 to 22 Days in Texas, 1995 ed., 192 pp. $11.95

2 to 22 Days in Thailand, 192 pp. $10.95

22 Days Around the World, 264 pp. $13.95

Other Terrific Travel Titles

The 100 Best Small Art Towns in America, 224 pp. $12.95

Elderhostels: The Students' Choice, 2nd ed., 304 pp. $15.95

Environmental Vacations: Volunteer Projects to Save the Planet, 2nd ed., 248 pp. $16.95

A Foreign Visitor's Guide to America, 224 pp. $12.95

Great Cities of Eastern Europe, 256 pp. $16.95

Indian America: A Traveler's Companion, 3rd ed., 432 pp. $18.95

Interior Furnishings Southwest, 256 pp. $19.95

Opera! The Guide to Western Europe's Great Houses, 296 pp. $18.95

Paintbrushes and Pistols:

How the Taos Artists Sold the West, 288 pp. $17.95

The People's Guide to Mexico, 9th ed., 608 pp. $18.95

Ranch Vacations: The Complete Guide to Guest and Resort, Fly-Fishing, and Cross-Country Skiing Ranches, 3rd ed., 512 pp. $19.95

The Shopper's Guide to Art and Crafts in the Hawaiian Islands, 272 pp. $13.95

The Shopper's Guide to Mexico, 224 pp. $9.95

Understanding Europeans, 272 pp. $14.95

A Viewer's Guide to Art: A Glossary of Gods, People, and Creatures, 144 pp. $10.95

Watch It Made in the U.S.A.: A Visitor's Guide to the Companies that Make Your Favorite Products, 272 pp. $16.95

Parenting Titles

Being a Father: Family, Work, and Self, 176 pp. $12.95

Preconception: A Woman's Guide to Preparing for Pregnancy and Parenthood, 232 pp. $14.95

Schooling at Home: Parents, Kids, and Learning, 264 pp., $14.95

Teens: A Fresh Look, 240 pp. $14.95

Automotive Titles

The Greaseless Guide to Car Care Confidence, 224 pp. $14.95

How to Keep Your Datsun/Nissan Alive, 544 pp. $21.95

How to Keep Your Subaru Alive, 480 pp. $21.95

How to Keep Your Toyota Pickup Alive, 392 pp. $21.95

How to Keep Your VW Alive, 25th Anniversary ed., 464 pp. spiral bound $25

TITLES FOR YOUNG READERS AGES 8 AND UP

American Origins Series
Each is 48 pages and $12.95 hardcover.
Tracing Our English Roots
Tracing Our French Roots
Tracing Our German Roots
Tracing Our Irish Roots
Tracing Our Italian Roots
Tracing Our Japanese Roots
Tracing Our Jewish Roots
Tracing Our Polish Roots

Bizarre & Beautiful Series
Each is 48 pages, $9.95 paperback, and $14.95 hardcover.
Bizarre & Beautiful Ears
Bizarre & Beautiful Eyes
Bizarre & Beautiful Feelers
Bizarre & Beautiful Noses
Bizarre & Beautiful Tongues

Environmental Titles
Habitats: Where the Wild Things Live, 48 pp. $9.95
The Indian Way: Learning to Communicate with Mother Earth, 114 pp. $9.95
Rads, Ergs, and Cheeseburgers: The Kids' Guide to Energy and the Environment, 108 pp. $13.95
The Kids' Environment Book: What's Awry and Why, 192 pp. $13.95

Extremely Weird Series
Each is 48 pages, $9.95 paperback, and $14.95 hardcover.
Extremely Weird Bats
Extremely Weird Birds
Extremely Weird Endangered Species
Extremely Weird Fishes
Extremely Weird Frogs
Extremely Weird Insects
Extremely Weird Mammals
Extremely Weird Micro Monsters
Extremely Weird Primates
Extremely Weird Reptiles
Extremely Weird Sea Creatures
Extremely Weird Snakes
Extremely Weird Spiders

Kidding Around Travel Series
All are 64 pages and $9.95 paperback, except for *Kidding Around Spain* and *Kidding Around the National Parks of the Southwest*, which are 108 pages and $12.95 paperback.
Kidding Around Atlanta
Kidding Around Boston, 2nd ed.
Kidding Around Chicago, 2nd ed.
Kidding Around the Hawaiian Islands
Kidding Around London
Kidding Around Los Angeles
Kidding Around the National Parks of the Southwest
Kidding Around New York City, 2nd ed.
Kidding Around Paris
Kidding Around Philadelphia
Kidding Around San Diego
Kidding Around San Francisco
Kidding Around Santa Fe
Kidding Around Seattle
Kidding Around Spain
Kidding Around Washington, D.C., 2nd ed.

Kids Explore Series
Written by kids for kids, all are $9.95 paperback.
Kids Explore America's African American Heritage, 128 pp.
Kids Explore the Gifts of Children with Special Needs, 128 pp.
Kids Explore America's Hispanic Heritage, 112 pp.
Kids Explore America's Japanese American Heritage, 144 pp.

Masters of Motion Series
Each is 48 pages and $9.95 paperback.
How to Drive an Indy Race Car
How to Fly a 747
How to Fly the Space Shuttle

Rainbow Warrior Artists Series
Each is 48 pages, $14.95 hardcover, and $9.95 paperback.
Native Artists of Africa
Native Artists of Europe
Native Artists of North America

Rough and Ready Series
Each is 48 pages, $12.95 hardcover, and $9.95 paperback.
Rough and Ready Cowboys
Rough and Ready Homesteaders
Rough and Ready Loggers
Rough and Ready Outlaws and Lawmen
Rough and Ready Prospectors
Rough and Ready Railroaders

X-ray Vision Series
Each is 48 pages and $9.95 paperback.
Looking Inside the Brain
Looking Inside Cartoon Animation
Looking Inside Caves and Caverns
Looking Inside Sports Aerodynamics
Looking Inside Sunken Treasures
Looking Inside Telescopes and the Night Sky

Ordering Information
Please check your local bookstore for our books, or call **1-800-888-7504** to order direct. All orders are shipped via UPS; see chart below to calculate your shipping charge for U.S. destinations. **No post office boxes please; we must have a street address to ensure delivery**. If the book you request is not available, we will hold your check until we can ship it. Foreign orders will be shipped surface rate unless otherwise requested; please enclose $3 for the first item and $1 for each additional item.

For U.S. Orders

Totaling	Add
Up to $15.00	$4.25
$15.01 to $45.00	$5.25
$45.01 to $75.00	$6.25
$75.01 or more	$7.25

Methods of Payment
Check, money order, American Express, MasterCard, or Visa. We cannot be responsible for cash sent through the mail. For credit card orders, include your card number, expiration date, and your signature, or call **1-800-888-7504**. American Express card orders can only be shipped to billing address of cardholder. Sorry, no C.O.D.'s. Residents of sunny New Mexico, add 6.25% tax to total.

Address all orders and inquiries to:

> John Muir Publications
> P.O. Box 613
> Santa Fe, NM 87504
> (505) 982-4078
> (800) 888-7504